AROUND <small>THE</small> FIRE

AROUND THE FIRE

RECIPES FOR INSPIRED GRILLING AND SEASONAL FEASTING FROM
OX RESTAURANT

GREG DENTON AND GABRIELLE QUIÑÓNEZ DENTON,
WITH STACY ADIMANDO

PHOTOGRAPHY BY EVAN SUNG

Ten Speed Press
Berkeley

CONTENTS

COAUTHOR'S NOTE

Dinner and a Pescatarian

I had only one night in Portland to find and eat the most incredible meal possible. One single dinner in this city my food-industry peers had for months been calling the new culinary capital of the country. And there I was, stuck dining with a pescatarian.

Out of the many restaurants that had been recommended to me, I had chosen this place called Ox upon a friend's insistence. And with its particularly carnivorous-sounding name and Argentinian grill concept in mind, I arrived ready to eat some meat.

When I walked through the doors at Ox, I felt a rush of warmth from the wood-fired grill, a 16-square-foot behemoth crackling and hissing away in the center of the room—not hidden in the kitchen like in most restaurants. And as the smoky scents and the buzz of the diners spiraled through the dining room, sparks flew around me in more ways than one.

Then I remembered my dining companion.

Don't get me wrong: I have nothing but love for you, non-meat-eating friend I speak of. But surely, I thought, the fire-cooked rib-eye and the onion-marinated skirt steak and the list of other grilled meats that ran down the center of this restaurant's menu must be the best dishes they offer. In this age of share-everything dining, I silently panicked.

It was partly through this "mishap" that I discovered the true genius of Greg and Gabi, the chefs and owners of Ox Restaurant and my coauthors of this book. That night, as our somewhat reluctant order of dishes like grilled halibut, mushrooms, and artichokes rolled out, I was floored by the magic these two chefs could work atop the fire with not just meat (though, of course, I snuck in a skirt steak . . . and a lamb shoulder chop) but these other foods as well. A heap of maitakes came off the flames glistening, chewy, and kissed with char plus a sprinkling of smoked sea salt and a brushstroke of a fruity extra-virgin olive oil. A deeply caramelized grilled onion tasted candylike beside rich and buttery diced beets. And a drippingly juicy fish "steak" was served thickly sliced, bone-in and skin on, smeared with toasted garlic oil and doused with a bright, citrusy sprinkling of chives. It lit up something inside me: an entirely new way of thinking about the grill.

Many of us likely grew up under the impression that "throwing something on the grill" meant applying the most minimal, summer-appropriate effort possible. While it may be true that it doesn't take much to make grilled food taste good, for better or for worse, we grew up lazy as a grilling culture—the easier, faster, and more straightforward grilled food could be, the better. And at my house, it all tasted the same: usually either slightly overcooked or totally overcooked (still love

you, Dad), and slathered with bottled barbecue sauce. But we loved it anyway, for the ritual of eating in the backyard with family, and those familiar, somehow comforting charred flavors. Only now do I realize how far I was from understanding the grill's potential.

I wasn't much of a dedicated griller before working on this book, probably for the reasons I just mentioned. But to witness grilling the way Greg and Gabi do it rendered the parts of grilling I once admittedly thought of as a hassle—the sometimes tedious process of lighting charcoal, the likelihood of going to sleep with smoke in my hair, and the rosy cheeks I acquire while tending a hot grill—worthwhile. Their food has proven to me that there is far more to grilling than convenience cookery, medium-rare meat and cover-up saucing. And once I was privy to their secrets, I looked at all food differently, wanting to take contrasts in ingredients to the extremes, pair dishes and plan grilled meals more deliberately, and surprise myself and my family and friends at every meal. Nowadays, I'd rather eat the food made from the recipes in this book than almost any food on the planet, and I look forward to any opportunity to light the grill.

Although part of what is romantic about grilled food is its rusticity, in reality, making grilled food as humblingly delicious as Greg and Gabi's takes an impressive amount of know-how. With their creative flavor pairings and perfectly honed fire-cooking techniques gleaned from years of cooking and traveling, they have taken the art of fire cookery to a level I had not realized existed.

As you will see, under Greg and Gabi's guidance, the grill's potential to transform ingredients does not just apply to meat. Pescatarians (and vegetarians) welcome.

—STACY ADIMANDO

INTRODUCTION

Igniting a Passion

A great grilled meal stays with you, as does the experience of cooking one around a fire. Some of the happiest times of our lives have been celebrated around a grill. The two of us—now the husband-and-wife chef-owners of Ox Restaurant in Portland, Oregon—fell in love while cooking over a wood-fired grill in Napa Valley. That was in 1999, and you might say we've been on a quest to share our passion for the grill ever since. Maybe our story makes us a little biased toward this style of cooking. But we have a strong feeling that you, too, have some good memories tied to gathering around a fire and grilling.

That first grill where we worked together was at chefs Hiro Sone and Lissa Doumani's restaurant Terra in St. Helena, California. This Michelin-starred wine country restaurant was also where we first met, and where we both cooked professionally for the first time over a mesquite-fueled fire. Our job was smoky, it was sweaty, and it was flat-out the most inspiring way either of us had ever prepared food. Any chance we had, we would daydream about and make plans for opening a restaurant with a wood-fired grill of our own someday.

In between our jobs at Terra, getting married, and opening Ox thirteen years later, the two of us cooked and ate in various parts of the world, Hawaii, Italy, and Spain among them. When creating our plans for our restaurant, Ox, we knew that—in addition to the influences we took home from these regions—we also wanted to incorporate flavors and inspirations from Gabi's Latin American roots. She spent almost every summer of her youth at her family's home in the Andean highlands of Quito, Ecuador, developing a love for local flavors and traditions while watching her grandmother cook foods like empanadas, hominy stew, and all kinds of seafood ceviches. We also knew we would build our menu around what's in season, as well as make sure we offered something for everybody—vegetarians, food-sensitive diners, everybody.

With our grill goals in mind, we studied the flavors and techniques of one of the best grilling regions in the world: Argentina. There, a simple grill grate propped over a fire and a dedication to using all parts of an animal yield dramatic, meaty masterpieces. Meals last hours, platters are always heaping, and dining companions are generous and hospitable. There is an idea among Argentinians that what comes from their own land is the best there is—and that it is all you need for a meal.

At Ox, we do Argentinian-style grilling with a Pacific Northwest approach. We cook over an open-fire Argentinian grill, known traditionally as a *parrilla* (pronounced pah-ree-sha), and much of our menu celebrates the bounty—vegetable, seafood, and meat—of the area surrounding Portland, our home since 2008. When we moved here, something about the community told us instantly it was the right place to open our restaurant. In this part of the country, people are passionate about ingredients and open-minded about cuisine. We are forever flattered and grateful that they embraced our concept with open arms—a South American–style grill with a Portland-esque respect for local ingredients and eating by the seasons.

While Portland and Ox are very special to us, we believe that what we do at Ox—and everything we have learned from our travels to South America and Europe—can be more or less replicated wherever you are. The pages of this book are designed to inspire you to have an affair with your own grill—be it wood-fired, charcoal-fueled or, yes, even gas—and bring people together around it. (In our Grilling Basics section on page 5, there are tips for maximizing the potential of whatever style of grill you have.)

Of course, there's a reason a gorgeous crackling fire often lures people to gather around and stay awhile. Besides being warm and giving nourishment, it's relaxing and enchanting, something that can intrigue and mesmerize you for hours. We hope that the ideas and recipes inside this book will tickle the same elemental urges and instincts as fire itself does, and ignite some adventure in both your backyard and kitchen cooking.

When we visited Argentina and Uruguay together, we were so moved by the resourcefulness and cleverness of the chefs and hosts we met. They can make a grill out of anything, and they apply the fire's magic to the most unlikely cuts of meat. Drawing inspiration from these traditions, we've taken a leap in using some lesser-known cuts and ingredients in this book. We promise they are worth your while to seek out. But even if you don't, there is plenty in these pages to suit and surprise you.

As for steaks, oh yes, they are here, and they are divine. But we've picked other proteins that we are almost more excited for you to try, like shoulder chops instead of rack of lamb, fish tails instead of fillets, and spiced morcilla sausages instead of spicy Italian. We are convinced these other types of protein will not only encourage you to think outside your grill routines but also might save you some cash and probably become why-didn't-I-think-of-that favorites. We don't like to be stuck in ruts as chefs, and we believe no home cook or host should suffer that fate either.

Of course, extraordinary grilling is not just about meat. At Ox, the grill grate is just as often covered with stunning seasonal vegetables—like enormous artichokes tenderizing to perfection and singeing on the ends, or halves of golden spaghetti squash or summer cantaloupes sliced down the center and left to soften and caramelize over the embers. These are the dishes that surprise many of our first-time restaurant diners, because we are not a traditional steak house, and these are not your traditional North American grill recipes.

Regarding the barbecue sauces and bottled condiments that are strategically missing from these pages, here's our take: grilled foods create their own natural, succulent, and luscious juices, so why waste them? We harness those drippings and season them with fresh, pungent herbs and spices, like bundles of rosemary and cloves of garlic; then we use these newly seasoned drippings to baste our grilled foods in their own amped-up natural juices. And when we need a condiment, we turn to the Argentinian classic: glistening, pungent chimichurri.

More than just give ideas, we'll teach you how to break down and prepare more flavorful cuts of protein, and provide seasonings, bastes, flavorings, and techniques that will hopefully allow you to expand the list of foods—not just familiar cuts of meat but also veggies, fruit, seafood, and offal—you get inspired to grill. We'll also share some fun finishing touches to try. We take pleasure in the look on diners' faces when they see fresh truffle shaved over their grilled leg of goat, or when they dip their spoon into the jalapeño-laced smoked marrow bone that sits atop our clam chowder. These flourishes can be omitted, but we urge you to try them since it is worth it to go the extra mile. This book is about sharing craft and creativity, inspiring new menus, and helping to create new associations with the grill and new memories around it.

A very important distinction we'd like to make—and one we think sets our book apart from other grilling books out there—is that not every dish that follows is cooked on the grill. To us, sautéed side dishes, crisp salads, creamy soups, chilled ceviches, and roasted and toasted elements of all kinds are essential accents that help bring balance to every meal, including grill-centric ones. We do not expect man to live off the grill alone. Though that would not be a tragic fate.

Our vision is that these recipes will help promote more than just cooking seriously good food but also the joy of sharing it, hosting with ease, and spending relaxed hours around the table. This kind of cooking and eating harkens back to our travel experiences in South America and Europe—some of our best memories ever of eating— where family-style feasts are everyday occurrences and where it seems the simpler the food, the more awe it inspires. It mirrors the technique, flavors, and heart of places where we have found so much inspiration: Argentina, Uruguay, and Ecuador. Their cooking is the epitome of simplicity and soul, and like the Europeans, they know how to execute and enjoy a long, lovely meal like the best of them. As the world gets closer and smaller—communication and travel are easier, and people are taking trips near and far to expand their food experiences— everybody seems to be on a quest to find and re-create that same feeling these far-flung places foster. Here's the secret we want to share: it's right in your own backyard.

—GREG AND GABI

GRILLING BASICS

Mastering the heat of the grill—building it, maintaining it, and enjoying being around its intensity—improves with practice. Unlike in your kitchen, where you may be so familiar with your tools and stove that you can cook almost without thinking, cooking over fire can push you slightly out of your comfort zone. Each grill is different, as is each piece of wood or charcoal, how the wind is blowing from one day to the next, and a list of other factors that will affect your outcome every time you grill. Using the tips in this section, however (and following the advice within each grilled recipe), you can and will be cooking at the grill with as much confidence—or perhaps more—than you do at your stove.

Learning the basics of great grilling can sometimes mean unlearning some of the things you think you already know. For example, many people have had a great medium-rare burger or rib-eye off the grill, leading them to assume medium-rare is always the ideal doneness for meat. Others may achieve an amazing crispy sear on grilled foods by preparing the grill to its highest heat setting, so they assume the best grilled foods are cooked over high heat. These things are not universal truths. And this section on grilling basics will help you better understand your grill, so you can prepare and tend it perfectly for every item you cook.

Styles of Grills

Our grill at the restaurant is not like most North American home grills. It is a Grillworks brand 48-inch grill modeled after Argentinian *parrillas*. The two 24-inch grates have slanted V-shaped channels that capture the juices from cooked foods. We then collect those juices in pans at the front of the grill that are lined with garlic, green onions, herbs, and lemon, and this magical mixture becomes what we baste our meats with all night. The V-shaped channels also help to prevent flare-ups that can occur when fats trickle down onto the embers. Our grill burns through 250 pounds of wood every night. We use its adjustable cranks to raise and lower food toward and away from the heat and allow easy access to the coals for direct cooking. The grill's large size enables us to feed hundreds of people and also to take advantage of many different heat zones within the space. We feel very lucky to have this amazing setup, but you do not need this kind of elaborate grill to cook delicious grilled food—all it really takes is heat, sometimes a grate, and always good ingredients.

WOOD, CHARCOAL, AND GAS

In all honesty, the woodsy, smoky aroma that comes forth from grilling over wood or charcoal cannot be matched. Even though you will never quite get that added dimension of smoky flavor with a gas grill, don't fret if that's what you have: most techniques and recipes in this book can still be perfected over gas. Gas grills, of course, have their own advantages over wood and charcoal grills. They can be divided into various heat zones quickly and with the turn of a knob, and you can keep them lit for long grill sessions without having to refuel.

GRILL SIZE

While you can grill most food on a tiny apparatus and achieve great results (at times we've even placed a grate atop the lit coals in a chimney starter and grilled on it), ideally, if you are feeding more than one to two people, you want ample room to create zones and move food around them. It is ideal to leave some space around foods as they grill. Crowding proteins or vegetables together may snuff out the fire or not allow the heat to access all parts of the food evenly, causing ingredients to steam rather than sear.

Ideally, a grill with 22 inches of grate will suffice for most jobs. That's large enough to fit four large pork chops or two large steaks on one side while leaving the other side clear for different heat zones (read more about this in Direct vs. Indirect Heat, page 11).

Types of Fuel

If you do have the capacity to grill with wood or charcoal, select a fuel that will burn as hotly and cleanly and for as long as possible before turning to ash. Hardwoods such as oak wood and fruitwoods are typically your best bet (as opposed to softwoods or highly resinous woods like pine and fir). With a few exceptions, their density and tight grains enable them to burn less rapidly and more steadily, keeping them in that ideal golden ember-y state for longer. We use mostly oak in our grills because it is the hardest and densest wood and also has a mild, lightly sweet aroma. Maple, mesquite, and cherry wood are good alternatives.

Most wood available for purchase will be seasoned (meaning partially dried out) and ready for grilling. As opposed to "green" or freshly cut wood, which retains the full moisture content of the live trees it comes from, seasoned wood will ignite easily and burn cleanly without excess smoke. Since factors such as a wood's age, sap content, and density can drastically affect the time it will take to season it (this can range from weeks to years), your best bet is to buy seasoned wood rather than cutting and seasoning your own.

If you are grilling with charcoal, be aware that each type of coal will produce a different result. For the most intense heat and longest burn, look for lump charcoal made with the same hardwoods as mentioned above. (Many high-quality charcoal pieces will actually still look like branches of a tree that have been converted to coal.) They will burn hotter and up to twice as long as other coals, such as briquettes. Our favorite brand is Lazzari, which is a mesquite charcoal, and you might have to seek it out at a gourmet grocery store or hardware store. But if you can't find it, the lump hardwood charcoals at most grocery stores will do the trick.

We completely understand why briquette charcoals are popular: they light easily, making the initial work of lighting the grill that much simpler. However, we do find that briquettes sometimes burn through faster, create more ash, and do not release as much flavorful smoke. (This may be because they are not necessarily all wood but rather a compressed compilation of combustible materials.) For a first-person glimpse into why we don't recommend them, give them a good smell. Much of the time—especially when the briquettes have been treated with lighter fluid—you will notice a chemical aroma that, in our opinion, is not desirable on food. If all you have on hand is briquettes, we suggest you avoid using lighter fluid to start or maintain the fire— to us, this is a double dose of chemical smell.

In the end, the choice of fuel is up to you. But what effort you spend on sourcing good wood or charcoal will come back to you in flavor.

Essential Grilling Tools

From an equipment perspective, grilling can be one of the most low-maintenance forms of cooking there is. You probably already have on hand any tools you will need, and if not, you don't have to look far to find a vast array of grill tools in almost any store.

Chimney starter The easiest way to start a fire in a non-gas grill is with a chimney starter. Chimney starters help to light wood or charcoal by cradling the fuels in a small but ventilated area so they can ignite quickly and evenly. A bonus to having one is that for smaller, one- or two-person grilling jobs, you can grill directly atop a chimney starter to avoid using the extra fuel required to fill a whole grill. Simply set the chimney starter inside your grill base, fill, and ignite it. Once the fuel has begun to glow red and the flames have subsided, balance a small grill grate atop the chimney and add your food. If you don't have a chimney starter, you can layer your fuel inside a small cardboard box or a large paper grocery bag, or build a fire in the base of your grill.

Tongs We like to have three different sizes of tongs within reach whenever we're grilling: a long set for managing food over especially hot fires; a medium-length set, our preferred size for control and stability; and a shorter pair that can be very useful for levering large pieces of meat, moving the grill grates, and collecting charcoal from the bag.

Spatula A large offset metal spatula is another tool we use quite often for turning and handling meat and other heavy-duty items.

Grill baskets We use grill baskets for managing small or delicate items atop the grill grate. For fish fillets or whole fish, we prefer the double-sided wire baskets that make flipping fish easy (for this reason, they are often marketed as fish grilling baskets in stores, but you can use them for other purposes too). For grilling petite items such as snap peas or small shrimp, we prefer the open-top grill baskets with small holes on the bottom. Buy the largest basket you can fit on your grill. If you don't have a grill basket or want to invest in one, you can place a sturdy metal cooling rack upside down on the grill so that the grates run in the opposite direction as those on the grill, forming a crosshatch pattern that will help prevent small foods from slipping through.

Grill brush For cleaning the grill, which you should do every time you heat it, have a standard grill brush handy. And for those times when a grill brush just won't do the trick to remove stubborn particles, also look for something flat with a somewhat sharp edge, like a wood chisel.

Towels We can't overemphasize how important towels are, but if you ever go to your grill without one, you will learn soon enough for yourself. Use towels for cleaning hands and tools, to grip something that is too hot to handle with an unprotected hand, and for wiping down the grill after cleaning it (dip the towel in oil, which helps season the grill).

A small shovel (or comparable tool) If you are cooking with charcoal or fire, you may need something to rake or shift around the coals at times. At the restaurant, we use a baker's bread peel that we bent so that it would grab onto the coals, but for home use we recommend a small shovel, a short metal rake, or a large metal spoon.

Tough fingertips Well, these will come with time . . .

How to Light the Fire

The ritual of lighting the fire is the most primal, satisfying part of grilling, and sometimes the most challenging. This very challenge is what created a commercial need for lighter fluids and quick-lighting briquettes, but those rob you of the sense of accomplishment you attain from building a good fire, and they often contribute a chemical taste to food. Here are the basic steps to lighting a natural fire, whether for a charcoal or wood-burning grill:

Step 1: Layer your fuel. Whether you plan to build and light the fire inside a chimney starter or the old-fashioned way—by layering paper

and wood in the bottom of your grill—start by placing the materials that will burn most easily on the bottommost layer. Depending on the size of your grill, for an average job you will want between 2 and 5 pounds of fuel to start.

- **Layer 1:** At Ox, we use a combination of cardboard and paper rolled into loose spirals, lining them up along the bottom rear of our wood-fired grill (but you can do this in the bottom of a chimney starter or your grill base). Loosely arrange the materials to allow proper airflow, but layer them sufficiently so they don't burn away too quickly. (You can cut some holes into a cardboard box to help with airflow.)

- **Layer 2:** If using wood or a variety of charcoal sizes, add any tinder or small pieces of wood or charcoal that will ignite quickly. These will help ignite whatever larger pieces of wood or charcoal you place on top. If you are using uniform-sized pieces of charcoal, skip this layer.

- **Layer 3:** Add some medium pieces of charcoal or wood atop the kindling and/or paper materials.

Step 2: Light from the bottom up. Light the paper and cardboard on fire using a match or, our preferred tool, a propane torch. As we mentioned previously, try to avoid lighter fluids or other aids, since these can release an unnatural chemical aroma onto food and on all the surfaces of your grill.

Step 3: Complete the heat (add a fourth layer). Once the fire is going, add the largest pieces of charcoal and more wood, doing so continually until you've reached the fire size you desire. Be sure to keep airflow in mind when stacking fuel: leave spaces and crevices among the piles, and set any wood pieces askew to allow the fire to keep breathing and building. For particularly long grill tasks such as large pieces of meat cooked slowly over indirect heat, gently add small pieces of wood or coal as needed during grilling to maintain the heat you want. No need to reignite the same amount of fuel you used originally; just top the existing source with about 20 percent of the initial amount.

Step 4: Direct the heat. The best state for grilling is when the fuel has turned to golden embers and flames are not really licking up anymore. At this point, redistribute the coals as needed to create the level of heat you want under certain areas of the grill.

Testing Grill Heat

All of our grill recipes specify an ideal heat to which you should prepare your grill, be it high, medium, low, or somewhere in between. Since gas grills are unlikely to get as hot as wood- or charcoal-fueled grills, and all grills and fuels are different, the best way to test the heat level is to rely on visual and tactile cues. First, look for signs of very high heat. One indication is that the flames have just died and the coals

Max Temperatures

If you prefer to rely on a device for some degree of reassurance, checking your grill thermometer can help you determine the relative heat level (most gas grills will have one, or you can purchase one for most styles of grills). At its highest heat, a good charcoal fire will achieve almost 700°F. Most gas grills will max out around 550°F or so. Anywhere between the 450°F to 500°F range would be considered medium-high. And after some time, you'll hit medium heat around 400°F. After that, temperatures drop down to low.

are glowing red but are still retaining their basic shape and density. That is the moment the heat will be at its most intense. As a second test, carefully lower your eye level to line up with the height of the grate. Look for heat rising from the coals—it will distort vision directly above the grill. Finally, do a hand test. Let the palm of your hand hover a few inches above the grill grate. If you have to move your hand away immediately, the grill is at its highest heat. Slightly less quickly, the heat is at medium-high, and so on.

At times in our recipes, we call for raising or lowering the heat of the grill midway through cooking. On a gas grill, you can of course adjust the knobs. On any grill, another option is to move the food nearer or farther from the heat to alter its contact with the heat (see Direct vs. Indirect Heat, below). If you are cooking over wood or coals, poke, scatter, or pull together the pieces of fuel as needed in order to concentrate or disperse the amount of heat beneath areas of the grate.

Direct vs. Indirect Heat

One of the keys to grilling is determining how intimately the foods should be in contact with the direct heat of the fire, and for how long. There are two ways the fire's heat can be applied: directly and indirectly. Really there are no hard and fast rules about which types of foods should be cooked over which type of heat. Rather, the end result you desire should dictate the techniques you use.

Having different heat zones on the grill also guarantees having options. When flare-ups start to happen or one ingredient is cooking faster than another, having a cooler zone designated on the grill will give you a place to shift the food. On the reverse end, when you want more heat or want to finish an ingredient over the fire to darken it more at the last minute, you can move it closer to the direct heat.

Direct heat application involves creating an even level of heat beneath the food (i.e., laying the coals evenly beneath it), then setting the food on the grate directly above it. This type of heat will have the strongest, most rapid impact on food. Depending on the intensity of direct heat, it can also create intense searing or grill marks and should be watched closely when done using fatty foods, because the dripping grease can easily create flare-ups.

Applying indirect heat on the grill can be similar to roasting. It involves setting the food on the periphery of the heat source so it is not directly above the heat. Indirect heat is useful for cooking food— especially larger or fattier ingredients—slowly and evenly, rather than aggressively applying heat only to one side of the food at a time. To grill using indirect heat, bank the coals or turn on the gas flame on only one side of the grill and place the food on the other side. You can close the lid to create an ovenlike effect, but if you do, remember

that this will affect the airflow and can snuff out your fire (even if the airflow valves are open). If this is the final item you will be grilling for the day, that may be okay. If not, propping the lid open with something like an extra pair of tongs or a brick works well to keep the heat contained but the fire going. If you don't have a lid on your grill but want an ovenlike effect, invest in a large metal bowl that you can invert over your grill to tent the food.

Cleaning and Seasoning the Grill

Brushing and oiling the grate before you grill is an integral part of the process. Most of the time, when food sticks to the grate, it is because the grill was not hot enough or clean enough in the first place. Throughout the grilled recipes in this book, you'll see the instruction to "prepare a grill." This should always include not only preheating but also brushing and oiling.

By far, the best way to clean your grill is with heat. A good time to clean your grill is right after you use it, if possible. If not, before you use it again, build a fire or turn on your gas grill. If you are using a gas grill, turn all the knobs to high and close the lid. When the temperature gauge reaches its highest point, you are ready to clean and season your grill. For wood or charcoal grills, prepare the fire and coals to a high heat, then place the grate over the coals and let it heat up for 5 minutes.

Next, applying some force, scrape the grate with a wire brush. For stubborn particles, use a long-handled, flat-edged tool (such as a wood chisel) to scrape more forcefully. Once the grill has been well brushed, roll up a small cloth kitchen towel—one that you won't mind throwing away after a few uses—and dip it lightly into vegetable oil. (The towel should not be dripping in oil, which can cause the fire to flare-up.) Using your hand or tongs, wipe the grill grates quickly and forcefully with the oiled rag, picking up the last of any carbon, rust, or old food bits that are still hanging around.

Your grill is now clean, seasoned, and ready for cooking.

Seasoning Food for the Grill

While we will use a marinade sometimes, our go-to seasonings are kosher salt, freshly ground black pepper, and a good, fruity extra-virgin olive oil or other vegetable oil. Besides transferring the heat from the grill and helping bring about the caramelization of the foods, the oil adds a fragrant, moisturizing gloss to grilled foods. It can also help the rest of the seasoning adhere. Seasoning the food ahead of time (depending on the delicateness of the ingredient, this could mean an hour or up to a day) brings out the food's juices, and the salt creates a mini brine or cure on the food.

Preventing Flare-Ups

Besides just being inconvenient (and momentarily scary), grease flare-ups can also lead to overcharring and its unfortunate side effect of bitterness. In the case of using briquettes as fuel, flare-ups can also bring about a bit of a chemical flavor to food as the grease strikes the hot coals.

The best way to prevent flare-ups is to plan ahead. Patient grilling is key to this process: by not placing extremely fatty items directly over the highest heat or overcrowding your grill, you can avoid the majority of flare-ups.

If flare-ups do happen, first try putting a cover on the grill temporarily to suffocate the flames. If they persist, shift the food away from the flare-up and into an indirect-heat zone as carefully as possible, using a flameproof tool. Wait until the flare-up subsides, then inch the foods back towards the heat. In some cases, basting the meat with some water-based salmuera (see page 245) can help keep potential flare-ups at bay as the moisture drips off the meat and onto the coals. Alternatively, use a squirt bottle filled with water on any areas that are flaring up.

Salt is your key to illuminating the natural flavors in foods and making your mouth fall in love. Home cooks are often astonished at how much seasoning restaurant chefs use. But most meats, if not previously brined, require a generous amount of seasoning. We prefer kosher salt because it has evenly sized crystals that are easy to pick up and release uniformly from your fingertips. In other words, it gives you the most control when seasoning.

Planning Doneness

Different pieces of meat or produce will not hit their perfect doneness at the exact same moment, even if you place them on the grill around the same time. That's because each of them varies from piece to piece, as does the fire beneath them. Use visual cues, temperature, and time cues to help determine the doneness, and follow the instructions within our recipes for more clues to gauging the doneness of various vegetables, fish, and cuts and types of meat.

Using a meat thermometer is another way of eliminating the guesswork, and it may offer some reassurance if you are still learning to understand the touch tests and visual cues. Taking temperature is best used for large items that take more than 10 minutes to cook.

Before we go any further, we must address the topic of carryover cooking. In short, even after you remove a protein such as a steak or piece of chicken from the grill, as the meat rests off the heat its internal temperature will continue to increase by 5 to 10 degrees. Take this into consideration when plotting the doneness you want. If you want a large steak to be medium-rare and you cook it to the final temperature we recommend for medium-rare, it may jump up to medium doneness as it rests due to carryover cooking. Always remove meat from the grill when its temperature measures 5°F lower than the final temperature you desire, or even up to 10°F or 15°F lower for larger, roast-size pieces like prime rib.

Letting protein rest—in other words, leaving it off the heat source but not slicing into it for the appropriate amount of resting time—is critical to keeping its juices and controlling its doneness. As a good rule of thumb, the larger the piece of protein is, the longer it needs to rest. For example, a 12-ounce steak needs about 5 minutes, and a whole (4- to 5-pound) chicken needs closer to 20 minutes.

In general, remember that foods with tougher interiors, like root vegetables or off-cuts of meat, are good matches for lower, slower cooking, and taste better at higher degrees of doneness. Their interiors need ample time to soften and tenderize as their exteriors darken and caramelize. Leaner or more delicate proteins are best cooked more quickly and served on the rarer side.

Basting

Basting grilled foods—brushing them with a seasoned oil or liquid while they cook—can help concentrate flavors and provide moisture during the grilling process. Much like using oil in a sauté pan, basting with oil is not only for imparting flavor but also for intensifying heat and concentrating color formation (see our recipe for "Black Gold" basting oil, opposite). Unlike basting with oil, basting with a brine (see Herbed Salmuera, page 245) will help prevent flare-ups and gradually distribute caramelization over the span of the grilling item (similarly to what happens when you deglaze a pan).

Simply put, when you want to add richness or fat to a leaner food, or add a quick hit of flavor to an ingredient, baste with oil. But for larger cuts of meat like whole legs or sides, which will release fat slowly as they cook, baste with brine. Remember: brine basting liquids contain a good amount of salt, so be careful not to overseason the meat before grilling and basting.

"BLACK GOLD"

While the intention of the V-slat grooves on an Argentine-style grill is to help prevent fat and oil from dripping into the coals and causing flare-ups, there is an added bonus to channeling these fats and juices off the grill. At the restaurant, we collect them and flavor them with aromatics, then use them as a basting liquid for grilled meats. We call this elixir "black gold" since it takes on a black tint from the meat juices, spices, smoke, and char.

While most home grills do not allow for collecting any meat drippings as food cooks, you can easily fake this seasoned basting oil by rendering any animal fat and warming it with fresh herbs and citrus. Olive oil also works in a pinch, though of course, neither of these options will have the same dark color as drippings off the grill.

This is less of a recipe and more of a suggestion for infusing a little more flavor into your grilled foods by basting with delicious aromatics. You can use any combination of the ingredients you like.

MAKES 1½ CUPS

1½ cups rendered fat, such as bacon fat, beef fat, good-quality lard, or duck fat, unsalted butter, or extra-virgin olive oil (or any combination of these)

8 to 10 sprigs assorted fresh herbs, such as basil, oregano, thyme, rosemary, and parsley (no more than 3 sprigs of each)

2 green onions

1 head garlic, halved crosswise

½ lemon

Place the fat in a small pot over low heat. Add the herbs, green onions, garlic, and lemon half and cook just until the herbs begin to wilt (but not sizzle), 140°F to 150°F. Remove from the heat and let sit for 15 minutes so the flavors can marry. When using to baste, keep in a warm spot on the grill. Strain before storing and refrigerate for up to a week. Add more fresh herbs upon rewarming.

Time, moisture level, and temperature will determine the flavors and intensity of smoked foods. In hot smoking, where temperatures register between 115°F and 185°F, you will cook *and* flavor foods at the same time. Cold smoking uses a gentler, lower heat (between 90°F and 115°F) and is intended for times when you don't want to cook a food (or intend to cook it later) but seek to infuse smoky flavor into it. Many proteins that are cold smoked have also been salted or cured.

To cold smoke, follow the same steps for setting up your grill, but use a minimal amount of charcoal. Place the food atop a metal pan filled with ice, then cover the ice with kosher salt, which will lower its temperature to below 32°F, maintaining a colder smoke for longer.

Regarding Crosshatching and Grill Marks

Crosshatch and grill marks can look attractive on food and can be functional for keeping track of timing, such as when you're organizing multiple pieces of meat being grilled to different doneness levels. But those classic television-ready grill marks on steaks and burgers are overrated from a skill and taste point of view. Caramelization, resting, and proper seasoning of the meat are truly what matter most.

How to Turn Your Grill into a Smoker

This method is intended for a standing charcoal grill or kettle grill with a fitted lid. If you have a gas grill, you can light one side of the grill and place your soaked wood chips directly on top of the grate (the lit side) in a perforated grill basket or in the wood chip box that comes with many models, then close the lid.

Step 1 Soak several cups of wood chips in water for at least 30 minutes. For a longer duration of smoking time, scale up the amount of chips as needed. You will need about 1 cup of wood chips for every 30 minutes of hot smoking, and about half that amount for cold smoking.

Step 2 Remove all grates from your charcoal grill. (At this point, be sure the small grate is relatively clean—you may be using it later to hold food.) Make sure the bottom airflow vents are open on the grill. Bundle up several sheets of newspaper or a paper bag and place it in the bottom of the grill barrel, pushing it off to one side. This will be used to light the coals in future steps.

Step 3 Place the small grate over the paper, then add a small pile of charcoal directly above where the paper sits, off to one side of the grill.

Step 4 Create a barrier between the two halves of the grill, with the goal of keeping the heat source out of direct contact with whatever food you are smoking. To do so, build a small wall down the center of the grill using a few bricks or a rectangular metal lid. If you have a small foil tray, stand it up lengthwise against the "wall" and secure it in place with another brick on the charcoal side. (Be sure the tray is not so tall that it gets in the way of your closing the grill lid.)

Step 5 Light the paper to ignite the fuel, then wait until the charcoal is largely covered with ashes, about 20 minutes.

Step 6 Add a small handful of the soaked wood chips to the ash pile, then place a few more pieces of fresh, unlit charcoal on top of the wood chips. You should perform this step at least every 30 minutes to guarantee that the wood chips continue to smolder.

Step 7 On the side opposite the charcoal, place your ingredients directly onto the small grate, or use a small grill basket to hold them on the small grate.

Step 8 Cover the grill, making sure right away that the vents are open and will be situated over the side opposite the fire. (If the vents lie over the fire, all of the smoke will go up and out.) Replenish with wood chips every 20 to 30 minutes as needed, then with charcoal, always in that order (regulate the temperature by using more or less charcoal). Remember never to let the charcoal completely die or the wood chips completely turn to ash without replenishing. Smoke until the desired effect is achieved.

HOW TO USE THIS BOOK

Recipes for delicious grilled foods are the cornerstone of this cookbook. But to us, what are even more crucial and exciting than the recipes are the seemingly endless possibilities of feasts you can make when you pair and serve them together. These particular recipes represent a moment in time in our restaurant and our food. Menus change, and just as we like to leave ourselves flexibility to progress and play with the dishes we serve, we want our diners and the users of this book to feel the same. Consider this book a choose-your-own-adventure concept, rather than a rigid or dictatorial manual of what dishes to make and in what order to serve them. We want you to be involved the moment you flip to page one, and to create and master your own dining destiny.

Although the two of us have both worked in restaurants with traditional main- and side-dish approaches (protein, vegetable, starch, and sauce), nowadays it seems like people aren't as drawn to that style of eating—they often prefer snacking their way to a full meal in order to try more things. That's part of the reason why in the restaurant (and in this book), we don't try to pair your mains and your sides for you. Instead, we encourage you to pick and choose what sounds complementary to you among the chapters. (Of course, we can't help but offer suggestions for some of our favorite combinations.)

We have structured the chapters in a way that makes sense to us—by clustering dishes of similar styles together, be they chilled seafood dishes that have similar cooling elements, or meats from the grill, in hopes that you will be able to efficiently compare and contrast them when creating a meal plan.

The dishes in this book are meant to be friendly for groups and family-style dining. At the Argentinian table, grilled meals are rarely portioned out onto individual plates. Everyone is encouraged to help themselves off family-style platters, which means no two persons' plates at the same table end up looking the same. Of course, you'll be able to find appropriately sized dishes for more intimate affairs, like date nights, weeknight meals, or family suppers. In most cases, you can use your judgment on scaling recipes up and down as needed to suit the occasion.

We believe that simplicity and elevation can coexist. At the heart of most of these recipes is a basic, everyday ingredient cooked using classical kitchen or grill techniques. But to make them three-dimensional dishes, we've given some a longer list of ingredients or multiple steps. Feel free to break them down as needed, and you will find tips everywhere for prepping and storing elements in advance. Some of the components you create for one dish might be great on other dishes as well. We do our best to point out places where dressings, sauces, garnishes, and other elements have such flexibility and should be made in larger batches, but you may also dream up even more ways to use these subrecipes on your own. Wherever possible, we offer optional shortcuts, like using high-quality store-bought products in place of homemade ones, or substituting them for hard-to-find ingredients.

Living and cooking in Portland, it can be easy for us to take for granted that most restaurants and maybe even home cooks use seasonality as the starting point for the way they cook. We are constantly changing what's on our menu at Ox and our table at home based on what's available and which types of produce are at their peak. Ingredients taste the best that way, and cooking seasonally has a lower impact on the environment. It also keeps you on your toes, urging you to be creative in the kitchen.

Finally, we are huge fans of balance through contrast—using an array of textures, flavors, and temperatures. When you are mixing and matching dishes on your own, try to think in terms of complementary flavors (sweet with salty, spicy with cooling), contrasting textures (delicate with crunchy, silky with firm), and even temperatures. But most importantly, remember to have fun with the planning and just cook food that excites you. After all, by taking risks and putting your own spin on things is how you become a truly empowered cook.

ODE TO ARGENTINA

It is difficult to leave the countryside of Capitán Sarmiento, Argentina—both physically and emotionally speaking. Located about one hundred miles northwest of the city of Buenos Aires but still in the Buenos Aires province, the area is a patchwork of family ranches and green fields that sprawl like oceans off the quiet country roads. The easiest way back to the city is by hiring a local driver. Ours had dropped us off here hours ago and wasn't returning until the following morning. Then again, as we stood around the fire that October evening, watching the sun turn from yellow to pink as it descended upon a fifty-hectare horse ranch in the peak of Argentina's spring season, we really didn't mind our isolation.

There were about twelve of us that night—we two chefs who were on a long-awaited first-time culinary pilgrimage to Argentina, plus our new friends who had generously opened their doors to us at their family *estancia*, or ranch. We stood in a circle, chatting and gazing upon the live coals at our feet with admiration, growing buzzed and hungry. The main event was Rafa, an elderly Argentinian from Córdoba with well-worn smile lines, sun-bronzed skin, and a newsboy hat, who was midway through cooking us an Argentinian *asado*. One of two grilling preparations in Argentina, *asado* typically consists of meat (usually beef) cooked on a spit or cross over an open fire. *Parrilla* grilling, the other style, uses a grate or rack.

"About three hours," Rafa had said in Spanish—his prediction of the cook time for the whole lamb he was slow-roasting over fire for dinner. The animal had been freshly killed and purchased from a neighboring farm that day. We had been gathered around for at least that long already, lusting for a taste of the fire-cooked meat but in the meantime happily filling our bellies with cheese, charcuterie, and Argentinian wine.

Despite having enjoyed various styles of fire-cooked meals in parts of North America, South America, and Europe before, this was our first *asado* in Argentina, and the matter-of-fact approach by which our cook built and used the fire was eye-opening. He bypassed any kind of formal fire pit and instead, carved a shallow pocket into the lawn and collected whatever wood was nearby to fill it. As we would learn, when you cook beside the fire instead of directly over it—as is often the case with *asado* as well as indirect grilling—you don't need perfect coals. Certain woods, like the eucalyptus he had sourced from the yard, would break down into embers that continued to release heat, but others just burned down to ash and provided heat to the food along the way. Here and in the countless *parrilla* restaurants we visited during the remainder of our trip, there was no rush to eat—cooking took however long it was going to take, and the chef and diners enjoyed the journey there, talking and laughing between sessions of refueling the fire.

The *cruz* (cross) is the go-to tool for cooking whole-animal *asado* in South America. A tall, cross-shaped metal apparatus that looks somewhat like a torture chamber mechanism, it acts as a sturdy vertical resting place on which to secure animals for slow-roasting by fire. Tonight, the butterflied lamb was hoisted across the *cruz*, barely fussed with by the cook except for a generous coating of salt and pepper and occasional basting with a bushel of mint and a saltwater mix (see Herbed Salmuera, page 245). On the opposite side of the fire, delicate innards from the same animal, like *tripa* and *tripa gorda* (the small and large intestines), roasted at equal distance away from the flames. Because they were beside rather than over the fire, the meats would cook almost painstakingly slowly, their juices cascading down little by little, basting each cut in more of its own fat and flavor. This, we would come to understand, was the regional cooks' secret to an ineffably juicy interior and a bronzed, crispy outside.

Even though Rafa's carefree approach made it all seem so simple, we knew better. As is usually true with expert cooks and grillers, experience had earned him the instinct and know-how he needed. That night, just after the four-hour mark, we were able to sit down to taste the fruits of his labor.

The fire had created a "skin" on the meat—a crystalline layer up and around the ribs that peeled off like sheets of nori in all their crackly-brown glory, and this was the most remarkable part of all. But the meat, tender and with fat caps that had mostly rendered into a lovely creamy gelatin, was the tastiest. As we started to eat, Rafa continued to come around with trays full of more meaty parts from other animals: veal sweetbreads from both the neck and the heart, strong-flavored beef kidneys, and an unbelievably moist and barely rare beef tenderloin that melted in our mouths. Our hosts served it all with two salads—a simple bowl of spinach with tomatoes and a delicate lettuce with raw mushrooms and grated cheese. This was the typical format of a grilled feast in Argentina—with fire-cooked proteins at the center and cooling vegetables and a house chimichurri as accompaniments.

From that very first night, we felt a deep connection to the region's culinary traditions and priorities, and the ingenuity and passion of the cooks. Many of the travel days that followed were spent eating our way through Buenos Aires as well as in Uruguay just across the border. Impeccable grilling and ardent generosity were abundant everywhere we went, as were countless examples of resourcefulness, ingenuity, and a use-everything, welcome-everyone attitude. We couldn't help but see the connections with our own kitchen at Ox.

Since the very conception of our restaurant, we set out to incorporate certain Argentinian foods into our menu. Initially these were based on Gabi's memories of growing up in Southern California and being

surrounded by Argentinian friends and their expat families. Weekends of her youth usually revolved around soccer games followed by meat- and organ-heavy Argentinian-style barbecues hosted in someone's backyard, at the park, or at a local restaurant. Her desire to revisit these flavors and culinary traditions was something she dreamed of sharing with Greg and learning more about.

Argentina is known for having the best fire cookery in the world, and we did our best to honor the country as our muse from afar. But once we found the opportunity to visit Argentina, we were able to not only verify but deepen that connection. The similarities between Argentinian tradition and the culture at Ox abound.

Though we can't cook outdoors every night or carve out fire pits on the fly wherever we go, we were thrilled and reassured to find that many of the other elements of Argentinian grilling and dining were certainly within reach. Just like in numerous restaurants in Argentina, our wood fire–fueled grill is at the center of our restaurant—both physically and philosophically. Like the meat-proud Argentinians, we make an effort to use and sing the praises of "those other cuts" beyond the loins and the rib-eyes. True to Latin American form, ceviches and chilled seafoods, salads, and vegetable dishes are part of our menu as well, intended to complement and contrast the flavors of our fire-cooked food. We have designed and labored over our very own versions of traditional Argentinian recipes—items like morcilla (blood sausages), chorizo, empanadas, and chimichurri—which we make with the bountiful seasonal ingredients available where we live. And finally, come time to gather around the table, we hope our family-style service at Ox also encourages the communal spirit that is the essence of Argentinian dining: long, satisfying meals; friends and family sharing off the same plates; and dining to the tune of a crackling fire in the background.

Although that is really as far as our ties to Argentina go—our restaurant and the recipes in this book are very much our own creations and not intended to exactly replicate authentic Argentinian cuisine—we hope the ways we have applied its influences would excite and delight any Argentine who comes through our door (and we certainly would welcome this opportunity to repay them the kindness and deliciousness they showed to us). Around those fires, we felt connected with our food and the land it came from, as well as the people who were making it and enjoying it with us. This is a feeling we strive to bring to our own kitchens each day.

CHIMICHURRI

When sitting down to dine in Argentina, a small jar or vessel of oily, deep-green chimichurri is often the first food to greet you at your table. A traditional condiment made of parsley and other herbs, sometimes speckled with dried red peppers, green onions, or garlic, chimichurri is the iconic sauce of the *parrilla* culture, delivering a welcome bolt of bright, sharp, herbaceous saltiness and acidity that takes fire-cooked foods to new heights.

In Argentina each restaurant and home cook has a signature recipe. And at Ox, we too have our own, made fresh daily and left upon each table along with some good crusty bread and butter, to stave off hunger as diners wait for their food—and later, to spoon over grilled meats, fish, and vegetables.

There is no "right" way to make a chimichurri—its proportions, flavors, and ingredients fluctuate from cook to cook. As you dip your nose into bowl after bowl of it, the differences are wonderfully interesting and inspiring. Some are more garlicky, higher in acidity, or even generously salted to deliver more impact and cut through intense gristly meats. Others have a milder taste in which the olive oil provides more of the flavor than the acid. And the different use of herbs is the most widespread factor of all. In Argentina, you'll often see a robust mix of strictly dried herbs: a parsley base with a dash of oregano or possibly thyme. In other versions, the herbs are a blend of dried and fresh. In some cases, they'll keep their deep-green color, while in others the cooks will allow their chimichurris to take on a brown tone as the herbs pickle inside the vinegar mixture, which tames their intensity.

At Ox, we go the fresh herb route, leading with bright, citrusy parsley and adding a hint of fresh oregano for depth and complexity. We also use red wine vinegar and oil in a 1:2 ratio to deliver freshness and cooling relief, and to complement and contrast our smoked and grilled items especially. And we add minced onion, which gets mellowed and lightly pickled by the vinegar, for the crisp and pungent bite it delivers.

You may very well develop your own proportions of chimichurri ingredients as time goes on—a process that is part of the fun of serving and making it. We are constantly adding to and experimenting with our chimichurri as the seasons change, adding fresh mint, diced tangerines, chopped hazelnuts, cooked lentils, or even cubed foie gras terrine into the mix. Feel free, too, to experiment with different acids. Meyer lemon juice is delicious, and we like to use verjus when we want to tone down the acidity.

It is very easy to get used to having a jar of chimichurri within reach at all times. Luckily, due to the simple, flexible nature of the recipe, that is an extremely achievable goal. To get some of the prep work out of the way, make the chimichurri up to 4 days in advance but do not add the vinegar; bring it to room temperature and add the vinegar a few hours before serving. At home you can use chimichurri on anything and almost everything, from eggs at breakfast to sandwich toppings at lunch, crudités and empanadas at hors d'oeuvres time, to cooked meats and vegetables at dinner.

OX'S CHIMICHURRI

In a medium bowl or jar, combine the onion, parsley, oregano, garlic, salt, black pepper, and red pepper. Add the oil and vinegar and mix well. Store covered for a couple of days and use before the herbs start to turn brown.

MAKES ABOUT 2 CUPS

½ cup minced yellow onion

½ cup chopped fresh flat-leaf parsley leaves

1 tablespoon chopped fresh oregano

1 teaspoon finely grated or minced garlic

1½ teaspoons kosher salt

1 teaspoon freshly ground black pepper

½ teaspoon red pepper flakes

1 cup extra-virgin olive oil

½ cup red wine vinegar

PART 1 **BEGINNINGS**

There's nothing quite like that moment when the first platter of food comes out of the kitchen, and friends begin toasting and tasting. The recipes in this section make a fantastic first impression and are just enough to take the edge off a crowd's hunger while the grill heats up for dinner.

Because no one wants to be in the kitchen plating finger food as the party is starting, many of these dishes can be prepared in advance, and you can get as rustic or refined as you want when it comes to the presentation. Our usual strategy is to set out a few dishes, napkins, and forks when—or even before—guests arrive, and let our hungry friends and family graze at will.

CHAPTER 1   # ENTRADAS

The evening's adventure and fun really begin with the starters you choose. If you know you are going to eat a fat steak as an entrée, the perfect starter could be a chilled seafood salad or some fresh oysters. Conversely, if you're going light with your main dishes, a fried, spicy beef empanada will start off the meal with a bang. Of course, any and all of the so-called starters in this chapter can be moved around on your menu, to be used as sides, snacks, or even light meals.

Let some components of these dishes inspire courses or meals to come. Toss some leftover Foie Gras Terrine (page 53) into hot pasta in lieu of butter or olive oil. Slice up extra portions of the Smoked Beef Tongue (page 60), top with Chimi Mayo (page 243), and use in lunch sandwiches the next day. Play around with these recipes and suggestions to suit your own personal style—we're all for it. If you're having fun, your guests will, too.

SPICED BEEF EMPANADAS
with olives and raisins

MAKES FIFTEEN 6-INCH-
LONG EMPANADAS

¼ cup unsalted butter

1 tablespoon chopped garlic

2 cups diced onion (from about
1 medium onion)

2 pounds ground beef chuck

2 teaspoons Hungarian sweet
paprika

2 teaspoons ají amarillo powder
(see Note), espelette pepper,
or a pinch of cayenne pepper

2 teaspoons ground annatto
seed (see Note) (optional)

2 teaspoons dried marjoram
or oregano, or a combination

1 teaspoon ground cumin

1½ teaspoons freshly ground
black pepper

1½ tablespoons kosher salt

1 tablespoon plus 1 teaspoon
red wine vinegar

½ cup sliced pimiento-stuffed
green olives

½ cup raisins

3½ pounds (2 batches)
Empanada Pastry (page 242)

1 egg

Neutral-flavored vegetable oil,
for deep-frying

It just feels right to kick off this book with a recipe for empanadas, not only because it is the first dish we planned for our restaurant menu but also because it epitomizes South American cooking and was a treat Gabi loved while spending summers in Ecuador as a child. Whether her grandmother made them in the late afternoon as a snack, or someone was selling them at a soccer game, the warm, hefty pockets of chopped beef or other fillings were irresistible.

Beef empanadas are the ultimate drinking food and ideal for keeping guests happy while you get the grill going. In Argentina, the beef is often hand-chopped and mixed with inexpensive fillers like hard-boiled eggs or potatoes. We make ours by using 100 percent ground beef chuck (and in the restaurant, we add a little smoked bone marrow fat to our filling to heighten the unctuousness). Cumin, paprika, and chiles add heat and smokiness, and raisins counterbalance with sweetness. Finally, a dash of vinegar helps cut the richness.

A small stock of either this filling (a *picadillo*, or minced beef hash) or this dough in the freezer is a host's secret weapon. You can freeze the filling for weeks in advance and serve with fried egg and potatoes, with rice and beans, or tucked into quesadillas. For greatest ease on the day of serving, do some advance prep work: One day—even a week before—roll out the dough and cut the disks. Another day, make the filling. When you're ready to party, all you have to do is stuff and fry. Speaking of which, you can make these easily without a deep-fryer—just heat the oil in a large pot.

In a wide, heavy pot over medium heat, melt the butter. Add the garlic and cook, stirring, until lightly toasted, 1 to 2 minutes. Immediately add the onion and cook, stirring occasionally, until softened, about 3 minutes. Add the beef and cook, stirring until broken up, until no pink remains, about 8 minutes. Add the paprika, chile, annatto seed, marjoram, cumin, black pepper, salt, and vinegar. Decrease the heat to low and simmer, stirring occasionally, until the liquid has been absorbed and the meat is tender, about 5 minutes more. Add the olives and raisins and simmer for 5 minutes more. Adjust the seasoning, if necessary, then let cool completely. Stir from time to time while it cools to disperse the fat throughout the mix. You should have about 5 cups of filling.

While the filling cools, roll out the empanada pastry on a lightly floured surface to about ⅛ inch thick. Using a round cutter or a small inverted bowl, cut out round disks about 6 inches in diameter. Stack the disks separated by parchment paper or waxed paper.

CONTINUED

Chill pastry for at least 20 minutes, until firm. If not using immediately, wrap the stack in plastic wrap and freeze for up to 1 month or refrigerate for up to 24 hours (after which the dough will start to oxidize and turn gray).

Crack the egg into a bowl and whisk briefly with a fork. Dip a pastry brush into the egg and paint a 1-inch circle around the outer edge of an empanada disk. Place ⅓ cup of filling onto the center of each dough round. Fold the dough in half around the filling; press the edges together. Working on a flat surface, crimp the edges with the tines of a fork or with your fingers (see photos at right). Transfer to a parchment paper–lined baking sheet and refrigerate the empanadas as you assemble them.

Pour about 3 inches of oil into a large pot and heat over medium heat to 375°F on a deep-fry thermometer. Set an oven to warm, about 200°F. Set a warm wet towel near the stove to wipe down any splattered oil.

Gently lower two or three empanadas at a time into the hot oil, being careful not to splash and avoiding crowding. Fry, turning over once, until the dough is browned and crispy and the inside is likely heated through, 4 to 5 minutes.

Using a slotted spoon, carefully remove empanadas from the fryer and blot with a kitchen towel or paper towel. Transfer to a baking sheet. Store in the warm oven until all the empanadas are ready to be served.

Note Ají amarillo powder, ground from a South American chile, has a medium level of heat—similar to a serrano—and a beautiful floral quality. If you can't find it, substitute espelette pepper or a small amount of cayenne pepper. Ground annatto seed is something you'll see all over South America. You warm up the seeds in oil and they leach out a brilliant orange color. (They call it *color* in Ecuador.)

HOW TO FILL AND SEAL EMPANADAS

Practice makes perfect, but don't worry about perfection. There's more than one way to do this (the simplest is crimping the edges of each empanada together with the tines of a fork). Empanadas are like snowflakes in that each one will be a little different no matter how well you've nailed down your technique. To start, try this traditional method before developing your own:

Step 1 Set the disks of pre-rolled dough near a clean work surface. Crack an egg into a bowl and whisk it briefly with a fork. Working with one disk at a time, dip a pastry brush into the egg and paint a 1-inch circle around the outer edge of the dough. Place ⅓ cup of filling into the center.

Step 2 Fold the dough in half to completely cover the filling, bringing the edges together and lining them up against one another. Press the edges of the dough together to seal.

Step 3 Raise the empanada off the work service and hold it in your nondominant hand with the flat side facing vertically (as pictured). Starting at the bottom pointy end, grab the empanada dough between your thumb and forefinger, pressing your fingers together and pulling slightly to thin out and stretch the dough a little in that spot. Fold the small piece of dough inward, pressing in with your thumb while bringing your forefinger around towards you, to make a wavy crimp.

Step 4 Continue pressing and crimping small sections of dough along the length of the curved side of the empanada. Transfer to a parchment-lined baking sheet and refrigerate the empanadas as you assemble them. Empanadas can be filled and rolled up to a day in advance before frying.

GRILLED CORN EMPANADAS
with poblano and gruyère

This is our summertime go-to. We wait all year for sweet corn to come back, then combine it with char from the grill and a little kick from the poblano chiles in this smoky, spicy filling. We like it with Gruyère cheese for the added touch of funk it lends, but any melty cheese will do.

A batch of these makes a stellar beginning to almost any menu. One of these empanadas and a couple of grilled sausages, and you can go to bed happy.

Prepare a grill to medium-high heat.

In a large bowl or on a baking sheet, toss the ears of corn with the oil; season with salt, then transfer to the grill. Let cook without disturbing until the kernels begin to look unevenly golden brown and roasted, 3 to 4 minutes. Rotate the corn slightly and continue cooking, rotating every 3 to 4 minutes, until all the sides of the corn are grilled, 12 to 15 minutes total; remove. Let cool to room temperature.

Let the poblanos cook undisturbed on the grill until the skin is completely blackened on the first side, 3 to 4 minutes, then continue cooking, rotating them every 3 to 4 minutes until they are completely charred black, about 12 minutes total. Transfer to a bowl, cover it tightly with plastic wrap, and let cool. Peel away the charred skin and remove the seeds and the stem. (Rinse under cold water if you are having a hard time cleaning off the charred skin.)

Slice the kernels off the corn using a sharp knife. Dice the poblanos into ¼-inch pieces. Set aside 1 cup of the corn kernels and ¾ cup of the diced poblanos for the filling; reserve the rest for another use.

In a large bowl, combine the 1 cup of the grilled corn kernels, ¾ cup diced poblano, and the cheeses; season with salt and pepper and toss to combine. Chill until ready to use; you should have 3½ cups of filling. Taste and adjust the seasonings, if necessary, before filling empanadas.

Fill and fry the empanadas following the instructions on page 34.

Seasonal Vegetable Variations

FALL, sweet potato: Substitute small cubes of roasted sweet potato for the corn; mix with Gruyère or cheddar.

WINTER, broccoli: Substitute small pieces of roasted broccoli for the corn; mix with equal parts ricotta and blue cheese.

SPRING, chard or morels: Substitute blanched, chopped Swiss chard (excess water squeezed out) or sautéed morel mushrooms for the corn; mix with Jack and chèvre cheeses.

MAKES ABOUT TEN 6-INCH-LONG EMPANADAS

2 ears fresh corn, husks and silks removed

2 tablespoons extra-virgin olive oil

Kosher salt

3 poblano chiles

4½ ounces Gruyère cheese, shredded (1½ cups)

2 ounces mild domestic Fontina cheese (or substitute Jack cheese), shredded (½ cup)

Kosher salt and freshly ground black pepper

1¾ pounds (1 batch) Empanada Pastry (page 242)

1 egg

Neutral-flavored vegetable oil, for deep-frying

GRILLED ARTICHOKES
with espelette mayo

Any artichoke lover would be more than happy to eat a boiled one accompanied by either a butter- or mayonnaise-based dip. But brushing a little olive oil on an artichoke and searing it on the grill makes it otherworldly, adding crispiness and smokiness that go even better with creamy dips.

You don't want to deal with boiling artichokes while guests are waiting. Precook these a day ahead, then reheat and char them on the grill just before serving.

Espelette, which adds kick to our creamy mayonnaise sauce, is a dried red chile from the southwestern region of France that's growing in popularity here in the States. It has a moderate level of heat and a nice citrus quality. You can find it at gourmet markets.

To make the espelette mayo, in a bowl, whisk together the mayonnaise, espelette pepper, lemon juice, garlic powder, and salt until combined. Chill until ready to serve.

To cook the artichokes, bring a large pot of salted water to a boil. Add the garlic cloves. Squeeze the lemon juice into the pot and drop in the halves. Add the artichokes, bring the water back to a simmer, and cook until the artichokes feel tender, about 25 minutes. Test for doneness by piercing the heart with a paring knife; the knife should release easily. Drain and transfer to a cutting board to cool. This can be done up to 2 days in advance. Store wrapped in the refrigerator.

To finish the artichokes, cut them in half lengthwise, then scoop out the choke and some of the soft inner leaves from around each heart. Liberally season the remaining parts with salt and pepper and drizzle with oil.

Prepare a grill to high heat and be sure to carefully oil the grates.

Transfer the artichokes flat side up to the grill; cook until golden brown and lightly charred on one side, about 10 minutes. Flip and continue to cook until grill marks appear, 5 minutes more. Remove, drizzle with more oil, and season with salt and pepper. Garnish with edible flowers and serve with the espelette mayo for dipping.

SERVES 4 TO 8

Espelette Mayo

1 cup mayonnaise, homemade (page 243) or store-bought

1 tablespoon ground espelette pepper

1 tablespoon fresh lemon juice

⅛ teaspoon garlic powder

⅛ teaspoon kosher salt

Artichokes

4 cloves garlic

1 lemon, halved

4 large artichokes

Kosher salt

Freshly ground black pepper

Extra-virgin olive oil

Edible flowers, for garnish (optional)

BROILED CANTALOUPE
with hand-stretched mozzarella curds and prosciutto

A fun take on the classic pairing of raw melon and prosciutto, this recipe works one of two ways. The first requires inferno-like heat levels, which you can achieve either under a kitchen broiler as instructed in the recipe, or by tucking the melon under the fire cage of an Argentinian-style grill. The high heat helps the cheese to start bubbling almost immediately, before the cantaloupe has a chance to get mushy.

If you're determined to start up the grill, though, try this second option, which will yield great results and similar flavor profiles: Prepare a grill to high heat, then slice the peeled melon into 2-inch-thick wedges. Brush the wedges with oil, season with salt and pepper, and grill them on both sides until lightly charred (about 4 minutes total). Plate and top with the prosciutto and ¾ pound thinly sliced fresh mozzarella (instead of the mozzarella curds—which you can find online or at specialty cheese chops— or dry pizza mozzarella listed in the recipe). Garnish as described.

Preheat a broiler and set a rack in the top of the oven. Place the cantaloupe on a cutting board and slice off the stem end and its opposite end to create two flat surfaces. Make a parallel slice to cut the melon in half; remove and discard the seeds.

Place each half, cut side down, on a work surface; trim away the skin with a sharp chef's knife. Flip the halves over and rub each inside and out with 2 tablespoons of the oil; season all over with salt and pepper.

Crumble the mozzarella curds (or break up the mozzarella cheese into small pieces, if substituting) into a bowl; season generously with salt, pepper, and ¼ cup of the oil and toss well. Fill the inside of the melon halves with the mixture. Place the melon in a 10-inch cast-iron pan (or any other heat-resistant pan) to fit snugly.

Set the pan that holds the cantaloupe on the top rack just below the broiler. Cook for 3 to 4 minutes, until the cheese curds start to brown. Stir with a spoon, flipping the melted part under and the uncooked cheese on top. Broil another 3 minutes, then stir again, pulling and stretching the cheese to look like melted mozzarella. If the curds are not melting in this time, flip the cheese inside the cantaloupe again and continue cooking and flipping the cheese as needed, no more than 12 minutes total.

Place the melon halves on a cutting board and let rest for 3 minutes so the cheese can firm up slightly. Slice each in half and transfer to four serving dishes. Drape each melon quarter with two to three slices of prosciutto, then drizzle with the remaining 2 tablespoons of oil. Garnish with parsley and serve.

SERVES 4

1 small, firm cantaloupe (about 4 pounds)

½ cup extra-virgin olive oil

Kosher salt and freshly ground black pepper

8 ounces mozzarella curds (or substitute low-moisture mozzarella)

4 ounces thinly sliced prosciutto

1 tablespoon chopped fresh flat-leaf parsley leaves

BAKED RICOTTA
with button mushroom confit and balsamic brown butter

We're big fans of any cheese plate, but a warm, roasted cheese dish offers an element of surprise and comfort that no standard cheese board could hope to deliver. This particular version is our spin on *provoleta*, an Argentinian starter that consists of a thick slice of provolone grilled or broiled until just gooey. We wanted a cheese that would stay creamy at any temperature and not get rubbery, which is why this recipe requires homemade ricotta (it is easier to make than it sounds and offers a better texture and flavor in this dish than any commercial version can deliver). Pop it under the broiler and watch it puff up until light and airy with a gorgeous golden-brown cap.

A drizzle of vinegary butter sauce makes this even more of a masterpiece for little effort. In the summer, try the ricotta and sauce topped with halved cherry tomatoes and basil. In the fall, replace the tomatoes and basil with diced roasted squash and sage. In the spring, try fresh favas or English peas. This dish works great not just as a starter or small meal but also as an accompaniment to any grilled protein.

SERVES 4

Button Mushroom Confit
½ cup extra-virgin olive oil

½ teaspoon red pepper flakes

2 tablespoons chopped garlic

1 pound button mushrooms

½ cup white wine

½ teaspoon kosher salt

¼ teaspoon freshly ground
black pepper

Balsamic Brown Butter Sauce
½ cup unsalted butter

2 tablespoons balsamic vinegar

¾ teaspoon kosher salt

¼ teaspoon freshly ground
black pepper

2 cups Homemade Ricotta
(page 251)

½ teaspoon flaked sea salt

1 tablespoon chopped fresh
flat-leaf parsley leaves,
for garnishing

Grilled Bread (page 250)
or sliced baguette, for serving

To make the button mushroom confit, in a nonreactive medium pot over medium heat, combine the oil, red pepper, and garlic. Cook, stirring, until the garlic is lightly toasted, 1 to 2 minutes. Add the mushrooms and wine and cover. Adjust the heat to medium-high and bring to a simmer; let cook for 5 minutes, until the mushrooms have softened. Uncover and let cook until the wine has evaporated, about 5 minutes. When the mushrooms start to sizzle and brown, remove from the heat. Stir in the salt and pepper and keep warm until ready to serve.

Preheat the broiler.

To make the balsamic brown butter sauce, in a small pot, melt the butter over low heat and cook, stirring, until deep brown, about 6 minutes. Remove from the heat and let cool for 2 minutes. Add the vinegar, salt, and pepper. Keep warm.

To serve, divide the ricotta among four small (2-cup) baking dishes or one large (2-quart) baking dish, slightly mounding the cheese in the center. Broil until browned across the top and heated all the way through, 5 to 8 minutes for the small dishes, and 14 to 20 minutes for the large baking dish. Sprinkle with the sea salt, top with the mushrooms, and drizzle each portion with a spoonful or two of the brown butter sauce. Garnish with parsley and serve with grilled bread and extra brown butter sauce on the side.

COAL-ROASTED OYSTERS ON THE HALF-SHELL
with chimi mayo and manchego

Put us near a raw bar, and Gabi will happily eat oysters by the dozen. Greg, not so much: he prefers the transformed texture of a cooked oyster. This grilled preparation is the best of both worlds—it maintains all of the fresh oceanic flavor of raw oysters and complements that inimitable flavor with satisfying char, fire, fat, and a meatier texture. Because of the richer flavor, you can get away with buying and shucking far fewer of these oysters to feed your clan.

For such a limited cook time on the grill, the oysters pick up an impressive amount of smokiness. But the real surprise is how well the Manchego cheese works with them. We recommend having some good crusty bread on hand to dab at the savory juices and bits left behind in the shell.

In a bowl, combine the chimi mayo, lemon juice, and Manchego and mix well.

Prepare a grill to high heat. Meanwhile, shuck the oysters (see How to Shuck an Oyster, below), preserving their juices in the shells.

Line the bottom of a cast-iron or other heavy-duty skillet with coarse rock salt and nestle the oysters on top. If you don't have rock salt, set down a bed of uncooked lentils or lightly crumble some aluminum foil and nestle the shells into it to keep them in place. Place a dollop of the mayo-Manchego mixture onto each.

Flatten the surface of the hot coals and place the pan directly on the coals. Close the lid of the grill. Roast the oysters until they are just warmed through and the mayo begins to brown, about 5 minutes. Serve immediately with oyster forks and crusty bread.

How to Shuck an Oyster

You'll need a shucking knife and a clean hand towel for this.

Place the oyster on a small folded towel with the flat side facing up. Grip the oyster on its wider end with your nondominant hand, using the towel to protect your hand. Dig the tip of the oyster knife into the hinge of the oyster shell (it's located on the narrower end), and apply firm, steady pressure, slowly wiggling the knife back and forth to help loosen the hinge. Once the shell cracks open, slide the knife between the top and bottom layers to completely separate them, pressing the knife along the top shell to detach the oyster cleanly. Discard the top shell and detach each oyster from its bottom shell using the oyster knife. Clean away any grit or broken shell, being careful not to spill the juices.

MAKES 24

1 cup Chimi Mayo (page 243)

2 tablespoons fresh lemon juice

2 ounces Manchego cheese, finely grated (½ cup firmly packed)

24 live oysters, scrubbed clean

Coarse rock salt, for lining the pan

Crusty bread, for serving

DUNGENESS CRAB BRUSCHETTA
with avocado, radish, and shiso

When December strikes in the Pacific Northwest, it's Dungeness crab season. Compared to Maryland blue crabs, Dungeness have huge bodies with unbelievable amounts of meat, all of which is good for cooking and eating. They are also, in our opinion, some of the sweetest and most delicious crabs anywhere. The season is long, so the meat is pretty consistently available wherever you are, but if you can't find it, you can substitute any lump crabmeat.

Here, we give the crab a hint of umami, then pair the crab with toasts, radishes, and cucumber for crunchy contrast. For a gluten-free option, omit the bruschetta and serve the crab salad atop a ripe avocado half or a bed of sliced avocado.

Shiso and tobiko are usually found in Japanese or other Asian markets. Make the soy dashi and vinaigrette before starting on the other elements.

SERVES 4

Dungeness Crab Salad

8 ounces fresh Dungeness crab, picked clean of shells

2 tablespoons finely chopped chives

2 fresh shiso leaves, thinly sliced (or substitute fresh basil)

1 tablespoon yuzu-flavored tobiko, mixed with 2 tablespoons extra-virgin olive oil

3 tablespoons Soy Dashi (page 244) (or substitute an additional 1 to 2 teaspoons soy sauce in the crab salad)

5 tablespoons Citrus-Soy Vinaigrette (page 244)

Bruschetta

Grilled Bread (page 250) or toasted, thickly sliced bread

12 very thin slices English cucumber

2 small radishes, thinly sliced

1 ripe avocado, pitted and diced

Kosher salt and freshly ground black pepper

To make the crab salad, combine the crabmeat, half of the chives, half of the shiso, and half of the tobiko mixture in a medium bowl. Add the dashi and vinaigrette; stir to combine. Adjust the seasoning as needed.

To make the bruschetta, while the bread is still warm, top with the crab salad, dividing evenly among the toasts. Overlap three slices of cucumber on top of each, then four to five slices of radish and some of the avocado (season it lightly with salt and pepper). Drizzle the remaining tobiko mixture over the top of each bruschetta. Garnish with the remaining chives and shiso.

CLAM CHOWDER

with smoked beef marrow bones, green onion, and jalapeño

SERVES 6

Chowder

6 tablespoons unsalted butter

½ cup diced bacon, homemade (page 246) or store-bought (from about 4 slices)

2½ teaspoons chopped garlic

½ teaspoon red pepper flakes

1 cup diced onion (¼-inch cubes)

½ cup peeled and diced carrot (¼-inch cubes)

½ cup diced celery (¼-inch cubes)

2 cups white wine

2 cups heavy cream

1 cup milk

2 teaspoons sambal olek (or substitute a few dashes hot sauce such as Tabasco)

Kosher salt and freshly ground black pepper

1½ cups peeled and diced russet potato (¼-inch cubes)

2½ pounds fresh, purged manila clams in the shell (see How to Purge Live Clams, at right)

Garnish

6 Smoked Beef Marrow Bones (recipe follows)

Flaked sea salt

Toasted Garlic Bread Crumbs (page 250) (optional)

1 large jalapeño pepper, very thinly sliced

⅓ cup thinly sliced green onion (green parts only)

2 tablespoons chopped fresh flat-leaf parsley leaves

People lose their minds over this chowder. Greg is from New England, so we wanted to serve a creamy version on our menu, and we sought to make a gluten-free version that still delivered on richness and texture. We go through a *lot* of this chowder, regardless of the time of year or weather.

The base starts off loose and brothy, so the clams can open inside the broth and release all their juices. To fortify the body of the chowder later, we add silky, unctuous smoked bone marrow.

At the restaurant, we garnish the marrow bones with toasted garlic bread crumbs for crunch, but you can leave them off to keep the soup gluten-free. For balance against all the richness, go heavy on the fresh herbs and green onions. Lacing each marrow bone with sliced jalapeño helps, too.

To make the chowder base, in a large, heavy pot over medium heat, combine the butter and bacon; cook until the bacon starts to brown, about 5 minutes. Add the garlic and red pepper flakes and cook, stirring occasionally, until the garlic is lightly browned, about 2 minutes. Immediately add the onion, carrot, and celery and cook, stirring occasionally, until the onion is translucent, about 5 minutes. Stir in the wine. Bring to a boil, skimming away any impurities or foam that rise to the top, then add the cream and milk. Bring to a boil, then add the sambal olek; season with 2½ teaspoons salt and ½ teaspoon pepper. Add the potatoes and bring the mixture up to a simmer. Taste and adjust the seasoning, if necessary, then remove from heat. At this point you can cool the chowder base in the pot and refrigerate for up to 4 days until ready to use.

To prepare to serve, preheat the oven to 450°F. Place the prepared smoked marrow bones on a baking sheet and roast until heated through, 10 to 15 minutes. (Watch carefully to avoid overheating, which would cause too much of the marrow to render out of the bones.) Keep warm.

Meanwhile, add the clams to the chowder base; cover and bring to a boil over medium heat. Reduce to a simmer and cook until the shells have all opened, about 5 minutes. (Discard any clams that do not open.) Taste and adjust the seasoning, if necessary.

To serve, divide the chowder among six warmed soup bowls. Sprinkle each warm marrow bone with sea salt, then sprinkle with the bread crumbs to cover. Line each bone with jalapeño slices, slightly overlapping. Place one bone on the side of each bowl, then garnish bowls with the green onions and parsley. Serve immediately, encouraging guests to scrape the marrow into the chowder before eating, jalapeños and all.

How to Purge Live Clams

Place the clams in a large bowl or container and run cold water over them, stirring them around with your hands; drain off the dirty water. Repeat two more times, then cover the clams with fresh cold water. Add enough salt to mimic the saltiness of the sea. Cover the container completely so that it's dark in the bowl and refrigerate for a couple of hours or up to 12 hours. Drain off the salty water, then rinse clams three more times to wash away any salty water or dirt that was purged from their shells.

MAKES 6

6 (4-inch) beef marrow bones, split lengthwise by your butcher (or substitute 2-inch pipe marrow bones)

SMOKED BEEF MARROW BONES

Cover the marrow bones in water and refrigerate overnight. The next day, remove from water and pat dry.

Prepare a smoker with mesquite wood chips and preheat to 200°F. Smoke the bones until caramel colored, about 1 hour. Refrigerate until ready to use.

GRILLED FOIE GRAS

with caramelized onion-sherry broth, savoy cabbage, and gruyère toasts

Lots of restaurants offer a French onion soup on their menu. But during a trip we took to Chamonix, France, we tasted what we found to be a slightly lighter, brothier alternative to the soup, made with silky pieces of green cabbage. The simplicity of it really struck us—especially the sweetness and texture that the cabbage added. We thought, what would make this even better? Some sherry and a piece of grilled foie gras just made sense. The soup keeps the foie warm as you eat it, so much so that the liver and its smoky flavors continue to render into the broth as you spoon away. The toast—which stays crispy because it's not overladen with cheese—helps soak up every last drop.

SERVES 4

Caramelized Onion-Sherry Broth

2 tablespoons unsalted butter

1 large onion, halved through the stem, then sliced into ¼-inch-thick slivers (about 3 cups)

1 teaspoon sugar

Kosher salt

1 cup Manzanilla sherry

4 cups water, plus more as needed

¼ teaspoon freshly ground black pepper, plus more to taste

4 sprigs fresh thyme

4 cups savoy cabbage leaves cut into 2-inch pieces (about half a head's worth)

Grilled Foie Gras and Gruyère Toasts

4 (1-inch-thick) slices sourdough bread, crusts removed

4 ounces Gruyère cheese, grated (1½ cups)

Kosher salt and freshly ground black pepper

4 (2-ounce) slices Grade A foie gras (about ½-inch thick)

To make the broth, melt the butter in a large, heavy nonreactive pot over high heat. Add the onion, sugar, and 1 tablespoon salt. Cook, stirring frequently, until softened, being careful to avoid burning, about 6 minutes. Reduce the heat to medium and cook until the mixture starts to brown and stick to the pot, 2 to 3 minutes more. Using a wooden spoon, stir vigorously, scraping up as much as you can off the bottom of the pot. Pour in ¼ cup of the sherry to deglaze, stirring to help loosen the brown bits from the bottom of the pan. Continue cooking until the onion begins to stick and grow darker, and deglaze with another ¼ cup of the sherry. Continue cooking and deglazing until the onion turns a uniform dark caramel color, 20 to 30 minutes total. (If you have used up all your sherry and the onions are still too pale, continue to deglaze using some water instead.)

Add the water and bring to a simmer, skimming off any foam with a spoon or ladle. Simmer until the liquid reduces by about 1 cup, about 15 minutes. Stir in the pepper and thyme sprigs; taste and adjust the seasoning, if necessary. Remove the pot from the heat and let sit for 20 to 30 minutes to help the new flavorings incorporate. Discard the thyme sprigs. The broth can be refrigerated for up to 5 days before serving.

Bring a medium pot of salted water to boil. Meanwhile, set a bowl of ice water next to the stove. Drop the cabbage pieces into the boiling water and cook until just tender, about 2 minutes. Remove and immediately drop into the ice water; let cool completely, then remove and squeeze out the excess water. Set aside.

Prepare a grill to medium-high heat. Preheat a broiler. Bring the onion-sherry broth to a simmer; add the cabbage and return to a simmer. Taste and adjust the seasoning, if needed. Keep warm.

Place the slices of bread on the grill and cook until lightly toasted on one side; flip and repeat. Transfer to a baking sheet and top with the Gruyère; broil until the cheese is melted. Sprinkle with pepper and keep warm.

To grill the foie gras, season the first two slices with salt and pepper. Carefully oil the grate, then immediately add the slices two at a time to prevent flare-ups, transferring them directly to the hottest section of the grill. Cook until grill marks form, about 30 seconds. Rotate 60 degrees (to form a crosshatch pattern) and cook for 30 seconds more. (If flare-ups do occur, don't be too concerned: the foie gras will render enough fat as it cooks that any acrid taste from flare-ups will render away.) Using long grill tongs, carefully flip and cook for about 30 seconds on the second side, then remove and keep warm while you season and grill the remaining two slices. Keep warm.

To serve, divide the broth among four warm serving bowls. Cut each of the toasts into three pieces, and place the three pieces over the top of the cabbage and broth in each bowl. Place one slice of grilled foie gras on top of the cheese toasts, and serve.

FOIE GRAS TERRINE

Foie gras terrine is the one food Greg must order if he sees it on a menu.

Commitment-wise, making foie gras terrine is definitely more of an advanced recipe. But if you're up for the challenge, it is a matchless way to dress up a dinner party and really is the gift that keeps on giving.

A terrine is a French country–style preparation in which chopped seasoned meat is preserved under a fat cap and served chilled or at room temperature (it is also the name for the ceramic dish in which the meat is classically cooked and preserved). This version is made with fattened duck liver, which you can purchase at a specialty market or online. Capping it with fat preserves it for at least two weeks, and a little goes a long way to satisfy your gluttonous desires.

Bring the foie gras to room temperature, about 1 hour; transfer to a large cutting board. Each lobe contains a large and a small section; separate the two. Turn each section so that the smooth side of the foie is facing down on the cutting board and the narrower end of the lobe is at the top of the cutting board. The goal is to remove the veins from the foie without completely melting the foie with the heat of your hands or breaking it up into too-small pieces. (You won't be able to avoid breaking some pieces off, but just handle it gently.) In each of the two sections of the lobe, there are two layers of veins webbing from the center outward. Begin by placing your fingers in the center of the lobe and pressing down gently to start to expose the web of veins. Press the foie away from the veins with your fingertips, attempting to leave the veins intact without breaking them. As you expose the veins, gently place your fingers underneath them and lift the veins away from the foie until separated. Continue exposing and separating as many veins as you can find.

Spread the pieces of foie out in a 9 by-12-inch (or rough equivalent) stainless steel or glass pan and evenly distribute the salt, pepper, sugar, nutmeg, bourbon, brandy, port, and maple syrup over the foie. Gently flip the foie pieces to help distribute the marinade. Cover with plastic wrap, pressing it directly against the foie. Wrap the pan tightly with plastic wrap and refrigerate for 24 hours.

Bring the foie to room temperature, about 1 hour.

Meanwhile, preheat the oven to 200°F and set a rack in the center. Place the pieces of foie gras into a 1½-quart terrine mold, starting with half of the larger pieces on the bottom, then the smaller pieces throughout the middle, and the rest of the larger pieces on top. Cover the terrine with its lid and place it in a larger deep pan that will allow you to create a water bath for the terrine. Pour hot water from the tap into the pan so that it

CONTINUED

**MAKES ABOUT 24 OUNCES;
SERVES 12 TO 16**

1½ pounds Grade A duck foie gras

1½ teaspoons kosher salt

½ teaspoon freshly ground white or black pepper

1 teaspoon sugar

Pinch freshly grated nutmeg

1½ teaspoons bourbon

1½ teaspoons brandy

1½ teaspoons port wine

1 teaspoon maple syrup, preferably Grade B

Grilled Bread (page 250), for serving

reaches three quarters of the way up the side of the terrine vessel. Gently place onto the middle oven rack. Cook until a thin layer of rendered fat visibly coats most of the foie gras (about ⅓ cup), 9 to 12 minutes. Remove from the water bath to stop the cooking process, then use a soup spoon to gently press on the foie and gather up the rendered fat; reserve the fat.

Loosely cover the terrine with plastic wrap so that it can be pressed into the corners. Measure the length and width of the inside of the top of the terrine. Cut a sheet of aluminum foil to those dimensions. Cover the foie with the aluminum foil, then place up to 2 pounds of weight evenly distributed across the top. (We use a few pounds of butter.) Refrigerate overnight.

The next day, remove the foie from the refrigerator and remove the weight, foil, and plastic wrap. Level the top of the foie gras by scraping away the remaining rendered fat and flattening the foie. Refrigerate the terrine again.

In a small pan, place the reserved fat and everything that was scraped off to level the foie over low heat; gently heat just to melt. Let cool slightly so that the fat mixture will not melt any more foie when placed over the top. Strain directly over the foie through a fine-mesh strainer, covering the whole terrine by slightly tipping it from one side to the other. This fat cap will help prevent the terrine from oxidizing. Place the lid back on top of the terrine and refrigerate until the fat has solidified, about 30 minutes. Wrap tightly with plastic wrap and place the lid over it. Store in the refrigerator for up to 2 weeks. (Be sure to tightly wrap any cut portions in plastic wrap, pressing the plastic wrap directly against the surface of the terrine to avoid oxidation.)

GRILLED LAMB HEART
with charred leek puree and toasted pine nuts

We are always trying to find ways to use lesser-appreciated cuts of meat and introduce more people to foods that may sound scary but are delicious. A lamb heart is one of the most tender, delicate, mild-flavored pieces of offal you could ever eat, and we're not just saying that: if someone weren't sure they liked lamb, we would actually give them lamb heart as a gateway cut. Of course, it's important to source the heart—like any offal—from a well-raised animal for the cleanest flavor.

Fire-cooked leeks are a magical pairing with this. We first cooked this dish in a fireplace in Provence after a trip to the local farmers' market, and it was good enough to take home halfway across the world. Use the leftovers as a dip for crusty bread, or for smearing on grilled cheese sandwiches.

Prepare a grill to medium-high heat. Preheat the oven to 325°F.

Place the pine nuts in a small baking dish or rimmed baking sheet and roast, stirring once, until golden brown, 8 to 10 minutes. Transfer to a plate; let cool.

Cut the lamb heart into four 2-ounce portions, trimming away any fat or ventricles that were not previously removed. Drizzle with 1 tablespoon of the oil and season each side with salt and pepper. Place on the hottest section of the grill and cook for about 2 minutes, then flip and repeat. (This will cook the heart slightly to the rare side of medium-rare, which is ideal for this tender and mild meat.) Remove from the heat and let rest for 1 to 2 minutes. Slice lengthwise as thinly as possible (about 1/8 inch).

Place a generous dollop (2 to 3 tablespoons) of Charred Leek Puree in the center of each of four serving plates. Fan out the thinly sliced heart around the leek puree. Drizzle with saba and the remaining 1 tablespoon of oil, then garnish with the toasted pine nuts and edible flowers.

CONTINUED

SERVES 4

3 tablespoons pine nuts

8 ounces trimmed, cleaned lamb heart

2 tablespoons extra-virgin olive oil

Kosher salt and freshly ground black pepper

3/4 cup Charred Leek Puree (recipe follows), at room temperature

1 tablespoon saba (reduced grape must) (or substitute store-bought balsamic vinegar glaze)

12 small edible flowers (optional)

MAKES A GENEROUS 1 CUP

1 pound leeks (about 4 large leeks), trimmed

½ cup extra-virgin olive oil

Kosher salt and freshly ground black pepper

1 head garlic, cloves separated and peeled

1 cup firmly packed basil leaves, coarsely chopped

1 tablespoon sherry vinegar, plus more to taste

CHARRED LEEK PUREE

Prepare a grill to medium-high heat. Preheat the oven to 375°F.

Meanwhile, halve the leeks lengthwise and clean thoroughly (see How to Clean Leeks, below).

Set the leeks on a flat surface with the cut side down so any excess water can drip out of them before grilling; drizzle with ¼ cup of the oil and season with salt and pepper. Transfer to the grill and cook until charred with dark grill marks, 3 to 5 minutes. Flip and repeat, then transfer the leeks to a long, deep baking pan. Cover tightly with aluminum foil and transfer to the oven; cook until just tender, 45 to 60 minutes. Uncover and let rest until cool enough to handle.

Meanwhile, put the garlic cloves in a small pot or baking dish and drizzle with enough of the remaining oil to barely cover them, about ¼ cup. Cover with aluminum foil and roast in the same oven as the leeks until the cloves soften and turn a golden color (do not brown fully), about 40 minutes. Remove from the oven and let cool to room temperature.

Place the leeks on a cutting board and slice into 1-inch pieces; discard the roots. Transfer to a food processor and add the garlic and the oil from the garlic; pulse until the leeks and garlic are coarsely chopped, then add the basil and continue to process until a paste forms. Taste and season with salt and pepper, if necessary. Mix in 1 tablespoon of the vinegar. Taste again and add more vinegar to taste. The puree can be made up to 3 days in advance. Refrigerate until ready to use, then bring to room temperature before serving (about 1 hour).

How to Clean Leeks

Leeks can harbor a lot of hidden dirt, so clean them carefully. First, cut the leeks in half down the middle. Hold them under cold running water and rinse thoroughly, spreading open the various layers and blasting out any dirt clods with water. Then, just to be safe, submerge the leeks completely under water for 10 minutes before rinsing one more time.

BEEF TENDERLOIN TARTARE
with fried squid and herb-caper emulsion

SERVES 4 TO 6

Herb-Caper Emulsion

1 egg yolk

3 tablespoons Dijon mustard

1 tablespoon ketchup, homemade (page 242) or store-bought

1 tablespoon soy sauce (gluten-free if desired)

1½ teaspoons sambal olek

2 teaspoons fresh lemon juice

¼ cup extra-virgin olive oil

¼ cup minced cornichons

2 tablespoons minced capers

2 tablespoons minced shallot

2 tablespoons minced onion

¼ cup chopped fresh flat-leaf parsley leaves

Tartare

¾ pound beef tenderloin, diced into ¼-inch pieces, trimmed of silver skin and fat

¼ cup extra-virgin olive oil

2 tablespoons chopped fresh flat-leaf parsley leaves

Flaked sea salt and freshly ground black pepper

Squid and Garnishes

Neutral-flavored vegetable oil, for deep-frying

24 whole flat-leaf parsley leaves

Kosher salt and freshly ground black pepper

1 lemon, sliced crosswise as thinly as possible

8 ounces cleaned squid, rings cut about ½ inch thick, and tentacles

1 cup all-purpose flour, for dredging

We love contrast in every dish we make, like raw items with fried, crispy things, and cooler items with something hot or spicy, which is why we think it's worth the extra effort to fry some squid and whip up our herb-caper emulsion reminiscent of tartar sauce. Store extra emulsion in a jar to use as a potato salad dressing; a sandwich, hot dog, or burger condiment; or as an accompaniment to fried fish. Use only the freshest, most beautiful, lean, and tender beef (preferably grass-fed) you can find. And when you're cutting the meat, keep it chilled by placing a larger bowl with ice underneath the bowl you're putting the diced meat into.

To make the herb-caper emulsion, in a bowl, whisk together the egg yolk, mustard, ketchup, soy sauce, sambal olek, and lemon juice. Slowly add the olive oil, whisking until completely emulsified. Stir in the cornichons, capers, shallot, onion, and parsley until combined. Chill until ready to serve.

No more than 10 minutes before serving, make the tartare by combining the beef, olive oil, and chopped parsley; season with sea salt and pepper and mix well. Taste and adjust the seasoning, if necessary.

To make the squid and garnishes, preheat the oven to 200°F. Set a paper towel–lined platter next to the stove. In a large pot over medium heat, heat the vegetable oil to 375°F on a deep-fry thermometer.

Add the whole parsley leaves to the hot oil and stir gently with a slotted spoon or spider skimmer. As soon as the leaves turn translucent and crisp, about 25 seconds, remove and transfer to the paper towels; season lightly with kosher salt.

Separate the lemon slices and gently lower into the hot oil. Fry for 30 seconds, then transfer to the paper towels to drain; season lightly with kosher salt and keep warm in the oven.

Working in batches to avoid overcrowding the pot, dredge about one-third of the squid with flour, then place it in a strainer and shake off the excess flour. Gently lower into the oil; fry until crispy, about 1 minute. Transfer to the paper towels, season with kosher salt, and keep warm. Repeat with the remaining squid.

As soon as all the squid is fried, mound a portion of the beef on each serving plate, and shape using a ring or square mold (if you don't have one, just mound it onto the plate, then flatten the top). Drizzle a couple of tablespoons herb-caper emulsion around each portion of the beef but not on it. Divide the fried squid, parsley leaves, and lemon slices among the plates, piling them on top of the chilled beef. Serve immediately.

SMOKED BEEF TONGUE

with ensalada rusa and sweetbread croutons

This dish is really just a version of smoked cold cuts and potato salad, but the details and complexity turn it into something special. We were inspired by a traditional Argentinian dish called *lengua a la vinagreta*, which is basically a pickled beef tongue. As delicious as the classic is, we wanted to transform it into something that would be more familiar and appealing to the American palate. We poach, then smoke, the tongue to give it a hammy flavor, then thinly slice and serve it with *ensalada rusa*, a richly embellished potato salad made and eaten all over Latin America. This salad can also be served as a side to any grilled meal. Our briny caper vinaigrette lends that classic pickle-y quality to the dish.

To find good sweetbreads, start by going to a butcher you trust. The sweetbreads should be relatively odorless, with a light pink–tan color and very little visible blood. The crispy sweetbread "croutons" can be eaten on their own—like nuggets with dipping sauce—or substituted for croutons on a hearty salad. Rice flour gives the crispiest results. Bonus: it's gluten-free.

There will be some leftover tongue, and luckily there is also plenty to do with it. You can thinly slice it and serve as a ham or cold-cut replacement on sandwiches, or dice it and toss it into a cobb or chef's salad, an omelet, soup, or fried rice. As for any leftover caper dressing, it's great drizzled over grilled fish or chicken, or as a dressing for potato, pasta, or beet salad.

SERVES 8 TO 10

Sweetbread Croutons

1 pound raw veal sweetbreads

½ cup unseasoned rice vinegar

Kosher salt and freshly ground black pepper

½ cup rice flour

Neutral-flavored vegetable oil, for deep-frying

Tongue and Potato Salad

1¼ pounds Cured and Smoked Beef Tongue (recipe follows), very thinly sliced against the grain

2½ cups Ensalada Rusa (recipe follows)

40 leaves arugula

1 cup Caper Vinaigrette (recipe follows)

Garnish

1 knob peeled horseradish root, for shaving

2 tablespoons chopped fresh flat-leaf parsley leaves

To prepare the croutons, soak the sweetbreads in cold water in the refrigerator for at least 8 hours and up to 24 hours; drain.

Set a bowl of ice water next to the stove. In a large nonreactive pot over medium heat, combine 10 cups water, the vinegar, and 1 tablespoon salt and bring to a simmer. Add the sweetbreads and return to a low simmer. Cook until they are just pink in the middle, 10 to 14 minutes. Transfer to the ice bath with a slotted spoon; let cool completely.

On a cutting board, peel away the white membranes and any fat from the sweetbreads, and cut away any gray spots. Keep chilled until ready to use.

In a large pot over medium-high heat, heat about 2 inches of the oil until it registers 375°F on a deep-fry thermometer. Line a plate with paper towels.

Cut the sweetbreads into ¾-inch chunks ("croutons"). Dredge them in the flour; then, shaking off any excess, transfer them to the hot oil. Cook, turning as needed, until crispy, 3 to 4 minutes. Transfer to

CONTINUED

the lined plate and season with salt and pepper. Keep warm until ready to serve.

To serve, divide the slices of beef tongue among eight to ten large plates, spreading them out so they just barely overlap. Top with dollops of the ensalada rusa, then garnish with the arugula leaves. Drizzle the caper vinaigrette over the tongue and around the plates. Using a grater, finely shave horseradish over each dish to taste, then sprinkle with the parsley. Divide the warm sweetbread croutons among the plates and serve immediately.

CURED AND SMOKED BEEF TONGUE

MAKES 1¾ TO 2½ POUNDS

1 beef tongue (2½ to 3 pounds)

⅓ cup Dry Cure (page 246)

Kosher salt

In a large bowl, toss the beef tongue with the dry cure to coat generously. Transfer the tongue a large sealable plastic bag and refrigerate for 3 days.

On the fourth day, rinse the seasonings from the tongue. Transfer the tongue to a medium pot and add water to cover; season lightly with salt. Bring to a simmer, then let cook until the tongue is tender, about 3 hours. Remove from the liquid and let rest until cool enough to handle; peel off the outer membrane while the tongue is still warm. Refrigerate the remainder overnight, uncovered, to dry out any excess moisture.

The next day, prepare a smoker with mesquite chips and heat to 110°F. Smoke the tongue for about 3 hours. Let cool completely. Store unsliced and wrapped tightly for up to 5 days in the refrigerator or 1 month in the freezer.

MAKES ABOUT 2½ CUPS

Kosher salt

1 cup peeled and diced russet
potato (⅓-inch cubes), soaked
in water to avoid oxidation

¼ cup finely diced celery
(⅓-inch cubes)

¼ cup peeled and finely diced
carrot (⅓-inch cubes)

¼ cup finely diced yellow onion
(⅓-inch cubes)

½ cup diced roasted golden
beets or Chioggia (pink) beets
(page 249), cut into ⅓-inch
cubes

2 tablespoons thinly sliced
cornichons

¼ cup mayonnaise, homemade
(page 243) or store-bought

2 tablespoons Dijon mustard

Freshly ground black pepper

ENSALADA RUSA

To prepare the vegetables, bring a large pot of water to a boil. Season
the water with enough salt so that it tastes like the sea. Set a large bowl
of ice water next to the stove and set a large strainer inside. Drain the
potatoes of their holding water, then toss in the boiling water. Boil until
just cooked through, 7 to 9 minutes; remove immediately with a slotted
spoon and transfer to the iced water.

Return the water to a boil and add the celery, carrot, and onion; boil until
the carrot is just crisp-tender, about 3 minutes. Remove the vegetables
using a slotted spoon and transfer to the ice water. Drain well and add to
the bowl with the potatoes.

Add the beets, cornichons, mayonnaise, and mustard and mix well to
combine; taste and adjust salt and pepper as needed. Keep chilled until
ready to serve. Store, refrigerated, for up to 4 days.

MAKES 1⅔ CUPS

½ teaspoon finely grated
or minced garlic

3 tablespoons Dijon mustard

¼ cup champagne vinegar

¼ teaspoon kosher salt

1 teaspoon freshly ground
black pepper

1 cup extra-virgin olive oil

⅓ cup capers, drained

CAPER VINAIGRETTE

In a bowl, whisk together the garlic, mustard, vinegar, salt, and pepper.
Slowly drizzle in the oil, whisking constantly. Stir in the capers. Store,
refrigerated, for up to 2 weeks.

SPICY TOMATO-BRAISED BEEF TRIPE

with poached octopus and mint aïoli

We love surf and turf, and we wanted to do a more unexpected take on the pairing. We start off with stewed tripe—or beef stomach lining—as the meaty element, inspired by our friend chef Hiro Sone's Florentine-style version. We add briny poached octopus and a dollop of brightly flavored mint aïoli. If you like octopus, this dish provides a friendly introduction to the world of offal: the tender octopus and bright, spicy flavors of the tomato stew help balance some of the inherent gaminess of the tripe. It's one of the most popular items on our menu and, no doubt, a dish your guests will talk about.

You want to think big when you're cooking this recipe—what's the point of slow-cooking anything in tiny batches? You can freeze the tripe once it's cooked and pull it out as you need it. Feel free to play around with garnishes other than the mint aïoli and octopus, swapping in fresh cilantro, chiles, and lime juice. Or follow Chef Sone's Italian-inspired lead and stir in white beans, grated cheese, and basil.

At Ox, we like to garnish this stew with crispy Sunchoke Chips (page 250) for textural contrast and crunch, but the dish is also great with grilled or toasted bread.

Tripe can be found at your trusted butcher or a Latin market. Octopus can be found at many grocery stores and fishmongers, or at Asian markets.

SERVES 4 TO 6

Tripe

2 pounds honeycomb beef tripe

½ cup unseasoned rice vinegar

Stew

2 tablespoons extra-virgin olive oil

¼ cup unsalted butter

¼ cup chopped garlic

1 teaspoon red pepper flakes

8 anchovies in oil, chopped

1 cup diced yellow onion

½ cup diced celery rib

½ cup peeled and diced carrot

1 teaspoon dried marjoram

½ teaspoon kosher salt

½ teaspoon freshly ground black pepper

2 cups white wine

4 cups canned chopped San Marzano tomatoes or other high-quality tomatoes

2 cups ¼-inch diagonally cut slices Poached Octopus (page 248)

8 leaves spearmint, thinly sliced into ribbons

4 leaves basil, thinly sliced into ribbons

1 tablespoon chopped fresh flat-leaf parsley leaves

¼ cup Mint Aïoli (page 243), for serving

To precook the tripe, combine the tripe and vinegar in a large pot and cover with water. Bring to a boil, then reduce to a simmer. Let cook, not stirring but skimming off foam and impurities occasionally, until the tripe is tender, about 90 minutes. (Test its tenderness by poking with the tip of a paring knife; the knife should feel no resistance.)

Transfer the tripe to a baking sheet and refrigerate until cool. Scrape or cut away any solidified fat. Slice into strips about ½ inch by 2 inches.

Preheat the oven to 325°F.

To prepare the stew, in a large ovenproof pot over medium heat, heat the oil and 2 tablespoons of the butter until the butter is melted. Add 2 tablespoons of the garlic, ½ teaspoon red pepper flakes, and the anchovies and stir, breaking up the anchovies with a wooden spoon. As soon as the garlic begins to brown, add the onion, celery, carrot, and marjoram; cook, stirring, until the onion begins to soften, 3 to 4 minutes. Add the tripe, season with the salt and pepper, and cook, stirring, a few minutes more. Stir in 1 cup of the wine, scraping up any browned bits from the bottom of the pan, then bring to a boil. Add the chopped tomatoes and bring to a simmer. Cover and bake for 90 minutes.

CONTINUED

Remove the pot from the oven and skim off any oil or impurities. At this point, you can cool the braised tripe or even freeze it for later use. (If frozen, allow the tripe stew to thaw completely, then resume the recipe as follows.)

Preheat the broiler.

In a small, heavy nonreactive pot over medium heat, heat the remaining 2 tablespoons butter until melted. Add the remaining 2 tablespoons garlic and remaining ½ teaspoon red pepper flakes. Cook, stirring constantly with a wooden spoon, until the garlic is toasted to a deep golden brown, 1 to 2 minutes, then stir in the remaining 1 cup wine. Cook until the wine reduces by about half, 1 to 2 minutes. Add this garlicky wine reduction to the tripe stew and bring the stew back up to a simmer. Add the sliced octopus and cook, stirring, to heat through, about 2 minutes more. Stir in the fresh herbs, then taste and adjust the seasoning, if necessary.

Divide the stew among four to six ovenproof dishes and finish each with a dollop of the mint aïoli. Broil until the aïoli is lightly browned on top, about 2 minutes, and serve.

One of us grew up eating frozen cod fillets, and the other grew up around fresh Ecuadorian ceviches and coastal California seafood. Whichever end of the spectrum your own seafood experience falls on, you'll find some exciting, approachable things to try in this chapter, which takes inspiration from the various places we've lived and cooking styles we love.

CHAPTER 2

CHILLED SEAFOOD

Having a chilled seafood section in this book is important to us because of its ties to Latin American cooking—and because we love to start a grilled meal with something light, cold, and zesty that provides a counterpoint to all the heat involved in grilling. Especially for rich or heavy meals, chilled seafood makes an ideal introduction or accompaniment. (It also doesn't hurt that our definition of a celebratory meal usually involves a glass of bubbly, and these plates are a perfect complement to—and excuse to drink—something sparkling.)

There's more to chilled seafood than the raw bar. In fact, very few items in this chapter are served raw. Some, like the Salmon Gravlax (page 74), which is cured slowly over four days, require more time and patience to "cook," but others you'll find simple and speedy. The portions are sized to whet appetites or offer fresh, vibrant accompaniment to a fire-cooked meal. Of course, though the portions are small, they don't skimp on flavor.

SHRIMP CEVICHE
with chiles, avocado, and popcorn

Making ceviche is more or less an act of pickling, and South Americans do it with gusto. You add a highly acidic liquid to seafood and wait for its proteins to become flaky and lightly "cooked." In Ecuador, ceviche joints are everywhere, and each has a signature recipe. Classic flavorings include orange and lime juice, chiles, onion, and sometimes a little hint of ketchup. We use tomato paste instead, and add lemon to amp up the acid. For heat, we go with an ají panca paste, which has a medium-plus spiciness—similar to sriracha (a good replacement if you can't find the jarred paste).

It's traditional to serve Ecuadorian ceviches with *cancha*, toasted corn nuts that add a salty, starchy contrast and give a little relief from the spice. Also traditional is popcorn, and this is our favorite garnish, because people are always happy to see popcorn on their plate.

While typically ceviche is cooked by its highly acidic liquid, it's not uncommon to precook the shrimp before combining them with the rest of the ingredients. You can buy bay shrimp already poached, or quickly cook any size peeled raw shrimp by pouring boiling water over them and removing them as soon as they start to curl up. (They'll continue to firm up in the citrus juices, so be careful not to overcook.)

SERVES 4

Ceviche Juice

1 cup fresh orange juice

¼ cup fresh lemon juice

¼ cup fresh lime juice

2 tablespoons ají panca paste (or substitute sriracha), plus up to 1 tablespoon more to taste

3 tablespoons tomato paste

1 tablespoon kosher salt

¼ teaspoon freshly ground black pepper

Sugar (optional)

Ceviche

12 ounces cooked shrimp (any size you like)

½ red onion, thinly sliced

½ red bell pepper, finely diced

2 jalapeño peppers, seeded and minced

½ cup coarsely chopped cilantro leaves

To Serve

1 ripe avocado, peeled and diced into ½-inch cubes

4 teaspoons extra-virgin olive oil

2 cups salted popcorn

To make the ceviche juice, in a nonreactive bowl, combine the orange, lemon, and lime juices; add the ají panca paste, tomato paste, salt, and pepper; whisk until smooth. Taste and adjust the seasoning, if necessary. If the orange juice isn't particularly sweet, feel free to add up to a teaspoon of sugar.

To make the ceviche, in a separate large nonreactive bowl, no more than 2 hours before serving the ceviche, combine the shrimp, onion, bell pepper, jalapeños, and cilantro. Pour in the ceviche juice. Refrigerate until ready to serve.

When ready to serve, taste the ceviche and adjust the seasoning, if necessary. Divide among four chilled serving bowls. Garnish with the avocado and drizzle with oil. Sprinkle the popcorn on top.

Clockwise, from bottom right: Shrimp Ceviche, Albacore Tuna Ceviche (page 79), Scallop Dynamite Salad (page 73), Salmon Gravlax (page 74), Mussel Poke (page 72)

MUSSEL POKE
with celery, ginger, and sesame

Poke is a traditional Hawaiian chilled seafood dish in which fish, most often tuna, is cured with a little bit of seaweed, then served tossed with sesame oil and green onion. During our five years of living and cooking in Maui, the most common way we'd eat poke was on the beach with some potato chips or crackers while waiting for our little hibachi grill to heat up.

We wanted to create a poke recipe that would represent our new home, so we steam and shell Pacific Northwest mussels and toss them in vinaigrette that has traditional poke ingredients, plus a bit of ginger and citrus. We still serve it chilled, and with taro, potato, or plantain chips.

For ease, you can prepare the vinaigrette and cook the mussels a couple of days in advance. Feel free to save the mussel juices after cooking for up to 4 days. Strain and use it to flavor a chowder or tomato sauce for pasta, or in a bloody Caesar cocktail in place of clam juice.

SERVES 6 TO 8

4 pounds fresh mussels

Poke Vinaigrette

⅓ cup toasted sesame oil

¼ cup fresh lemon juice

¼ cup unseasoned rice vinegar

5 tablespoons soy sauce (gluten-free if desired)

1 tablespoon sambal olek (or substitute diced fresh jalapeños or sriracha sauce)

½ teaspoon finely grated or minced garlic

½ teaspoon finely grated fresh ginger

2 teaspoons sugar

To Serve

½ cup macadamia nuts

½ small sweet onion, such as Walla Walla, Vidalia, or Maui, halved through the stem and thinly sliced into half-moons

5 tablespoons thinly sliced green onion (both white and green parts)

¼ cup finely diced celery

1 tablespoon toasted sesame seeds (see Note, page 246)

Sort, scrub, and rinse the mussels. Discard any with cracked shells or any whose shells don't close when you handle them. Grab ahold of the beard of each (the seaweed-like threads that are coming out of the shell), and gently pull back and forth along the length of the shell to loosen. Remove the beard by pulling it towards the hinge of the mussel until it releases; discard.

Fill a large nonreactive pot with ½ inch of water and bring to a strong simmer over medium heat. Add the mussels, cover the pot, and cook until all of the shells have opened, 4 to 7 minutes; discard any that do not open. Strain through a fine-mesh strainer, reserving the cooking liquid. Let cool, then remove the mussels from their shells. (You should have 3 to 4 cups of "meat.") Transfer to a storage container, pour the cooking liquid over the top, and refrigerate until chilled. The mussels can be stored up to 3 days.

To make the vinaigrette, in a medium bowl, whisk together the sesame oil, lemon juice, vinegar, soy sauce, sambal olek, garlic, ginger, and sugar until well combined. Set aside.

To roast the macadamia nuts, preheat the oven to 375°F. Place the raw nuts on a baking sheet and roast until light golden brown, 8 to 10 minutes. Remove and let cool to room temperature, then chop roughly.

Add the onion to the vinaigrette and let sit for 20 minutes to mellow its flavors. Strain the mussels from the liquid and place them in a serving bowl. Add half of the green onions, the celery, the vinaigrette, and the sesame seeds; toss, then taste and adjust the seasonings, if necessary. Garnish with the remaining green onion and the macadamia nuts. Serve immediately.

SCALLOP DYNAMITE SALAD
with avocado, nori, and tobiko

Maybe you've seen a variation of this dish on a sushi menu. Sometimes served raw and sometimes baked as a gratin, dynamite salads are usually seafood mixed with a spicy mayonnaise-based sauce. Argentina also has a version of this dynamite sauce called *salsa golf*, a zesty mayonnaise- and ketchup-based condiment that you might see served with chilled shrimp or other shellfish (or nowadays french fries).

We love this creamy, spicy salad because it provides a nice counterpoint to the highly acidic ceviches we serve. To riff off that classic sushi bar flavor, we garnish the salad with nori, which has a great savory flavor to complement the sweetness of the seafood.

If you can't find bay scallops, you can substitute sea scallops. Poach them until just cooked, then dice them before tossing with the rest of the ingredients.

SERVES 4

12 ounces bay scallops, cleaned

2 green onions, thinly sliced on the bias (about ⅓ cup)

2 tablespoons yuzu-flavored tobiko (or any similar tobiko)

¾ to 1 cup Dynamite Sauce (recipe follows)

1 large firm-ripe avocado, peeled and diced into ½-inch cubes

Flaked sea salt

Freshly ground white pepper

½ sheet nori, cut into 1-inch strips and thinly sliced

Fill a medium pot two-thirds full with lightly salted water and bring to a boil. Meanwhile, set an ice water bath next to the stove. Add the scallops to the boiling water and remove the pot from the heat. Let sit for 15 seconds, then remove the scallops from the water and transfer to the ice bath to chill. Drain, then blot the scallops dry with a paper towel.

In a bowl, combine the chilled scallops, green onions, and tobiko. Drizzle with about ¾ cup of the dynamite sauce and toss gently to combine. Taste, then add more sauce, if desired. Divide among four chilled serving bowls.

Season the avocado with a light sprinkling of salt and white pepper, then divide among the serving bowls. Garnish with the nori strips.

DYNAMITE SAUCE

MAKES 1 CUP

3 to 4 fresh fresno chiles, stemmed, seeded, and coarsely chopped

¾ cup mayonnaise, homemade (page 243) or store-bought

1 tablespoon soy sauce (gluten-free if desired)

1 tablespoon yuzu juice (or substitute fresh lime juice)

In a blender, combine half the chiles, the mayonnaise, soy sauce, and yuzu juice. Puree on high speed until smooth, then taste for spiciness. If your fresno chiles are mild or you want more spice, add the rest of the chiles, then puree again until smooth. Strain through a fine-mesh strainer or chinois and refrigerate until ready to use (or for up to 4 days).

SALMON GRAVLAX

with orange-chile oil, cucumber, and shiso

We have been huge fans of DIY food preservation for a long time. We love the idea that you can create something nourishing, delicious, beautiful, and long-lasting by preserving something that might otherwise have a short shelf life. Gravlax was once prepared in Scandinavia by curing the fish with salt, fermenting it, and often burying it beneath the ground for months. Our recipe keeps alive parts of that age-old technique, by substituting your refrigerator for that hole in the ground and lightly salt-curing the salmon.

The somewhat slow preserving process (most of which is hands-off time in the fridge) concentrates the flavors of fresh fish and, in this case, infuses it with bright, fresh herb flavor. Almost any seasoning works well with gravlax, from dill or fennel to cumin, coriander, smoked paprika, or smoke itself. You can even substitute miso for some of the salt. At the end, when much of the moisture has dripped away, the fish becomes a chewy, candied jewel.

Serve the finished gravlax on a bagel with cream cheese, or as we have here, as a starter with chilled cucumber and a lightly spicy vinaigrette.

Cut a slice off the top and bottom of the orange so it lies flat on your cutting board. Slice away the skin and pith in pieces. Slice in between each membrane—as close to the membranes as possible—to remove the segments of fruit.

In a large bowl, combine the orange segments, gravlax, cucumber, shiso, dill, chives, vinaigrette, and orange-chile oil. Taste and adjust the seasoning, if necessary. Serve within 30 minutes to prevent the gravlax from cooking in the vinaigrette.

Note Shiso, an Asian herb that tastes like a basil-mint-cinnamon hybrid, is available at most Japanese markets near the fish section. If you can't find it, use equal amounts of basil and mint.

SERVES 4

2 oranges

6 ounces Cured Salmon Gravlax (recipe follows), thinly sliced into 2-inch-long pieces

2 cups peeled and diced English cucumber (½-inch cubes) (from about 1 large cucumber)

4 leaves shiso (see Note), halved and very thinly sliced

1 tablespoon chopped fresh dill

¼ cup thinly sliced chives

½ cup Citrus-Soy Vinaigrette (page 244)

3 tablespoons Orange-Chile Oil (page 244)

4 cups kosher salt

3 cups sugar

4 garlic cloves, finely grated or minced

4 ounces dill fronds and stems (about 6 bunches), finely chopped

4 ounces fennel fronds and stems (from about 1 bulb fennel), finely chopped

Zest of 4 lemons, peeled into wide strips (do not include the pith) and finely chopped

Zest of 2 oranges, peeled into wide strips (do not include the pith) and finely chopped

Zest of 2 grapefruits, peeled into wide strips (do not include the pith) and finely chopped

2 tablespoons black peppercorns

12 bay leaves

5 pounds wild skin-on salmon fillet, pin bones removed

CURED SALMON GRAVLAX

In a small bowl, combine the salt, sugar, and garlic. In a separate bowl, combine the dill, fennel, and citrus zests; mix well.

In a spice grinder, grind the peppercorns and bay leaves. (If the bay leaves do not break down, add a pinch of salt and try again.) Add to the salt-sugar mixture and toss well with your fingers. Pour over the herbs and citrus and toss well again, using your fingers to break up and disperse the flavorings.

Using a sharp knife, score the salmon skin, making 2- to 3-inch-long, ¼-inch-deep cuts every 3 inches.

Measure out 5 feet of cheesecloth and lay out as much as you can on a clean table. (The steps that follow can get sticky, but the mess will be easy to clean.) Starting about 10 inches from one end, lay half the salt mixture onto the cheesecloth in the shape of the salmon fillet. Place the salmon on top, skin side down, pressing gently into the salt mixture to coat. Spread the other half of the salt mixture on top of the fillet, pressing gently to help it adhere. Fold the 10 inches of cheesecloth over the salmon to cover, then do the same with the sides and edges of the cheesecloth. Place one hand under each end of the salmon. In one smooth, quick motion, turn the fish from one side over to the other, wrapping it tightly in the cheesecloth. Repeat, tightening the cloth with each roll, until the fillet is completely wrapped.

Set a drying rack on a rimmed baking sheet and place the fish on it. Cover with another baking sheet. Top with a heavy weight (such as a filled 1-gallon milk jug) and refrigerate for 4 days.

Remove the bundle, being mindful of any juices that have dripped into the pan. Unwrap the fish and rinse with cold water (you may want to do this over a sink with a drain stopper to catch the spices); pat dry.

To serve, trim away any skin and bloodline, then thinly slice against the grain to create narrow strips. Extra portions can be tightly sealed in plastic wrap, then stored in the refrigerator for up to 5 days or in the freezer for up to 1 month.

POACHED SQUID AND OCTOPUS SALAD
with fennel, orange, and celeriac

If the idea of cooking octopus at home sounds intimidating, rest assured: using the frozen version (available in many grocery stores) is not only easy but ideal. The process of freezing and thawing can help tenderize the octopus. Plus, you can cook it up to 4 days in advance and store it in its poaching liquid until serving time.

We garnish this salad with a light drizzle of squid ink puree because it adds an additional essence of the sea, and also because it's just downright beautiful in its appearance. Squid ink is a specialty item, but your fish purveyors should carry it. Alone, the flavor can be pretty strong, so we sauté it with garlic and onions in olive oil, then simmer it with a little white wine and water before using. That said, this component may be omitted if the squid ink is hard to come by.

Big, fresh flavors from fennel and orange, plus the heat from pickled chiles, really complement the fresh briny seafood, and the addition of poached celeriac adds the texture and flavor of artichoke heart. Feel free to serve it as a party dish or turn it into a lunch by serving it with grilled bread or potato chips.

SERVES 6

Squid and Octopus Salad

1 medium-large celeriac

1 tablespoon extra-virgin olive oil

1 lemon, halved

12 ounces cleaned squid rings and tentacles, large tentacles halved vertically

8 ounces Poached Octopus (page 248)

1 cup diced celery (¼-inch pieces)

¾ cup diced fennel bulb (¼-inch pieces)

¼ cup chopped pickled red peppers, such as Mama Lil's Mildly Spicy Peppers in Olive Oil

4 basil leaves, thinly sliced

Spanish Croutons

1 clove garlic, lightly smashed

2 tablespoons extra-virgin olive oil

1 cup cubed crustless baguette or levain bread (¼-inch pieces)

Pinch kosher salt

¼ teaspoon smoked sweet Spanish paprika (also called pimentón dulce)

Dressing and Garnishes

1 cup Orange-Sherry Vinaigrette (recipe follows)

¼ cup thinly sliced chives

1 tablespoon Squid Ink Puree (recipe follows) (optional)

To prepare the salad, peel the celeriac by cutting off both the top and root end, then shaving away the skin with a chef's knife. Slice crosswise into six rounds ½ to ¾ inch thick; transfer to a small pot. Add water to cover plus the oil; season with about 1 tablespoon salt. Reduce the heat to low and cover the celeriac with a round of parchment paper to keep it submerged. Simmer until cooked through and tender when poked with the tip of a knife, about 20 minutes. Let cool in its cooking liquid and refrigerate until ready to serve.

Meanwhile, fill a small pot with 8 cups water; bring to a boil. Season with a few tablespoons of salt and squeeze the juice of both lemon halves through a strainer into the pot; drop the lemon halves into the pot. Lower the heat to bring the mixture to a simmer. Add the squid and poach until just cooked through, 45 to 60 seconds. Remove with a spider skimmer or slotted spoon and transfer to a mixing bowl to cool; refrigerate until chilled.

Preheat the oven to 325°F. Line a plate or baking sheet with paper towels.

To make the croutons, warm an ovenproof sauté pan over medium heat. Add the garlic and oil and cook until the garlic is lightly browned on one side, about 2 minutes. Flip the garlic, then add the bread cubes to the pan. Turn the heat to low and cook the bread, stirring occasionally, until it starts to toast, about 5 minutes.

CONTINUED

Transfer the pan to the oven and bake, stirring occasionally and checking often to prevent burning, until the croutons are toasted evenly on all sides, 6 to 8 minutes. Remove from the oven, sprinkle with the salt and paprika, and stir well. Transfer the croutons to the lined plate. Remove and discard (or eat) the garlic. Let the croutons cool to room temperature before serving.

To finish the salad, slice the poached octopus tentacles into ¼-inch-thick coins. Add to the bowl with the squid. Add the celery, fennel, pickled peppers, and basil. Drizzle with the vinaigrette; toss well to combine. Taste and adjust the seasoning, if necessary.

To serve, place one disk of chilled celeriac in the middle of each serving plate. Divide the seafood salad among the plates, spooning it on top of the celeriac. Garnish each with chives, the Spanish croutons, and a drizzle of the squid ink puree.

ORANGE-SHERRY VINAIGRETTE

MAKES 1½ CUPS

Finely grated zest of ½ orange

½ cup fresh orange juice

¼ cup sherry vinegar

1½ teaspoons kosher salt

¼ teaspoon freshly ground black pepper

¾ cups extra-virgin olive oil

In a bowl, combine the orange zest and juice, vinegar, salt, pepper, and oil; whisk until well blended. Refrigerate for up to 2 weeks.

SQUID INK PUREE

MAKES ABOUT 3 CUPS

3 tablespoons extra-virgin olive oil

1 teaspoon chopped garlic

1 small white or yellow onion, minced

1 cup white wine

1 (17.5-ounce) jar squid ink

½ cup water

Kosher salt

In a small saucepan over medium heat, combine the oil and garlic and cook until the garlic is lightly browned, about 1 minute. Add the onion and cook, stirring occasionally, until softened slightly, about 2 minutes more. Add the wine, stirring to deglaze the pan, and bring to a simmer. Add the squid ink to the pot, then pour the water into the empty ink container; swirl to remove any remaining ink, and add the water mixture to the pan. Bring to a simmer and let cook for 3 to 4 minutes to allow the flavors to blend. Taste and season with salt, if needed.

Transfer the mixture to a blender and puree. Strain through a fine-mesh strainer. Refrigerate what you plan to use in the next several days, and freeze the remainder for later use.

ALBACORE TUNA CEVICHE
with yuzu, white soy, and tomato

When it's albacore tuna season here in the Pacific Northwest, from June through October, everyone goes crazy for it. Served cold on a hot day, it totally hits the spot. We love albacore because the texture and density of the fish gives it a rich mouthfeel, even though it's fairly lean. Albacore is also sustainable right now, and when it comes into season, there is so much available that you can buy superhigh-quality fish quite inexpensively. But really, any sushi-grade tuna will do.

We serve big chunks of it, and use white soy sauce to keep the color from going murky (although the flavor is similar to that of classic soy sauce). We also add fish sauce for an extra savory boost.

Be aware that you should serve this within 10 minutes of preparing it if you appreciate the texture of raw or very lightly cooked tuna, as we do. Within this amount of time, the fish will straddle the line between being a crudo (raw by definition) and a ceviche. Marinate it any longer and the effects of the acidity will render it a true ceviche.

To make the ceviche juice, in a large bowl, combine the ají amarillo paste, soy sauce, lime juice, yuzu juice, fish sauce, and sugar; whisk to combine. Add the albacore, tomatoes, cucumber, cilantro, onion, oil, and spearmint; season with salt to taste, then stir well to combine. Serve immediately.

SERVES 4

Yuzu-Soy Ceviche Juice

2 tablespoons ají amarillo paste (or substitute ají panca paste for a spicier kick, see page 79)

¼ cup white soy sauce (or substitute classic or gluten-free soy sauce)

6 tablespoons fresh lime juice

2 tablespoons yuzu juice

2 tablespoons fish sauce

2 teaspoons sugar

Albacore Ceviche

12 ounces fresh albacore tuna loin, cut into 1-inch cubes (or substitute any sushi-grade tuna)

1 cup halved cherry or grape tomatoes

1 cup peeled and diced English cucumber (½-inch pieces)

⅓ cup packed fresh cilantro leaves

¼ sweet onion, such as Maui, Walla Walla or Vidalia, very thinly sliced

2 tablespoons extra-virgin olive oil

4 spearmint leaves, very thinly sliced

Kosher salt

PART 2 **FROM THE GRILL**

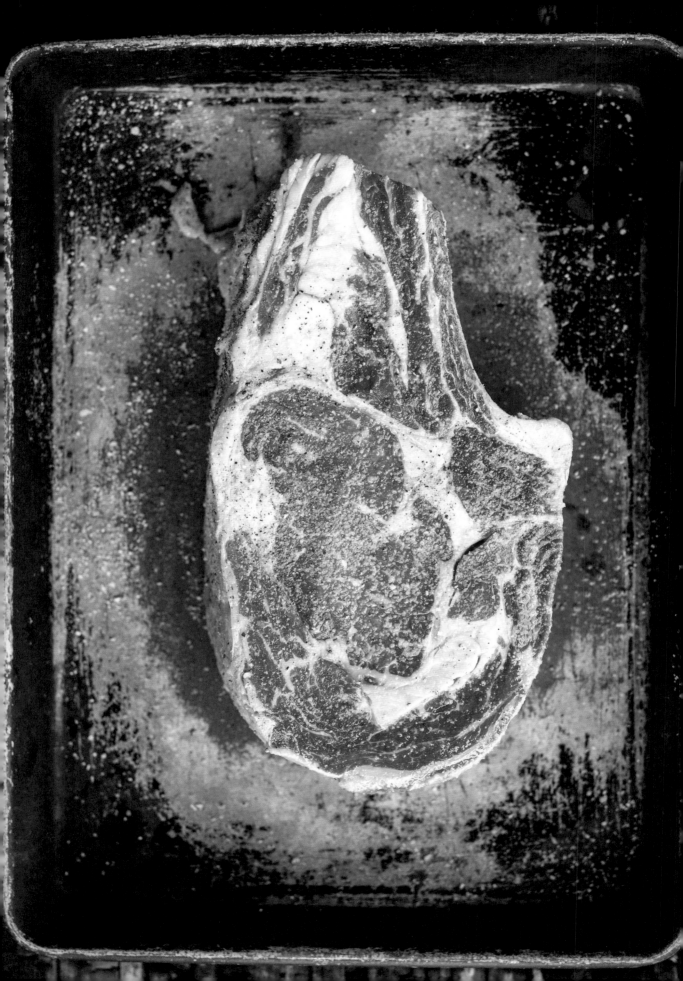

Meat is utterly central to the Argentinian diet. And beyond that, raising meat and cooking it at gatherings are defining parts of the culture. During our travels in Argentina, we couldn't help but notice the ubiquity of grilled beef—perched all over grills from fine dining restaurants to roadside stops, and at the center of every meal.

What left an even deeper impression on us was the harmony and connection between the land and animals and the butchers and cooks. In the countryside, vast pastures produce what seem to be the happiest cattle, as well as inspire the most wonderful, spontaneous cooking. Locals build small fires with whatever wood is around, then hoist up the meat to be grilled or roasted to perfection.

At our restaurant and at home, we try to be thoughtful about the way we use meat. We do our best to source it from places that treat the animals well and raise them healthfully, and to actually think about the meat we prepare from start to finish. Not every cut merits the same seasoning, technique, or time. Is it a leaner cut that needs quick searing at high temperatures and some richer accompaniments? Is it a stronger-flavored meat that can stand up to equally pungent herbs and flavorings? Will what we add to the dish enhance the grilled meat or detract from it? After all, a recipe is equal parts ingredients and how you treat them.

CHAPTER 3 GRILLED MEATS

You can't really have a restaurant that serves fire-cooked meats without some fan favorites on the menu like rib-eye steaks and pork chops. And we do love these cuts. But we also like to buy and cook cuts that aren't as high in demand or common to find on menus. An animal only has so many tenderloins and ribs, after all, so working with the other cuts is really a way to honor that animal. It also challenges us as chefs: what fun it is to hear our guests say "Wow!" to something they had never tried before.

One thing that's interesting about meat is that you really will never eat the same piece twice. The animals differ subtly, and at times greatly, from farm to farm and diet to diet, and at times even the same cut can differ from one end of the animal to the other. For example, the fat patterns and content of a rib-eye at the shoulder end of the animal will be different from those at its tail end. When you incorporate meats into a meal and how much meat you serve can also vary each time you come to the table. But using the techniques in this chapter, you can achieve consistency in how meats turn out and the level of flavor you impart to them.

GRILLED BEEF SKIRT STEAK
with onion marinade

This is one of those recipes that will make you look like an incredible cook for very little effort. Because of skirt steak's relatively loose grain, it soaks up marinade incredibly well and is one of the few meats we ever marinate before grilling.

There are a few tricks, though, to making skirt steak the best it can be. First, you want to transfer the meat straight from the refrigerator to the grill. This will prevent the inside from overcooking by the time the outside is well seared. Second, honor the variations in a skirt steak's thickness. From end to end, there will be thicker parts requiring more prolonged heat, and you should adjust the placement and time on the grill accordingly. Third, ideally you should serve skirt steak somewhere between medium-rare and medium. At rare, the muscle fibers haven't had their full chance to break down, and the meat can be slightly chewy. And finally, always slice skirt steak against the grain; the lines of muscle fiber are particularly easy to find on this cut (they run across the width of the steak).

To make the onion marinade, combine the onion, garlic, ¼ cup of the oil, and water in a blender; blend until smooth. Put the skirt steak in a large resealable plastic bag or baking dish and pour in the onion mixture, coating both sides. Cover or wrap the meat well so the onion scent does not permeate your refrigerator; chill for at least 4 hours and up to 24 hours.

Prepare a grill to medium-high heat.

Remove the steak from the marinade and season both sides with the kosher salt and pepper. Transfer the meat to the grill and let cook until one side is well seared, 3 minutes. Flip and cook for 2 minutes more, for rare to medium-rare. At this point, remove the steak from the grill and let rest for 2 minutes to allow the carryover heat to give it a more even doneness. Finally, return the steak to the grill and cook for 1 minute more per side (this guarantees this thin cut of steak will be served hot). (Add another minute of cooking on the second side for medium doneness.) Remove the skirt steak from the grill and let rest 1 to 2 minutes before slicing and serving.

Cut each steak with the grain into three sections. Turn each piece to slice against the grain at a 45-degree angle. Slice into ¼-inch pieces on a slight bias against the grain. You should get about 5 slices per cut piece, about 15 slices total. Transfer the meat to a warmed plate. Garnish with the remaining 1 tablespoon oil and smoked sea salt and serve with the chimichurri.

SERVES 4

Onion Marinade

½ medium yellow onion, coarsely chopped

1 small garlic clove, peeled

¼ cup plus 1 tablespoon extra-virgin olive oil

2 tablespoons water

Skirt Steak

2 pounds skirt steak, silver skin trimmed away

1 teaspoon kosher salt

¼ teaspoon freshly ground black pepper

Smoked sea salt, homemade (page 242) or store-bought, for finishing

Chimichurri (page 27), for serving (optional)

GRILLED BONE-IN BEEF RIB-EYE STEAK
with "Black Gold"

Grilling rib-eye steak this way is an act of love: this is a splurge cut that takes a while to cook, so it's worth spending the extra time and effort to season it ahead of time, baste it while it grills, and really nurse the searing of the outside to get a deeply caramelized exterior and juicy, tender interior. Ideally, you want to season a large steak heavily at least 2 hours before cooking. This allows the flavorings to penetrate more deeply into the flesh, so that they won't fully fall away as the fat renders on the grill. To be sure the pieces are evenly seasoned, we garnish with flaky finishing salt after cooking.

Practice makes perfect when it comes to checking a rib-eye for doneness, but you can use our timing below as a reliable starting point. With a steak as thick as this recipe calls for (or any steak thicker than 1¼ inches), bring the meat to room temperature before grilling to help the heat penetrate through. (For steaks any thinner, we take them straight from the fridge to the grill.) Keep in mind that the parts nearest the bone typically will be the most rare, and the edges may cook more quickly. We always feel that the bone should be the chef's treat—it's the source of the tastiest meat.

At least 2 hours, or up to 24 hours, before cooking, rub the rib-eye with the oil and season lightly with the salt and pepper. Store in the refrigerator until 1 hour before serving; let come to room temperature.

Prepare a grill to medium-high heat.

Remove the rib eye and season again with kosher salt and pepper. Transfer to the grill and cook on one side until well caramelized, 5 to 8 minutes. If flare-ups happen, move the rib-eye to a new area of the grill to avoid the flames. Begin basting. Flip the steak and repeat on the other side for rare doneness. For medium-rare doneness, flip the steak back over to the first side and cook an additional 3 minutes. For medium doneness, flip again and cook 3 minutes more.

Transfer the steak to a platter or cutting board and let rest for 5 to 8 minutes before slicing and serving. Brush with a fresh tablespoonful of "Black Gold," and sprinkle with sea salt.

SERVES 2 TO 4

1 (2¼-pound) bone-in beef rib-eye steak

2 tablespoons extra-virgin olive oil

Kosher salt and freshly ground black pepper

¼ cup "Black Gold" (page 15), for basting

Flaked sea salt, for garnishing

GRILLED FLANKEN-STYLE BEEF SHORT RIBS

The flanken-style rib is a very traditional cut of beef that you see all over the grills of Latin America. As you probably know if you've ever eaten braised short ribs, they're fatty, rich, and intensely flavored. When they're cooked on the grill, the meat develops a wonderful intensity but without the gelatinous consistency and very rich sauce. The result is a bit chewier; the meat takes more effort to eat but in a satisfying way. The teeth act as juicers to extract every last drop of flavor.

There are a few differences between grilling and serving a short rib versus grilling and serving a steak. First, you don't need to serve as much short rib as you do steak. And second, you want to take your time when grilling. Cook short ribs slowly and at low temperatures, taking the doneness to medium-well in order to break down some of the tough connective tissue and render some of the fat.

This is a great cut for basting with "Black Gold" (page 15) in order to continuously impart more flavor while grilling.

At least 2 hours or up to 24 hours ahead, rub the short ribs with ¼ cup of the oil and season with kosher salt and pepper; refrigerate until ready to grill.

Prepare a grill to medium-low heat.

Remove the short ribs from the refrigerator and apply another 2 tablespoons of the oil and more kosher salt and pepper. Transfer the ribs to the grill and cook low and slow until well caramelized on one side, about 15 minutes. If flare-ups happen, move the ribs to another area of the grill to avoid the flames. Flip and repeat on the other side. (If you will be basting the meat with "Black Gold," this is a good time to start.) The ribs should be cooked to at least a medium-plus temperature (the meat and tendon should be shrunken and pulling away from the bone, and the outer layer should be completely caramelized). Transfer to the cooler edge of the grill and let rest for about 4 minutes before serving. Serve whole, or cut between the small bones to separate the ribs. Garnish with the remaining 2 tablespoons oil and sea salt to taste.

SERVES 4

3 pounds flanken-style (or cross-cut) beef short ribs, cut to 1-inch thickness (across the bone)

½ cup extra-virgin olive oil, plus more for garnishing

Kosher salt and freshly ground black pepper

1 cup "Black Gold" (page 15), for basting (optional)

Flaked sea salt, for garnishing

GRILLED VEAL CHOPS
with chanterelle mushroom stroganoff

Some people love veal for its flavor and tenderness and the fact that it's a little less fatty than cuts like a beef rib-eye. Others disdain it for being a little less intense in flavor than beef. We like to pair something with it that adds to the meat's impact without diminishing its delicateness.

Our answer is a stroganoff sauce, a version that is light-bodied, satisfying, and made from scratch. The sauce calls for veal stock, which is delicious when it's homemade but also something you can buy if in a hurry, as well as shallot and madeira for sweetness and tang. The sauce is intentionally thin, ideal for keeping the dish from becoming too rich (and for potentially serving over some egg noodles). Here it's made with golden chanterelles, but morels would be a delicious seasonal alternative, and button or shiitake mushrooms also work perfectly well.

Keep in mind that, because of its leanness, veal tends to dry out if overcooked. But if you play your cards right atop the grill, it's one of the most tender meats you can buy.

SERVES 4

Chanterelle Mushroom Stroganoff

3 tablespoons unsalted butter

½ cup minced shallots

1 pound chanterelle mushrooms

Kosher salt and freshly ground black pepper

1 cup madeira (or substitute marsala)

2 teaspoons fresh thyme leaves

3 cups brown veal or beef stock, homemade (page 245) or store-bought

1 cup heavy cream or crème fraîche

Grilled Veal Chops

4 (12-ounce) bone-in veal chops

2 tablespoons extra-virgin olive oil

2 tablespoons kosher salt

2 teaspoons freshly ground black pepper

¼ cup dill sprigs, for garnish

To make the stroganoff, in a medium-large nonreactive saucepan over medium-high heat, melt the butter. Add the shallots and cook, stirring with a wooden spoon, until they just begin to brown in places, 2 to 3 minutes. Stir in the chanterelles and cook for a couple of minutes; season with salt and pepper. If the mushrooms continue to release considerable moisture, continue to cook, stirring occasionally, until all the moisture has evaporated and they begin to sizzle in the butter. Add the madeira and decrease the heat to maintain a simmer. Add the thyme leaves and cook until the madeira is reduced by about two-thirds, about 5 minutes. Add the veal stock and continue to cook until reduced by half, 12 to 15 minutes more. Stir in the cream. Bring the sauce to a simmer and cook for 2 minutes more. Taste and adjust the seasoning, if necessary. Keep warm until ready to serve.

To grill the veal chops, prepare a grill to medium-high heat.

Remove the chops from the refrigerator and brush with oil; season with salt and pepper. Grill until the first side turns golden brown, 4 to 5 minutes. Flip the chops and repeat on the other side. The veal chops should be close to the desired doneness (medium). Turn the chops so that they are vertical on the grill and facing bone side down (you may need to lean the chops on each other to keep them standing), and cook for 1 to 2 minutes more. Flip chops so the bone is facing up and repeat.

Transfer the veal to four plates and let rest for about 4 minutes. Drizzle with the stroganoff sauce, making sure to distribute the chanterelles among the servings, and garnish with the dill.

GRILL-ROASTED VEAL SWEETBREADS

with spring crudités and anchoïade

In Argentina and Uruguay, grilled sweetbreads is one of the most common, unpretentious dishes there is. Every restaurant with a *parrilla* serves its own smoky grilled version. Our take features the sweetbreads as an embellishment to a plate of baby vegetable crudités for a more refined dish, but the elements couldn't be more rustic.

Naturally tender, flavorful, and rich, veal sweetbreads (technically, the thymus and pancreas of a calf) need very little done to them, but while grilling, you can baste them with "Black Gold" (page 15) or Herbed Salmuera (page 245) for added flavor. As with any dish, you want contrast and variety when serving sweetbreads. The crisp spring vegetables are just that, providing an antidote to the offal's natural richness. A garlicky, vinegary anchoïade—a Provençal anchovy dip that goes great with grilled meats and chilled vegetables alike—delivers juiciness and brightness.

You can scale this dish up and serve it for a party on a large platter. Use any leftovers the next day to make a really good tossed salad.

SERVES 4

1 pound veal sweetbreads, soaked overnight in ice water

2 tablespoons extra-virgin olive oil

Kosher salt and freshly ground black pepper

4 breakfast radishes, trimmed

8 baby new potatoes

4 baby carrots, trimmed and peeled

4 baby artichokes, trimmed, stems peeled

24 small cauliflower florets

8 snap peas or snow peas, stemmed, fibrous strings peeled away

12 thin asparagus spears, woody stems snapped off

2 hard-boiled eggs
(see Note, page 149)

12 green olives, such as Castelvetrano and/or Lucques

4 caper berries

1 cup Anchoïade (recipe follows)

Prepare a grill to medium-low heat.

Remove the sweetbreads from the water and pat dry. Drizzle with oil and season generously with salt and pepper. Transfer the sweetbreads to the grill. Let cook until deep golden brown on one side, 20 to 25 minutes. (If they cook too quickly or are charring, move to a cooler section of the grill.) Flip and repeat on the other side. Remove and let rest for 4 to 5 minutes.

Meanwhile, blanch those vegetables that you prefer to eat cooked rather than raw (we blanch the potatoes, artichokes, cauliflower, and asparagus). Bring a medium pot of water to a boil over high heat and set a bowl of ice water next to the stove. Season the boiling water with a small fistful of salt (2 to 3 tablespoons) and add the vegetables, one kind at a time, until they are just cooked through to your liking. Using a slotted spoon, quickly transfer them to the ice water to stop the cooking; drain and pat dry if needed.

Slice the sweetbreads into ½-inch-thick medallions. Divide among four plates or serve on one large platter. Surround the sweetbreads with the vegetables, eggs, olives, and caper berries, and drizzle with the anchoïade. Serve any remaining anchoïade on the side for dipping.

MAKES ABOUT 1½ CUPS

1 (2-ounce) tin oil-packed anchovy fillets

2 tablespoons red wine vinegar

1 large clove garlic

½ teaspoon freshly ground black pepper

1 cup extra-virgin olive oil

ANCHOÏADE

In a food processor or blender, combine the anchovies, vinegar, garlic, and pepper; pulse to chop. Slowly stream in the oil and continue processing. Transfer to a bowl and serve at room temperature or store, covered, in the refrigerator for up to 1 week. To serve, bring to room temperature.

GRILLED MAPLE-BRINED PORK CHOPS

Even if you buy the most expensive, well-raised, and fanciest butcher pork chop there is, it is dangerously easy to end up with a dry, flavorless piece of meat. We always brine ours before grilling, because a brine locks in the juiciness even when the chops are cooked to a medium or medium-well doneness.

Other secrets to juiciness are buying bone-in chops—because the bone can help protect the meat from overcooking—and choosing loin parts that are as close to the shoulder end of the animal as possible. As you move in that direction, the chops tend to have more fat mixed with their meat, which typically leads to more flavor and overall moisture.

Our brine uses maple syrup, which, aside from being delicious with pork and thyme and all the other flavors in this dish, helps the meat caramelize on the outside while it grills.

Arrange the pork chops in a baking dish, plastic storage container, or 1-gallon plastic bag so that they fit snugly; pour the maple brine over them to cover completely. Cover and refrigerate for at least 24 hours and ideally up to 48 hours.

Remove the pork chops from the brine and discard the brine.

Prepare a grill to medium-high heat.

Rub or brush the pork chops with oil and season with salt and pepper, being sure to season the bones as well. Cook on the grill, undisturbed, just long enough for the pork to pick up some color and grill marks, 4 to 5 minutes for medium doneness. Flip and repeat on the other flat side. (If flare-ups happen during this phase of cooking, shift the chops to an area that's not flaring up, then shift back after the flames subside.) Shift the pork chops to a cooler portion of the grill. Turn each onto its rounded, fatty edge, either propping the chops against each other to cook them all together or taking turns holding them up with tongs. Cook until the fatty edge is golden and crispy, about 3 minutes, then repeat the same technique on the other narrow side (the bone side).

Test for doneness by checking the firmness of the meat next to the bone. If it still has some give at the bone but is firmer around the edges, then it's ready to come off the grill. Remove and let rest for 4 to 5 minutes before serving. Drizzle lightly with maple syrup, if desired.

SERVES 4

4 (14- to 16-ounce) bone-in pork loin chops (each about 1½ inches thick)

Maple Brine (page 246)

2 tablespoons extra-virgin olive oil

Kosher salt and freshly ground black pepper

Maple syrup, preferably Grade B, for drizzling (optional)

GRILLED CHORIZO SAUSAGES

During our travels in Argentina, we noticed that "chorizo" is used as a generic name for sausage that ranges very much in flavor and ingredients. Some are mild with a simple base of beef, pork fat, and salt, while others are heavily spiced and seasoned. Ours combines beef and pork like the classic, as well as garlic, oregano, and various types of chile. We give ours a little Italian influence and flavor by adding toasted fennel seed, and we balance out the spiciness with a touch of maple syrup. Our spice mixture makes quite a bit more than you will need, but if you make it once and store it, you can use it as a spice on so many dishes. Try sprinkling the chorizo spice on burgers, shrimp, pork chops, or fish before grilling, or use it as a blackening spice before sautéing or roasting any meat.

Grinding your own meat is fun and the results are delicious, but you can also buy it preground and mix in the seasonings at home. If stuffing it into casings seems daunting, form the meat into patties, like burgers, for grilling. Extras keep perfectly well in the freezer.

MAKES 25 TO 30 LINKS

2½ pounds pork shoulder, cut into 1-inch cubes (or whatever size fits through your meat grinder)

1 pound beef chuck, cut into 1-inch cubes

1 pound pork fatback, cut into 1-inch cubes

2 tablespoons kosher salt

4.5 grams (about ¾ teaspoon) pink salt (also known as Insta Cure No. 1 or sodium nitrite) (optional, see Note)

1 teaspoon finely grated or minced garlic

7 tablespoons Chorizo Spice (recipe follows)

⅓ cup red wine

3 tablespoons maple syrup, preferably Grade B

About 10 feet of hog casings, rinsed

Extra-virgin olive oil, for grilling

Making sure that the meat stays very cold while you work with it, separate the leaner-looking meat from the fattier meat and the fatback. In the bowl of a standing mixer, toss the lean meat with the kosher salt, pink salt, garlic, and chorizo spice; refrigerate for at least 8 hours and up to 24 hours. (The fattier meat and fatback stays in the refrigerator.)

Chill the components of a meat grinder in the refrigerator or freezer before grinding the meat. Make sure the meat mixture is also as cold as possible without being frozen. Grind all the lean meat, then return to the bowl and refrigerate. Then grind all of the fat and fattier meat pieces together.

Combine the lean, seasoned meat with the wine and maple syrup. Using the stand mixer with the paddle attachment, beat on medium speed for 5 minutes. Add the fatty mixture and beat just until well incorporated, about 1 minute.

In a skillet, fry up a small patty of the sausage mixture in order to taste it; adjust any seasonings if necessary and remix just long enough to incorporate any additions.

Thread the hog casings onto a sausage stuffer, leaving a small length of casing untied at the end of the tube so air can escape. Fill the canister with the sausage mixture and pack it in, a handful at a time, pressing out the air bubbles with your fingers to be sure there is very little air packed in with the sausage. Pipe the meat into the casings, coiling it into one large coil on a baking sheet as you work. Afterward, section off the sausages into 5- or 6-inch links, twisting one link in one direction, then the next in the opposite direction, to seal the ends. For best results, refrigerate for 2 days before cooking (though these can be stored up to 5 days in the refrigerator or for 1 month in the freezer). This helps give the casing a better snap, and dries out the sausage slightly to help prevent its contents from exploding during cooking.

When ready to serve, prepare a grill to medium heat and be sure to carefully oil the grate.

Lightly oil the sausages and transfer to the grill; let cook until grill marks have formed on one side, 3 to 5 minutes. Turn and repeat on the other side. Transfer to a cooler section of the grill and cook until the sausages feel firm and the meat is cooked through, 2 to 3 minutes more. Remove from the grill and let rest for 2 to 3 minutes before serving or slicing.

Note The pink salt used as a preservative in this recipe is optional. Since our sausages are fresh—not smoked or hung at temperatures above refrigeration level—it is not required. Curing salt is antimicrobial, enhances flavor, and it preserves the pink color in the sausage to keep it from turning grayish when cooked. But curing salt is also potentially toxic if not handled within the proper ratios. If you are going to use it, be sure to weigh out the measurement.

Sausage Making Tips

- Make sure there is plenty of water in the casing to help glide the casing easily over the stem of the machine and avoid tearing or sticking.

- Each link should be full but not too tightly packed. Remember, the casing will naturally attach itself to the meat while it sits in your refrigerator, so while it shouldn't be saggy, it doesn't have to be perfectly tight and fitted.

- To seal off the links while they're still strung together, twist one link clockwise, then spin the next link counterclockwise to seal. This will prevent them from coming undone.

- If you notice any major air pockets in the links once they're sealed off, poke them with a pin. The casing will seal itself back up.

CHORIZO SPICE

MAKES ABOUT 4 CUPS

1½ cups ground ancho chile

¾ cup Hungarian sweet paprika

⅓ cup smoked sweet Spanish paprika (also called pimentón dulce)

¼ cup onion powder

¼ cup dried marjoram

¼ cup toasted fennel seed

¼ cup cayenne pepper

¼ cup ají amarillo powder (see Note, page 34)

3 tablespoons dried oregano

3 tablespoons freshly ground black pepper

1 teaspoon freshly grated nutmeg

In a small bowl or medium jar, combine the ancho, both paprikas, the onion powder, marjoram, fennel seed, cayenne, ají chile, oregano, black pepper, and nutmeg; stir well to blend. The spice mix can be stored in an airtight container for up to 6 months.

GRILLED MORCILLA SAUSAGES

Another sausage that is ubiquitous around Argentina, Uruguay, and other parts of South America, traditional morcilla (or blood sausage) has less of the crumbly, meaty texture than might come to mind when you think of sausage. Instead, the filling is wetter, jammier, and all-around sweeter—almost like a pudding inside a casing—and the pork blood is bulked up with grains or potatoes, onions or apples, or nuts and dried fruits. For ours, we went with more of a meaty consistency, and cherry-picked all our favorite spices and seasonings from European and South American blood sausages. We mirror the South American version in our use of nuts, sweet spices, and raisins, but we add savory spices for balance.

This morcilla is delicious served on a roll with chimichurri (page 27); in Argentina this style of sandwich is called a *morcipán*. Or you can serve it simply with Dijon mustard, mashed potatoes, and roasted or grilled apples, playing off the sausages' sweetness.

MAKES 20 TO 25 LINKS

2 tablespoons neutral-flavored vegetable oil

4 cups diced yellow onions

About 2 cups water

2½ pounds pork shoulder, cut into 1-inch cubes (or whatever size fits through your meat grinder)

¼ cup plus 2 tablespoons Morcilla Spice (recipe follows)

3 tablespoons kosher salt

5 grams (about 1 teaspoon) pink salt (see Note, page 97)

1 pound pork fatback, cut into 1-inch cubes

4 cups fresh pork blood

½ cup red wine vinegar

⅔ cup toasted chopped walnuts

½ cup chopped golden raisins

⅓ cup chopped fresh flat-leaf parsley leaves

2 teaspoons chopped fresh oregano

About 15 feet of hog casings, rinsed

Extra-virgin olive oil, for grilling

In a large pan over medium heat, combine the vegetable oil and the onions; cook, stirring occasionally, until softened and lightly caramelized, about 15 minutes. When the onions start to stick or the pan starts to get dark, deglaze with ¼ cup water at a time, continuing to cook until it evaporates, until you've used about 2 cups. Transfer the onions to a baking sheet and spread them into a single layer; refrigerate until completely chilled.

Chill the components of a meat grinder and a stand mixer (bowl and paddle attachment) in the refrigerator or freezer before grinding the meat. Toss the pork shoulder with the morcilla spice, kosher salt, and pink salt, and chill until ready to grind. (Keep the pork fatback in the refrigerator.)

Grind the pork shoulder, then refrigerate. Grind the fatback, then refrigerate separately. Strain the blood through a fine-mesh strainer.

In the chilled bowl of a stand mixer fitted with the chilled paddle attachment, mix the ground seasoned pork shoulder on medium-high speed for 5 minutes. Turn the mixer off and scrape down the sides of the bowl and the paddle; turn the machine to low speed and slowly pour in the blood and the vinegar. Once the liquid is incorporated, increase the speed to medium and add the reserved onions, walnuts, raisins, parsley, and oregano. Mix well until fully incorporated, about 2 minutes, then add the fatback, a handful at a time. Mix until well incorporated and the mixture forms a thick paste, about 5 minutes.

In a skillet, cook a small patty of the sausage mixture in order to taste it, and adjust the seasoning if necessary.

Thread the hog casings onto a sausage stuffer, leaving a small length of casing untied at the end of the tube so air can escape. Fill the canister with the sausage mixture and pack it in, a handful at a time, pressing out the air bubbles with your fingers to be sure there is very little air packed in with the sausage. Pipe the meat into the casings, coiling it into one large coil on a baking sheet as you work. Afterward, section off the sausages into 5- or 6-inch links, twisting one link in one direction, then the next in the opposite direction, to seal the ends.

Heat a large stockpot of water to 185°F. Set a large bowl of ice water next to the stove. Maintain the temperature of the water over low heat while gently lowering in as many sausages as can fit in the pot. Poach the sausages for 8 minutes, until just cooked through, then remove and transfer to the ice water. Repeat as needed until all the sausages are poached and chilled. Refrigerate for up to 5 days before grilling.

When ready to serve, prepare a grill to medium heat and be sure to carefully oil the grate.

Lightly oil the sausages, and season lightly with kosher salt. Grill until grill marks have formed on one side, 3 to 5 minutes. Turn and repeat on the other side. Transfer to a cooler section of the grill and cook until the sausages feel firm and the meat is heated through, 2 to 3 minutes more. Remove from the grill and let rest for 2 to 3 minutes before serving or slicing.

MORCILLA SPICE

MAKES 1¼ CUPS

1 cup Hungarian sweet paprika

¼ cup ají amarillo powder (see Note, page 34)

3 tablespoons dried oregano

3 tablespoons ground cumin

2 tablespoons ground ginger

2½ tablespoons ground coriander

1½ tablespoons freshly ground black pepper

1½ tablespoons freshly ground white pepper

1½ tablespoons freshly grated nutmeg

1½ tablespoons dried thyme

In a medium bowl or large jar, combine the paprika, ají chile, oregano, cumin, ginger, coriander, black and white pepper, nutmeg, and thyme. The spice can be stored in an airtight container for up to 6 months.

ASH-SEARED LAMB LOIN

with celery, cilantro, charred orange, and cumin-chile oil

For those nights when you want to be liberated from the grill while the festivities are going on, this lamb loin can be finished in advance and served chilled or at room temperature. It's light enough to serve on the hottest summer nights, but the easy-to-find components (like celery, an unsung favorite of ours) make it friendly for year-round eating.

Think of the charred orange as a trick up your sleeve. The burning sugars of the orange lend a crème brûlée–like sweetness, making the orange amazing on everything from sweetened yogurt to a smoky Old-Fashioned.

Coat the lamb loin with the kosher salt, pepper, and cocoa powder, rubbing with your fingers to help the spices adhere. Wrap and refrigerate for at least 4 hours and up to 24 hours.

Prepare a grill to high heat. Meanwhile, to make the cumin-chile oil, in a small bowl, whisk the Orange-Chile Oil with the soy sauce and vinegar. In a small pan over medium heat, toast the cumin seeds until fragrant and starting to pop, about 1 minute. Remove and add to the chile-soy mixture.

Using a sharp knife, cut away the orange rinds and reserve the fruit.

While the grill is at its hottest, grill the lamb and the oranges: Unwrap the lamb loin and place it on the hottest part of the grill (if it's a gas grill), or—if using coals—set a metal cooling rack directly atop the coals and place the lamb loin on top. Cook for about 1 minute, until seared, then flip and cook the other side for 1 minute. (If your lamb loin is more round than oblong, give it a one-quarter turn every 30 seconds so that it cooks evenly.) Remove the loin from the heat (it will still be rare to medium-rare) and wrap it tightly in fresh plastic wrap to allow it to keep cooking while you grill the orange. At this point, you can store the cooked, wrapped lamb loin up to 3 days.

To finish the dish, place the oranges on the hottest part of the grill and cook, rotating until charred—and almost burnt—around the outside, 4 to 8 minutes. Remove from the heat and let rest until cool enough to handle; slice into ½-inch-thick rounds.

To serve, divide the orange slices among four plates. Unwrap the lamb loin and slice it into ¼-inch medallions; divide among plates. Garnish each slice with a light sprinkling of sea salt. Garnish with the celery, chives, and cilantro leaves. Drizzle the toasted cumin-chile oil over the meat and vegetables, stirring between each spoonful to properly distribute all of its ingredients. Sprinkle a small amount of cocoa across each plate and serve.

SERVES 4

1 (12-ounce) boneless lamb loin

1 tablespoon kosher salt

½ teaspoon freshly ground black pepper

2 tablespoons unsweetened cocoa powder, plus about 1 teaspoon more to garnish plates

¼ cup Orange-Chile Oil (page 244)

2 tablespoons soy sauce (gluten-free if desired)

2 tablespoons unseasoned rice vinegar

½ teaspoon cumin seeds

3 oranges

Flaked sea salt, for garnishing

1 large rib celery, sliced thinly on a diagonal

6 chives, sliced into 2-inch pieces

1 cup cilantro leaves

GRILLED LAMB SHOULDER CHOPS
with rosemary marinade

This is a cut for the carnivorous person who doesn't mind eating around a bone, or eating a little bit of fat, and really just enjoys the flavor of lamb. Lamb and rosemary go hand in hand, and because the shoulder has a bigger flavor, we amped up the rosemary flavor, too, applying it in a few different ways. The dish starts with a rosemary marinade, and the grilled chop is set atop a bed of fresh rosemary to release the herb's aromas. At Ox, we also send this out to the table garnished with a smoking sprig of rosemary lit from the fire.

This is an inexpensive cut relative to other cuts of lamb, so it's a great option for scaling up for larger groups.

In a blender, combine the oil, onion, garlic, rosemary, salt, and pepper; puree until smooth.

Generously coat the lamb chops with the marinade and chill, covered or wrapped tightly, for at least 4 hours and up to 24 hours. Before grilling, let the meat come up to room temperature, about 30 minutes.

Meanwhile, prepare a grill to medium heat.

Season the lamb chops with more salt and pepper and transfer to the grill. Cook, turning once, until both sides are golden brown and the meat is cooked to medium or medium-well, about 12 minutes total. Remove and let rest for 5 minutes before cutting or serving. Serve on a bed of rosemary sprigs and garnished with radish and flowers, if desired.

SERVES 4

½ cup extra-virgin olive oil

½ yellow onion, chopped

1 clove garlic

Leaves from 2 sprigs rosemary, plus more sprigs for garnishing (optional)

1 teaspoon kosher salt, plus more to taste

1 teaspoon freshly ground black pepper, plus more to taste

4 (12-ounce) bone-in lamb shoulder chops, about 1 inch thick

Thinly sliced radishes, for garnish (optional)

Edible flowers, for garnish (optional)

GRILL-ROASTED LEG OF GOAT
with white truffle, button mushroom, and fresh ricotta salad

This recipe is another case in which a large bone-in cut and slower cooking helps to develop flavors effortlessly. The goat is seasoned simply and basted while it cooks with an herbed *salmuera*—a simple water-based brine that's often used to baste fire-cooked meats in South America. We sometimes substitute a little beer for some of the water.

Served atop a mushroom salad, the goat meat releases its juices and they become a component of the salad's dressing. The warmth of the meat helps to release the fragrant aroma of the shaved truffle.

Prepare a grill to medium-low heat, banking the coals to one side for indirect grilling (if using a gas grill, only light one side).

Season the goat leg all over with kosher salt and pepper and place it over the cooler side of the grill so that the flat side is facing down (the side that is less meaty and closer to the bone; it may appear to have a seam running down it). Let cook for 15 to 20 minutes until just barely browned. If the meat has not taken on any color at all at this point, move it a bit closer to the heat. It should be slowly and lightly browning but not charring or taking on dark or heavy grill marks. Baste with the salmuera, beginning on the top, raw side of the meat. Then, using a kitchen towel, flip the leg to briefly baste the bottom side. Continue cooking on the flat side, basting every 10 to 15 minutes. After about 1½ hours, when the first side is a deep golden brown, flip the leg to begin cooking on its rounded, meatier side. Continue to baste every 10 to 15 minutes, for another 1½ hours or so, until a thermometer inserted into the thickest part registers 125°F to 130°F for medium-rare or 140°F for medium-well. You will be able to tell the leg is close to ready when you see the meat on the smaller end (the shank) begin to pull away from the bone, after about 3 hours. Carefully remove the meat from the grill and let rest in a warm spot for 20 to 25 minutes.

Meanwhile, prepare the mushroom salad. Thinly slice the button mushrooms about ⅛ inch thick and transfer to a bowl with the lemon juice, olive oil, and oregano; toss gently, then mound onto a serving platter. Garnish with small pieces of the ricotta. Using a truffle slicer or mandoline, slice the truffle thinly over the entire salad. Finish with a generous sprinkling of sea salt and black pepper.

Thinly slice the goat meat against the grain and season with sea salt; fan the slices out atop the salad. If you have any truffle left, slice it over the goat meat and serve.

SERVES 6 TO 8

Goat Leg

1 (6-pound) bone-in leg of goat

Kosher salt and freshly ground black pepper

4 cups Herbed Salmuera (page 245)

White Truffle and Button Mushroom Salad

1½ pounds button mushrooms, as fresh and white as possible

¼ cup fresh lemon juice

½ cup extra-virgin olive oil

2 tablespoons fresh oregano leaves

1 cup ricotta, homemade (page 251) or store-bought

2 ounces fresh white truffle (or substitute a couple of teaspoons truffle oil or truffle salt)

Flaked sea salt and freshly ground black pepper

GRILLED WHEY-BRINED QUAIL
with sage-roasted grapes

We strive to put every potential ingredient in our kitchen to good use, and marinating proteins in whey—the seasoned liquid left over from making ricotta—was a use-it-all-up experiment gone right. Because of the salt and vinegar contained in the ricotta and the lactic acid that occurs naturally in the milk, a whey brine helps tenderize lean quail meat and bring forth its inherent flavor and sweetness. The naturally occurring sugars also help its outermost layer to caramelize on the grill.

Birds go beautifully with stronger herbs like marjoram, rosemary, sage, and lavender. In this case, we cook some sage in butter to give it a delicious nutty flavor without the medicinal quality sage can have when raw. We roast some grapes to release their juices and form an effortless sauce, which we then enrich with butter and verjus (the pressed juice of unfermented grapes, which you can find in specialty shops or online). If needed, you can substitute unsweetened white grape juice for the verjus, but the sauce will turn out a touch sweeter.

Try this preparation with other similar proteins, like chicken thighs or breasts, or even pork tenderloin or chops.

SERVES 4 AS A STARTER OR 2 AS A MAIN DISH

Whey-Brined Quail

4 quail, glove-boned (or partially deboned) by your butcher

2 cups whey (see Homemade Ricotta, page 251)

2 tablespoons extra-virgin olive oil

Kosher salt and freshly ground black pepper

Sage-Roasted Grapes

3 tablespoons cold unsalted butter, cut into ½-inch cubes

8 fresh sage leaves

1½ cups seedless red grapes (8 ounces)

¾ teaspoon kosher salt

¼ teaspoon freshly ground black pepper

¼ cup white verjus

Sugar (optional)

Prepare the quail by bending their wings at the joints and tucking the wings behind their necks. Take a thin knife and cut a small slit on one of the inside "ankles" of each quail, cutting right behind the bone and all the way through the outside skin. Take the other leg and push its "ankle" through the hole, so that the quail looks like it's crossing its legs at the ankle. This will prevent the legs from splaying open as the quail cook.

Put the quail into a large resealable plastic bag or a plastic storage container and pour in the whey; refrigerate for at least 8 hours and up to 12 hours. Remove the quail, discarding the whey, and rinse quickly, just enough to rinse the whey from the skin; pat dry with paper towels.

Preheat the oven to 400°F and set a rack in the center. Prepare a grill to medium heat.

To prepare the grapes, warm an oven-safe sauté pan over medium heat. Melt 2 teaspoons of the butter in the pan, then add the sage leaves. Cook until the leaves and the butter start to brown lightly and become aromatic, about 3 minutes. Add the grapes, salt, and pepper, swirling them around the pan to coat. Transfer the pan to the middle rack of the oven and roast until the grapes just start to wrinkle, 8 to 10 minutes. Remove the pan and let sit at room temperature.

Brush the quail with the oil and season both sides with salt and pepper. Be sure to carefully oil the grate, then place the quail breast side down on the hot grill. Cook for 2 minutes, then flip and cook 2 minutes more.

Return to the breast side, rotating the angle about 70 degrees to get a nice crosshatch mark; cook for about 2 minutes. Flip one final time and cook until the quail are just cooked through but still pink, 3 minutes more. Test for doneness by making a small cut in the center of the back and checking the breast from the inside. The meat should be barely pink in the center yet firm. Remove from the grill and keep warm.

Quickly finish the sauce by placing the sauté pan back on the stove over medium heat. Add the verjus and bring to a simmer, then reduce the heat to maintain the simmer (do not boil). Add the remaining butter, one small knob at a time, swirling the pan constantly to help the butter emulsify into the sauce. Taste and adjust the seasoning, if necessary. If the grapes are particularly tart, add a pinch or two of sugar (the sauce should be both sweet and sour).

Spoon the sauce over the grilled quail and serve immediately.

GRILLED BUTTERFLIED WHOLE CHICKEN
with grilled figs, manouri cheese, and lentil chimichurri

If you've been to a backyard barbecue, chances are you've been served some burnt chicken. This is common and even understandable, because prolonged, direct contact between flames and delicate, fatty chicken skin can easily lead to flare-ups and over-blackening. The two tricks to tender, juicy chicken are indirect heat and a willingness to wait.

The indirect heat method used here is one of the foundations of open-fire cooking in South America. Seasoned cooks there know exactly how far away to position different cuts and meats from the coals for optimum results. That's why we turn chicken skin-side-up so that the skin never even touches the grate of a grill, and yet the skin and outermost layer of the meat still crisps and browns beautifully.

You can make and serve this chicken on its own, of course, but we love the fruit and cheese accompaniments when figs are in season. Along with the creamy manouri cheese and herbaceous lentil chimichurri, the sweet figs are the ideal contrast to the bird's smoky flavor and crispy skin. Likewise, you can serve the accompanying salad on its own as a light meal.

If figs are not in season, try peeled, seeded pears, fresh apricots, or thin slices of delicata squash.

Put the lentils in a small pot and add enough water to cover by about 1 inch. Cover the pot and bring to a boil over medium heat (you will see steam start to escape from the lid). Decrease to a simmer and cook until the lentils are just tender, about 18 minutes; drain. Add 1 tablespoon of the oil to the lentils and season with salt and pepper. Spread the lentils out on a flat dish and refrigerate until cool. Transfer to a small bowl and combine with the chimichurri; taste and adjust the seasoning, if necessary. Store covered at room temperature until ready to use.

Prepare a grill to medium heat, building the fire—or turning on the gas—on one side of the grill and leaving the other side open for indirect-heat cooking. (If using charcoal, start with a larger batch since you need it to last a little over an hour.)

To butterfly the chicken, place the chicken breast-side-up on a cutting board. Working from the tail end, insert a sturdy, sharp knife into the body cavity and make a straight cut through the ribs along one side of the backbone. Turn the chicken around on the cutting board so that the neck side is facing you (leave it breast-side-up). Starting at the neck cavity, cut along the same side of the backbone in order to connect to the previous cut and split the bird open down its back (but leaving the

CONTINUED

SERVES 4

½ cup lentils du Puy (French green lentils), rinsed and picked through

¼ cup extra-virgin olive oil

Kosher salt and freshly ground black pepper

1½ cups Chimichurri (page 15)

1 (4- to 5-pound) chicken

8 fresh firm-ripe figs, halved lengthwise

1 (3-ounce) wheel manouri cheese (or substitute a block of halloumi, cut ¾ inch thick)

backbone attached on one side). Turn the chicken over so that the breast side is now against the cutting board. Carefully splay the legs open and apply strong pressure onto the inner cavity with your palms to flatten the bird as much as possible. Season the inner cavity with a generous amount of salt and pepper, then gently flip the chicken and season the skin side, being sure to season under the legs and wings, too.

Transfer the chicken, breast side up, onto the grill in an area that is next to the coals but not directly atop them. Cover the grill, either with its own lid or by placing a large metal bowl over the chicken. Cook for 5 minutes, keeping watch for any flare-ups, until you hear sizzling sounds and the underside of the bird begins to brown lightly. (If flare-ups do happen, move the bird a little farther from the heat and cover it again. If it is not beginning to brown after 5 minutes, move it closer to the coals.) Cook for another 10 minutes, then rotate the bird 180 degrees, keeping the breast side up. Continue to grill, rotating the bird every 15 minutes but never turning it over onto its skin side, until the chicken is just cooked through, 1 to 1¼ hours. To test for doneness, make a small cut where the thigh meets the breast and be sure the juices run clear; keep cooking if you see any pink. Remove from the grill and let rest for 15 minutes before carving.

Meanwhile, brush the manouri cheese and figs with some of the remaining oil and season with salt and pepper. Transfer the cheese and the figs, cut side down, onto the hottest area of the grill. Cook just until grill marks form, about 3 minutes; turn and repeat on the remaining sides. Gently remove from the grill and keep warm.

To serve the cheese and figs, place the grilled cheese wheel on a large round plate. Distribute the figs atop and around it, then spoon half of the lentil chimichurri on top.

To carve the bird, place it, breast side up, on a cutting board. Remove the legs at the thigh. Separate the thighs from the legs, and separate the two breasts by cutting down in between them through the chest plate. Cut each breast in half horizontally, just under the wing. Pile the pieces onto a large plate or platter and serve with a small bowl of the remaining lentil chimichurri.

GRILL-ROASTED TURKEY BUTTS

with cilantro-peanut relish and watermelon

To get your hands on a turkey's butt (also known as a turkey tail), you sort of have to know someone. This might mean making a special order from your butcher, but it's not at all expensive and at least one of the more interesting orders they'll get all day. What we like about this part of the bird is its high skin-to-meat ratio. There is a bit of bone, but it's similar to that of a rib, and fun to nibble around.

We love what happens to this part of the turkey after hours of low and slow cooking. Though the method does require patience, the turkey meat begins to taste a lot like pork—taking on a gelatinous quality similar to that of a pork trotter. If you don't have 2 to 3 hours to see this recipe through—or if you can't make it to a butcher to score turkey butts—an easy substitute would be bone-in, skin-on chicken thighs. Cook them 35 to 45 minutes as directed, then skip the long indirect-heat cooking.

Served with fresh watermelon, this dish has a juiciness, coolness, and freshness that helps cut through the fattiness of the poultry skin. It all pairs inexplicably well with the cilantro-peanut relish, which isn't really spicy but is definitely zesty due to a bit of yellow mustard.

SERVES 6 TO 8

8 (6- to 8-ounce) turkey butts or tails (about 4 pounds total) (or substitute 4 pounds bone-in, skin-on chicken thighs)

Maple Brine (page 246)

2 tablespoons extra-virgin olive oil

Kosher salt and freshly ground black pepper

1 small seedless watermelon

Cilantro-Peanut Relish (recipe follows)

Put the turkey butts in a resealable 1-gallon bag and pour in the maple brine; refrigerate for at least 12 hours and up to 24 hours. Remove from the brine and pat dry with a clean kitchen or paper towel.

Prepare a grill to medium-low heat.

Rub the turkey butts with the oil and season with salt and pepper. Transfer to the grill and cook, turning the butts to a new side every 5 to 6 minutes, until golden brown with light spots of char all over, 35 to 45 minutes total. If flare-ups occur at any time during this phase, move the butts to a different spot on the grill to avoid the flames.

Shift the turkey butts to the outside edges of the grill, where the heat is less direct (if using chicken thighs, skip this step). Let cook until the meat is ultratender and the skin is well browned, 2 to 2½ hours more.

When ready to serve, peel and cut the watermelon by slicing off both ends, turning the watermelon onto one of the cut sides and removing the skin with a knife. Cut the flesh into ¾-inch by 3-inch rectangles; season with salt and pepper. Spread out the watermelon pieces on a serving platter, then place the grilled turkey butts on top. Drizzle each piece of turkey with a heaping tablespoon or more of the cilantro-peanut relish, then drizzle the rest of the relish on the watermelon.

CONTINUED

1 cup raw skinless peanuts

2 cups tightly packed cilantro leaves

1 cup extra-virgin olive oil

¼ cup lemon juice, preferably from Meyer lemons

Finely grated zest of ½ lemon, preferably Meyer lemon

2 teaspoons yellow mustard

1 teaspoon finely grated or minced garlic (from about 1 small clove)

2 teaspoons kosher salt

1 teaspoon freshly ground black pepper

CILANTRO-PEANUT RELISH

Preheat the oven to 325°F. Spread the peanuts in a single layer on a flat baking dish or small baking sheet and roast until lightly browned and aromatic, 14 to 18 minutes. Let cool to room temperature; coarsely chop and transfer to a small bowl.

Finely chop the cilantro and add it to the bowl with the peanuts. Add the oil, lemon juice and zest, mustard, garlic, salt, and pepper; mix well with a fork. Let rest at room temperature until ready to use. Serve within an hour or two, before the peanuts lose their crunch and the cilantro turns brown from the acid.

GRILLED SQUAB "AL DIABLO"
with sesame-chile oil

Squab is a decadent little game bird that features a delicious ratio of crispy skin to rosy, succulent meat. Here we brush it with a spicy and nutty-flavored chile oil to counterbalance its sweet dark-meat flavor.

As is the case when grilling many birds, butterflying the squab before grilling it helps all of its parts to cook evenly. But unlike our butterflied chicken recipe, which cooks skin-side-up, the squab should cook with its skin against the grill, giving the skin a chance to crisp while the meat cooks through. Squab is best cooked rare to medium-rare. Beyond that, the meat can take on a toughness and even a liverlike flavor.

While the sesame-chile oil will seem very spicy if you taste it on its own, once you brush it onto the birds, the flavoring mellows. Don't be afraid to drizzle a bit more onto the birds after grilling. Sesame-chile oil is very versatile: drizzle it over steamed greens, stir-fried vegetables, or fried eggs for heat and nuttiness, or rub it onto other poultry, meat (especially pork belly), or fish before grilling or roasting.

To make the sesame-chile oil, in a small pot over medium heat, heat the vegetable oil until a deep-fry thermometer registers 225°F. Remove from the heat and add the red pepper, sesame seeds, garlic, and 1 teaspoon salt. Let cool to room temperature, then transfer to a blender with the sesame oil. Blend at low speed until the mixture forms a gritty paste. Keep stored in the refrigerator for up to 2 weeks.

To butterfly the squab, place them one at a time on a cutting board, breast side up. Entering from the tail end, insert a sturdy, sharp knife into the body cavity. Pressing the knife against the backbone, cut straight down through the ribs along the backbone. Rotate the bird so the neck side is now facing you (it should still be breast-side-up). Insert a knife into the neck cavity and cut along the same side of the backbone in order to connect to the previous cut. This should split the bird open down its back (do not remove the backbone). Turn the bird over so that the breast side is now facing down. Carefully splay the legs open and apply pressure on the inner cavity with your palms to flatten the bird as much as possible.

Season the inner cavity of the squab with salt, then rub about 1 teaspoon of the sesame-chile oil onto the flesh and bone. Turn the squab over and season the skin side with salt, making sure to season under the legs and wings, too. Drizzle ½ teaspoon of the sesame-chile oil onto the skin and rub it in, but try to avoid using too many of the solid particles at the bottom of the bowl (they may burn with prolonged contact with the grill).

SERVES 4

Sesame-Chile Oil

1 cup neutral-flavored vegetable oil

2 tablespoons red pepper flakes

¼ cup toasted sesame seeds (see Note, page 246)

2 cloves garlic

2 teaspoons kosher salt

2 tablespoons toasted sesame oil

Butterflied Squab

4 squab, about 1 pound each

Kosher salt

Prepare a grill to medium-high heat and set up for indirect-heat cooking. (If using a gas grill, prepare one side to medium-high and leave the other side off. If using charcoal, bank the coals slightly to one side.)

Place the squab, skin side down and breast toward the heat, onto the grill in an area that is close to the heat but not directly over it. Cook until the skin in the breast area starts to turn golden brown, 4 to 5 minutes. (If the skin has not begun to brown after 5 minutes, inch it closer to the hot side and keep an eye out for flare-ups while the fat renders. If flare-ups occur, temporarily move the squab to another area of the grill to avoid the flames.) Rotate the bird 180 degrees so that the legs are now facing the heat. Cook until the skin is golden brown and crispy (including the skin under the legs) but the meat is still rare or medium-rare, 5 to 7 minutes. Turn the squab over, skin side up, and place it directly on the hottest part of the grill. Brush more of the chile oil, this time including the sesame seed paste, onto the skin side, and cook about 3 minutes more, until the breast bones are warmed through.

To serve, lay the squab skin-side-down. Cut the bird in half vertically between the two breasts so that there is one breast and one leg per piece. Then separate each half by cutting between the breast and the thigh. Drizzle with some of the sesame-chile oil, making sure to stir well and bring up some of the solids when you do. Serve with extra sesame-chile oil on the side. Encourage your guests to pick up and eat the birds with their hands, and offer wet napkins with lemon wedges for cleaning up afterwards.

GRILLED DUCK BREASTS
with brandied cherries

Much like bacon, duck skin is at its best when deeply browned and as crisp as a cracker. But the meat beneath the skin is at its best when cooked medium-rare and juicy. The secret to achieving both is the same on the grill as it is in a pan: render the fat over low heat. This simple method—and equally simple accompaniments—makes for an elegant and impressive main course.

Fruit is a classic pairing with duck, as its sweet-and-sour qualities help cut the richness of the skin and savoriness of the flesh. Adding rice vinegar, a liquor, and a bit of sugar to the cherries serves to intensify those qualities. The end result is a juicy preserve that beautifully complements not only duck breast but also pork, foie gras, or a bowl of vanilla ice cream.

To make the brandied cherries, in a large nonreactive skillet, combine the cherries, sugar, vinegar, and 1 tablespoon of the brandy; bring to a boil over medium-high heat. Reduce the heat to medium and simmer until the sauce has thickened slightly, about 3 minutes. Add the remaining 1 tablespoon brandy, the salt, and a pinch of pepper. Bring back up to a simmer, then remove from the heat. Serve slightly warm but not hot, or cool and refrigerate for up to 3 weeks. Rewarm before serving.

Prepare a grill to medium-low heat.

Using a small, sharp knife, score the skin of the duck by making ⅛-inch-deep cuts along the skin every ⅛ inch down the length of the breast (do not cut through to the flesh). Season both sides of each breast generously with salt and pepper and place, skin side down, on the grill. Grill until the skin is crispy and a deep, even golden brown, 10 to 12 minutes. If flare-ups occur while the fat renders, temporarily remove the duck breasts and pat the skin sides with a paper towel to absorb any excess fat. Place the breast back on the grill but in another spot that isn't flaring up. Flip and grill until the outside of the breast is just barely cooked, about 1 minute for medium-rare. Remove and let rest in a warm spot 2 to 3 minutes.

To serve, place the duck breast-skin-side down on a cutting board. Using a sharp knife, slice against the grain into ¼- to ½-inch pieces. Fan out the slices, drizzle the breasts or the plate with the warm cherry sauce, and serve immediately.

SERVES 4

Brandied Cherries

1 cup large fresh sweet cherries, stemmed and pitted

¼ cup sugar

3 tablespoons unseasoned rice vinegar

2 tablespoons brandy

1 teaspoon kosher salt

Freshly ground black pepper

Duck

2 large (12- to 16-ounce) duck breasts, preferably Moulard, silver skin carefully trimmed away

Kosher salt and freshly ground black pepper

Apart from the ubiquitous grilled shrimp, seafood seems always to play second fiddle to meat when it comes to home grilling—a fact that remains a mystery to us. Our only theory is that many home cooks have had a bad experience with fish sticking to the grill or falling apart. And maybe others aren't sure how to get creative with it beyond the classic squeeze of lemon, or worry that delicate seafood can't stand up to the intensity of the grill. Either way, it's a shame. If we're going to push you anywhere in this book, let it be in this section: you simply must discover the wonderful, heartier side of fish cooked over fire.

What made us believers? Our inspiration, it turns out, first came not from the grill fires of Argentina but during our honeymoon in Europe. We were staying on the Atlantic coast in Getaria, Spain, and everywhere we went, there was fish. Grilled fish. It was usually whole or bone-in, and almost always still covered in skin while it cooked. Even though the flesh itself was rarely in direct contact with the grill, the transformation of its mild white meat into the most unctuous, rich, gelatinous flesh as it sizzled away under that skin was astonishing. We paid attention to that—that bones and skin can help naturally protect the fish so the flesh stays moist—and took the theory all the way home. As you'll see, the same holds true for shellfish and crustaceans: grilling lobsters, whole crab, shrimp, or crayfish right in their own shells works wonders for concentrating and enhancing their natural flavors.

CHAPTER 4   # GRILLED SEAFOOD

It turns out that skin and shells actually simplify things: thanks to these protective and flavor-filled layers, grilling restaurant-worthy fish barely requires any preseasoning, skinning, or shelling at all. All you really have to do is make sure the grill is hot. Maybe as hot as it gets. Clean the grates and season them with vegetable oil just before adding the fish. And don't mess with the fish too much. It's naturally delicious, delicate, and often preseasoned by the very water it swims in, so you don't need a bunch of intense blackening, salting, or special techniques to turn it into something attention-worthy. The fire does most of the work.

Once it's off the grill and onto your plate, that's another story. Although many fish taste delicate when raw, poached, or sautéed, the unparalleled smoky flavor that seafood picks up on the grill means it can stand up to some remarkably intense accompaniments: spicy things, salty things, and rich and fatty things, like our highly addictive Bacon-Sherry Cream (page 166). Within this chapter, you'll find ideas for applying bold, interesting seasonings and techniques to a range of seafood styles, from strong-flavored fillets to delicate bivalves.

Between the beauty of fresh seafood itself and the flavors we've concocted for it, these recipes will make a fish lover out of anyone.

GRILLED HEAD-ON SPOT PRAWNS

with garlic, green onion, and sumac

The meat of spot prawns or jumbo shrimp is tasty on its own, but the best flavor comes from the shells. Compared to their peeled counterparts, there's a toastiness to shell-on, head-on grilled versions that's totally unparalleled. And what's hidden under the heads—especially the sweet spot where the head meets the body—has so much umami. We call it the foie gras of the sea.

We play up that savory flavor here with smoked sea salt, toasted garlic, and ground sumac, a Middle Eastern spice that imparts a bright citrusy flavor. Sumac is worth seeking out for its intensity and flexibility; it's very inexpensive and also delicious on rice or steak. But if you want to keep your dish simple, the garlic-lemon dressing will do the trick on its own.

To eat the spot prawns or jumbo shrimp, tear away the head first and—trust us—slurp the juices out of the head before putting it aside. Then go at the rest with either your fingers or a steak knife. We suggest you eat the shell; it's usually tender enough and is really where the true flavor resides.

With a sharp paring knife or pair of kitchen shears, make a shallow cut on the back of each spot prawn starting under the head and ending near the tail (do not remove the shells). Using your fingers, pry the cut open slightly and rinse under cold water, then pull out the dark digestive tract with your fingers or a toothpick.

Prepare a grill to high heat, leaving one area of the grill at low heat.

Season the prawns with salt and pepper and coat in oil. Place on a grill rack or in a grill basket if you have one, and transfer directly onto the hot coals or over the hottest part of the grill. Cook until the prawns turn from gray or light pink to a deeper, reddish pink, 30 to 60 seconds. Flip the prawns on the rack or in the grill basket and repeat the cooking on the other side. Transfer to the low-heat area of the grill and let rest for 2 minutes.

Serve the prawns whole and shell-on, drizzled with the garlic-lemon oil and garnished with the green onions, sumac, and smoked sea salt to taste.

SERVES 4 TO 5

20 large (U-10 count) head-on spot prawns (1½ to 2 ounces each) (or substitute jumbo shrimp)

2 teaspoons kosher salt

1 teaspoon freshly ground black pepper

¼ cup extra-virgin olive oil

1 cup Toasted Garlic–Lemon Oil (page 244)

½ cup thinly sliced green onions

2 tablespoons ground sumac

Smoked sea salt, homemade (page 242) or store-bought

GRILLED SEA SCALLOPS
with english peas and orange-pastis butter

Scallops taste heavenly with smoky flavors, and when it comes to grilling them, the bigger the size, the better. Because they don't take long to cook, larger scallops can stand up to the grill heat without drying out.

Aside from being one of the first things to show you you're heading out of winter, fresh peas have a nice bright flavor and a balance of starchiness and sweetness that goes well with a mildly flavored protein like scallops. Peas are often paired with ham or bacon, so we substitute salami for a salty, chewy dimension.

Prepare one side of a grill to high heat and the other side to medium heat. (Set the scallops, oil, salt, and white pepper nearby so they are ready to go on the grill before the ragoût is done cooking.)

To make the ragoût, warm a medium cast-iron pan over medium heat on the grill (alternately, warm a skillet on the stove over medium-high heat to cook the ragoût there). Melt the butter, then add the leek and fennel. Cook, stirring occasionally, until the leek has softened, about 2 minutes. Add the peas and salami; season with salt and white pepper. Cook until everything is just warmed through, about 2 minutes. Add a few dollops (one per person) of the orange-pastis butter and remove from the heat; serve hot.

Meanwhile, to cook the scallops, coat them with oil, then season with salt and white pepper. Be sure to carefully oil the grate over the hottest area of the grill, then place the scallops on that area and cook, without disturbing, for 2 minutes. Flip carefully to prevent sticking. (If the scallops don't release easily, use a thin metal spatula to gently scrape between the scallop and the grill to separate.) Cook until the center is just barely cooked through, 1 to 2 minutes more.

To serve, place the scallops atop the warm pea ragoût. Brush the scallops with some of the orange-pastis butter.

ORANGE-PASTIS BUTTER

In a medium bowl, using a rubber spatula, mix together the butter, pastis, orange zest, salt, and white pepper until well combined. Keep at room temperature until ready to use, or freeze for up to 3 weeks.

SERVES 4

English Pea Ragoût

¼ cup unsalted butter

1 small leek (½-inch dice)

1 small bulb fennel, (½-inch dice) (about 2 cups)

3 cups fresh English peas (from 2½ to 3 pounds unshucked peas)

6 ounces unsliced fennel salami, diced into ½-inch pieces

Kosher salt and freshly ground white or black pepper

2 to 3 tablespoons Orange-Pastis Butter, softened to room temperature, plus more for serving (recipe follows)

Grilled Sea Scallops

1¼ pounds large sea scallops (12 to 16), cleaned

2 tablespoons extra-virgin olive oil

Kosher salt and freshly ground white pepper

MAKES ABOUT ½ CUP

½ cup unsalted butter, softened to room temperature

4 teaspoons pastis liqueur (or another anise-flavored liqueur, such as Pernod or Sambuca)

¾ teaspoon grated orange zest (from about ½ orange)

¾ teaspoon kosher salt

⅛ teaspoon freshly ground white pepper

GRILLED WHOLE DUNGENESS CRAB
with smoked tomato-ancho chile butter

There's something beautifully family-oriented and ritualistic about eating whole shellfish. You end up around the table for what seems like hours, and everyone gets messy. Not to mention, there are silly-looking bibs to bond over.

Native to the Pacific Northwest waters, the Dungeness crab is available from November to late spring, and you can find it until the season closes in mid-August. It's kind of awesome to fire up the grill and serve seafood in the wintertime. You taste the flavor of the ocean when you come in contact with any fish served in the shell—it's like a flash of summer.

Feel free to use this same crab grilling technique and skip the Smoked Tomato–Ancho Chile Sauce in favor of melted butter. If you do decide to make the ancho sauce, the recipe will make more than you need, but you'll want to have extra for future use. It makes a great base for a barbecue sauce or a smoky vinaigrette, or—with the addition of cream—a delicious pasta sauce. And if you can't get ahold of any crabs, this sauce goes just as well with grilled crayfish or shrimp. If you don't have a smoker, you can skip the smoking step and just add a tablespoon of smoked sweet Spanish paprika at the tomato-roasting stage.

Prepare a grill to high heat.

Place the lemons, cut side down, on the grill and cook until grill marks appear, about 2 minutes. Remove and set aside.

In a medium pan, bring the tomato-chile sauce to a gentle simmer. Add the butter 1 tablespoon at a time, whisking until incorporated after each addition. (Do not boil, or the emulsion will break.) Remove from heat and set aside.

Place the crabs on the hot grill (or directly over the hot coals, if using). They will move for a second or two but will die very quickly. Alternately, you can kill the crabs first by plunging a knife deeply into their ventral nerve cord, which lies at the tip of the triangle-like shape on the belly. Cook for 6 minutes, then flip and cook for 6 to 7 minutes more, until the juices are boiling inside of the shell and sputtering around the edges. Cook for 1 minute more, then remove. Drizzle or toss with copious amounts of the warm sauce and serve with the extra sauce on the side and the grilled lemon halves for squeezing.

CONTINUED

SERVES 6

3 lemons, halved

3 cups Smoked Tomato–Ancho Chile Sauce (recipe follows)

1 cup unsalted butter

6 live Dungeness crabs (1½ to 2 pounds each)

MAKES ABOUT 4 CUPS

1 pound tomatoes (about
3 medium tomatoes)

3 ounces dried ancho chiles
(about 3 large chiles), stemmed
and seeded

¼ cup extra-virgin olive oil

3 tablespoons chopped garlic,
plus 1 medium clove

1 teaspoon red pepper flakes

2 cups white wine

1 tablespoon kosher salt

1 teaspoon freshly ground
black pepper

1 tablespoon smoked sweet
Spanish paprika (also called
pimentón dulce) (use only if you
are not smoking the tomatoes)

SMOKED TOMATO–ANCHO CHILE SAUCE

Prepare a smoker with mesquite wood chips and preheat to 120°F.

Cut each tomato into quarters and remove the core. Transfer to the smoker and smoke for 1 hour. (If you don't have a smoker, simply roast the cored and quartered tomatoes as directed in the next step, adding 1 tablespoon Spanish paprika.) Transfer the smoked tomatoes to a shallow oven-safe dish.

Meanwhile, preheat the oven to 400°F. Roast the tomatoes (and the paprika, if using) until slightly shriveled and dehydrated, about 30 minutes. Remove from the oven and set aside.

Warm a medium stainless steel pot over medium heat. Add the chiles and toast, stirring occasionally, until lightly smoking, 3 minutes. Remove from the heat and add warm water to the pot to cover. Bring to a simmer and cook for 10 minutes, or until softened; drain and set the chiles aside.

Rinse out the pot and place it back over medium heat. Add the oil, garlic, and red pepper flakes; cook, stirring, until the garlic is lightly browned, 1 to 2 minutes. Remove from the heat and carefully pour in the wine. Return to the stove and bring to a simmer over low heat. Reduce the wine by about half, then add the smoked tomatoes (or, if you just roasted the tomatoes, the tomatoes with the smoked paprika) and the rehydrated ancho chiles. Bring to a simmer and stir in the salt and black pepper. Cook for 5 minutes.

Transfer the tomato mixture to a blender and add the garlic clove. Start the blender on low, then slowly increase the speed and blend until the sauce is pureed. Taste and adjust the seasoning, if necessary. (If the sauce isn't velvety smooth, pass through a strainer and push through with the back of a small ladle.) Keep warm, or store refrigerated for up to 1 week, or frozen for up to 3 months.

GRILLED ALBACORE TUNA AND MOREL MUSHROOMS
with nettle and green garlic salsa verde

To us, serving morels with tuna is a not-so-common—and we think lovely—contrast that tastes a bit like surf and turf. The zesty salsa verde is a nice bridge between the mild fish and sturdy mushrooms. It's also delicious with boiled or roasted potatoes, grilled chicken, or as a dressing for pasta salad.

For the best results, you want a superhot, searing grill. Since the fish does not have much natural fat, high heat will cause caramelization on the outside without drying out its center.

This dish may look fancy, but it's totally bluffing: the sauce can be done in advance, the mushrooms can be cooked in advance, and none of it (not even the tuna) needs to be served hot. You can prep all of the components the day before and not even break a sweat come time to serve.

Prepare a grill to high heat.

Bring a small pot of lightly salted water to a boil and add the morels; cook until moistened and softened, about 30 seconds. Drain, dry the mushrooms gently on a towel, then drizzle with 2 tablespoons of the oil and season with kosher salt and pepper.

Season the albacore on all sides with a generous amount of kosher salt and pepper. Wait a few minutes, then rub it with the remaining 2 tablespoons of oil to coat.

Be sure to carefully oil the grate, then place the albacore on the hottest area of the grill. Cook, turning the tuna pieces every 30 to 45 seconds, until the insides are warm but still rare, 3 to 5 minutes total depending on the thickness of the tuna pieces. Once the albacore is on the grill, add the morels to the grill. Cook on one side until they begin to char, about 2 minutes, then flip and repeat. Remove from the grill and keep warm.

To serve, cut the tuna in half on the diagonal. Place 3 tablespoons of sauce on each plate and top with the tuna and morels. Garnish the cut side of the tuna pieces with sea salt. Serve extra sauce on the side.

CONTINUED

SERVES 4

Kosher salt

8 ounces fresh morel mushrooms

¼ cup extra-virgin olive oil

Freshly ground black pepper

4 (5-ounce) cubes albacore tuna loin (each about 2 inches square)

¾ cup Nettle and Green Garlic Salsa Verde (recipe follows), plus more for serving

Flaked sea salt, for garnishing

MAKES ABOUT 3 CUPS

3½ tablespoons kosher salt

4 cups firmly packed stinging nettle leaves (2 ounces)

1½ cups thinly sliced green garlic (from 1 medium stem)

10 medium-large basil leaves

½ cup extra-virgin olive oil

2 tablespoons capers

3 oil-packed anchovy fillets

1 tablespoon finely grated lemon zest

1 tablespoon fresh lemon juice

2 hard-boiled eggs (see Note, page 149), peeled and coarsely chopped

½ teaspoon freshly ground black pepper

½ cup water, plus more as needed

NETTLE AND GREEN GARLIC SALSA VERDE

Bring a medium-large pot of water to a boil over high heat; season with 3 tablespoons salt. Prepare an ice bath by filling a large bowl with ice then filling it two-thirds of the way to the top with water. Nestle a strainer into the ice water bath, then set it next to the stove.

Drop the nettle leaves into the boiling water and blanch for 30 seconds, then remove using a slotted spoon and transfer to the ice bath. Once the nettles have completely cooled, squeeze the excess water out of them and set aside. (You should have about ⅓ cup nettles.)

Next, add the green garlic to the boiling water and let cook 90 seconds; transfer to the ice bath. Once the garlic has completely cooled, squeeze the excess water out of it and transfer to a blender. (You should have about 1¼ cups garlic.) Coarsely chop the blanched nettles, then add them to the blender. Add the basil, oil, capers, anchovies, lemon zest and juice, eggs, the remaining 1½ teaspoons salt, pepper, and water and blend, starting slowly and increasing the speed of the blender to high until the mixture is completely smooth. If the sauce is too thick to blend properly, add more water 1 tablespoon at a time (do not exceed 4 tablespoons total). Taste and adjust the seasoning, if necessary. Keep chilled until ready to use. The sauce will keep, refrigerated, for up to 4 days.

GRILLED WILD HALIBUT ON THE BONE
with toasted garlic–lemon oil

People love eating meat off the bone. So why not fish? (We're not talking about those tiny pin bones.) From the crispy outer skin to the tender innermost flesh, cutting bulkier, bone-in portions allows you to cascade through layers of flavor as you eat. You'll see what we mean: in comparison, a fillet just seems so one-note.

The bonus is that bone and skin make your job easy: they naturally protect the fish flesh from both ends so it stays moist atop the hot grill. We garnish our halibut with a garlicky lemon oil, and we don't skimp on the big pieces of caramelized garlic. Afterwards, we shower the fish with chives for brightness and a little texture. This halibut is one of our best sellers and may be a different way of experiencing a fish you have had many times before.

You could possibly ask your fishmonger to reserve some halibut tails for you, but the best way to secure both the tail and steaks is to butcher the fish yourself (see How to Break Down Halibut, pages 134–137). We recommend using a grill basket to prevent the skin from sticking to the grate and tearing away the delicate, flaky flesh.

Prepare a grill to high heat, with one area heated to warm. If using charcoal, once the coals are glowing, spread them evenly to flatten. Then place a grill grate or metal cooling rack directly atop the coals.

Season the halibut with the olive oil, salt, and pepper; transfer to an oiled grill basket and place it on top of the grate. If using tails, cook one side for about 4 minutes, then flip and repeat. If using steaks, cook for 7 to 8 minutes on the first side, then flip and cook 5 minutes more. Transfer the tails or steaks to a warm spot on the grill to rest for about 3 minutes.

To serve, transfer the fish to plates. Drizzle with the garlic-lemon oil and garnish with the chives, sliced radishes or ice lettuce, and sea salt.

SERVES 4

4 halibut tails, or 4 halibut steaks, sliced 1 to 1¼ inches thick (10 to 12 ounces each)

2 tablespoons extra-virgin olive oil

Kosher salt and freshly ground black pepper

1½ cups Toasted Garlic–Lemon Oil (page 244)

2 tablespoons thinly sliced chives

3 small radishes, trimmed and thinly sliced, or 12 sprigs ice lettuce (fiocoide glaciale) (optional), for garnish

Flaked sea salt, for garnishing

HOW TO BREAK DOWN HALIBUT

Pacific halibut is a flatfish with big, meaty fillets. Usually you find it at a fishmonger or grocery counter already cut into four "sides," or boneless skinless fillets. We like the bone and skin intact—it creates juicier meat and crispy skin on the grill—so we portion the halibut instead into two (bone-in) sides, then slice the sides into thick steaks for the grill. This method yields 12 to 15 steak portions and one tail portion (they freeze pretty well). But if you don't need that much, ask the fishmonger to sell you half. Here's how it is done.

You'll need 1 whole halibut (around 15 pounds), bone in and skin on, head and guts removed.

Step 1 Place the whole halibut, dark side up, on a clean cutting board that measures at least three-quarters the size of your fish. Pat the halibut dry as much as possible with a clean kitchen towel.

Step 2 Remove the collar on the side facing you. Keeping your knife close to the collar fins, make a U-shape cut from the belly side of the fish towards the neck side. You will end up near the backbone where the head was. Disconnect the collar completely and reserve for grilling.

Step 3 Keeping the fish on the same side, find the neck bone at the top. Press firmly on the skin near the neck to help feel exactly where you will need to cut. Make the cut from the open side (where the head was originally removed) to the back side. You will hit the backbone. With some effort and force, cut through the backbone, stopping as soon as it is broken.

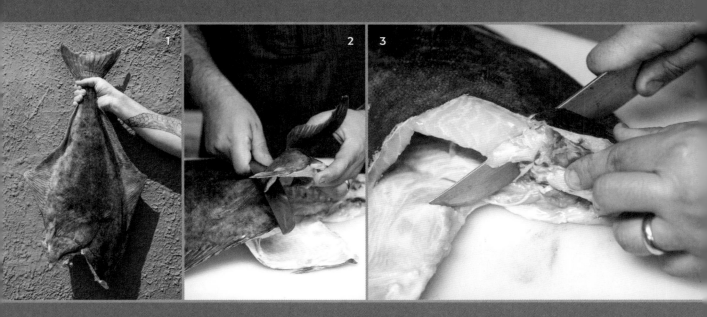

Step 4 Flip the fish over. Repeat the same collar cut as you did before (in Step 2) and remove the collar.

Step 5 Repeat the neck cut as in Step 3. This side will be much easier. Make the same cut in order to connect to the cut on the other side. Set aside.

Step 6 Find where the tail of the halibut goes from thick to thin (where it starts to hourglass). Using force, cut the tail off where it starts to thin out; reserve.

Step 7 Wipe down the fish again. You will notice a natural line that runs from the tail to the head on the fish, about midway between the fins. Plan to make a cut the entire length of the fish, down to the vertebrae, to one side of that "line" in the skin. Starting 2 to 3 inches from where the tail ends, make an incision with your knife along one side of the line. Cut all the way down to the vertebrae and towards the end of the tail. Turn the fish 180 degrees, and make a similar cut on the opposite side, connecting it to your original cut.

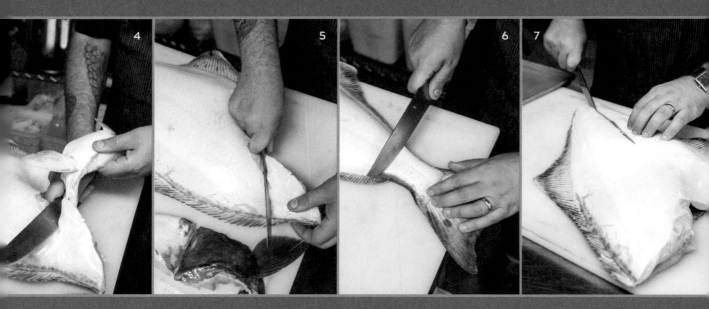

Step 8 When you have exposed the vertebrae completely, you will notice a thick side of the fish and a thin side. We will call the thinner side the belly, because that is where the guts were removed. You will need to cut the fish in half eventually, but cutting through a vertebrae is very difficult without using a saw. Instead, cut through the smaller bones that are connected to the vertebrae. Since we have to choose a side to leave more bone on than the other, we prefer to leave the majority of the bone and vertebrae on the thinner, belly side. Why? Because the bones will help protect the thinner flesh while cooking. To expose these smaller bones, use the vertebrae as a guide and slowly cut and push some flesh away from the vertebrae on the nonbelly side (about a half inch).

Step 9 Turn the fish over and repeat on the remaining side. Starting on the tail side of the fish and, cutting towards the head, make a cut that breaks the bones off the vertebrae but does not cut through the other side of the fish. Stop once you have broken the bone. Continue this style of cutting and breaking until one side is complete.

Step 10 Flip the fish so that the tail end is still on the same side of the cutting board, and gently cut the flesh away from the vertebrae and bone on the other side. (It should be easier because the bones are already broken.) You now will have cut your fish in half.

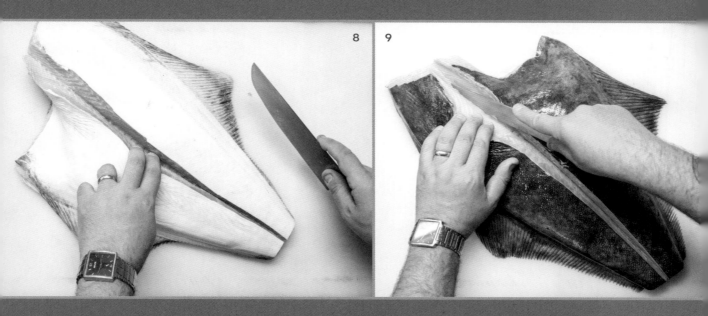

Step 11 Place the thicker nonvertebrae half of the fish in front of you with the cut side facing away. We cut our portions into about 12-ounce pieces, about 1 to 1¼ inches thick (but as you cut closer to the thinner tail end, those pieces will get shorter and wider). Make a 1-inch cut starting on the top side and cut all the way through the bottom side.

Step 12 To cut the other side of the fish, identify the white, thicker part of the vertebrae. When making the cut, start at that white section (where the vertebrae joins) so your knife will not get stuck. Cut all the way through. If you have trouble getting through the fin with a single cut, pick up your portion with your other hand and let the fin bones guide your knife through them.

Step 13 Store the fish portions on paper towels in a bin or large baking sheet to help soak up extra moisture. Use fresh within 3 days or until fish no longer smells fresh. Freeze any extra portions vacuum-sealed or wrapped tightly for up to 2 months.

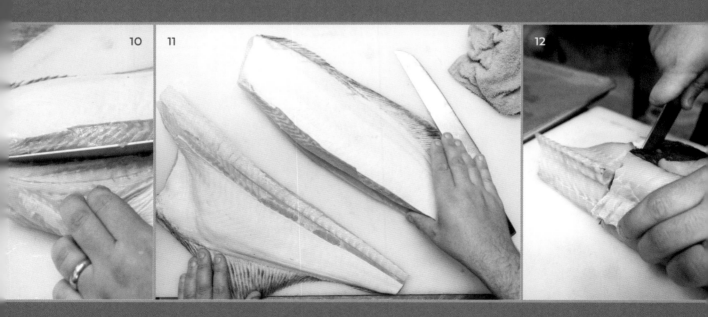

GRILLED MACKEREL
with charred poblano romesco and pickled red onion

Mackerel, much like sardine, is a strong-flavored and oily fish, so it's great with the smokiness from the grill and fun to pair with strong-flavored accompaniments. We love it, too, because it's healthy, sustainable, and holds up well to freezing, so you can usually find it year-round.

In Spain, romesco is a traditional sauce containing red chiles, sherry vinegar, garlic, bread crumbs, and usually ground hazelnuts or almonds. Our own version echoes a lot of those same flavors and ingredients but has a green color from poblano peppers. Try it on roasted green beans or asparagus in the spring, and Brussels sprouts or butternut squash in the fall or winter. It's great with grilled poultry, too, or spread on toast with a fried egg on top.

SERVES 4 AS A MAIN DISH OR 8 AS A STARTER

8 skin-on mackerel fillets (about 3 ounces each), pin bones removed

4 teaspoons kosher salt

2 teaspoons freshly ground black pepper

3 tablespoons extra-virgin olive oil

Charred Poblano Romesco (recipe follows)

16 to 20 rings Pickled Red Onion (page 249)

⅓ cup Toasted Garlic Bread Crumbs (page 250) (optional)

Prepare a grill to medium-high heat.

Season the mackerel fillets with salt and pepper, then rub with oil. Be sure to carefully oil the grate, then place the mackerel, skin side down, on the grill. Let cook, without disturbing, until the flesh is mostly opaque and the fish is more than halfway cooked through, 3 to 4 minutes. Flip the fillets and sear quickly on the flesh side to finish, about 15 seconds.

Spoon some of the Charred Poblano Romesco onto a platter. Place the fish on the platter, skin side up (this will help keep the skin crispy). Garnish with some pickled red onion rings and a sprinkling of the toasted bread crumbs. Serve the extra romesco on the side.

MAKES ABOUT 1¼ CUPS

¼ cup raw pecans

2 poblano chile peppers

6 fresh oregano leaves

2 teaspoons kosher salt

1 teaspoon sherry vinegar

¼ cup water

¼ cup extra-virgin olive oil

CHARRED POBLANO ROMESCO

Preheat the oven to 350°F.

Place the pecans on a rimmed baking sheet and roast until toasted and sweet, 6 to 9 minutes. Remove from the oven and let cool completely.

Prepare a grill to high heat.

Place the poblanos on the grill and cook, turning every few minutes, until charred and softened, 8 to 10 minutes. Seed and stem them but leave the skins on.

In a blender, combine the pecans, chiles, oregano, salt, vinegar, and water; puree until smooth. With the motor running, slowly drizzle in the oil to emulsify. The sauce can be refrigerated for up to 1 week. Bring to room temperature 2 hours before serving.

GRILLED SIDE OF SALMON

Serving a whole side of salmon rather than individually portioned fillets has its benefits. Besides being impressive looking, this presentation allows guests to serve themselves as much or as little of the fish as they want.

We typically like to grill salmon (and most other fish) with the skin still on. Not only does the skin help seal in the fish's juices to protect it from drying it out; it is also the source of much of the fish's flavor and imparts it into the flesh as it cooks. This is especially important when grilling wild salmon, which can be milder in flavor than its farm-raised counterparts.

Oyster leaves, which you can use as a garnish here, are blue-green-colored, lightly crunchy, succulent greens that taste uncannily like oysters. If you can't find them, either substitute edible flowers or proudly serve the fish ungarnished. It is pictured here with Blistered Snap Peas (page 152).

Prepare a grill to medium-high heat.

Place the salmon fillet, skin side up, on a cutting board, and score the fish by cutting three to four shallow slits through the skin about ⅛ inch deep and 3 inches long (do not pierce through the flesh). Season the fish on both sides with salt and pepper, and rub it with the oil.

Be sure to carefully oil the grate, then place the fish, skin side down, on the hot grill. (This is the only side that will come in contact with the grill.) Close the lid on the grill or cover the fish with a large metal bowl; cook, without disturbing, until the skin starts to shrink and natural juices start to bubble near the skin, 5 to 7 minutes.

Carefully remove the fillet (the very top of it will still look rare) with two metal spatulas and turn it over onto a platter, flesh-side-down. Let it rest for 3 to 5 minutes so that carryover heat can help cook the fish to the proper temperature (it should be cooked through on the thinner sections and medium-rare at its thickest parts). Garnish with oyster leaves.

SERVES 6

3 pounds wild salmon fillet, skin on, scales and bones removed by your fishmonger

Kosher salt

1 to 2 teaspoons freshly ground black pepper

¼ cup extra-virgin olive oil

Oyster leaves and/or edible flowers (optional)

CAST-IRON GRILLED WHOLE TROUT
with "black gold" fingerling potatoes and capers

Smoke is famously good with trout, and this preparation takes advantage of that. This particular whole fish can also be a good gateway if the idea of whole fish freaks you out: most seafood shops and grocery counters sell trout already gutted and deboned, so you can enjoy all of the drama of presenting a whole fish but without the messiness of the guts or paranoia about swallowing bones.

Primarily the pleasure of a whole trout or any grilled whole fish is the bronzed, crispy skin. Done properly, the skin takes on the texture of a thin, well-done slice of bacon and a little of its saltiness, too—a nice contrast to the tender, mild-flavored flesh. We balance out the richness of the skin with plenty of lemon, some briny capers, and fresh herbs.

It is very important that you have all the ingredients for the recipe prepped in advance and at the ready beside the grill, since the fish takes just a few minutes to cook.

Put the potatoes in a small pot and cover with water; season with salt. Bring to a boil, then simmer the potatoes until tender, about 10 minutes. Drain well and let cool enough to handle. Slice into ¼-inch rounds, then chill.

Prepare a grill to high heat. Preheat a cast-iron pan or any pan that can withstand high heat from the grill by placing it directly on the coals or over the hottest area of the grill.

Meanwhile, using paper towels, pat away any excess moisture from the trout. Brush the outside and inside of the cavity with the oil and season with salt and pepper. Close the fish cavity.

Add the "Black Gold" to the preheated pan, then add the fish. Cook until browned on one side, 3 to 4 minutes. Gently flip the fish using a metal spatula. Add the potatoes and capers (removing the pan from the heat and then returning it to the heat, if needed). Cook until the potatoes have started to brown, 3 to 4 minutes more. Squeeze the lemon into the pan, then add most of the parsley and all of the marjoram.

Remove the fish from the pan and transfer to a platter or two plates; divide the potatoes and capers between the plates. Taste the pan juices and adjust the seasoning, if necessary. Spoon it generously over the fish. Garnish with the remaining parsley leaves.

SERVES 2 AS A MAIN DISH OR 4 AS A STARTER

5 medium fingerling potatoes

Kosher salt

2 (12-ounce) whole boneless trout (preferably head-on, tail-on), fins removed

2 tablespoons extra-virgin olive oil

Freshly ground black pepper

2 tablespoons "Black Gold" (page 15)

2 tablespoons drained capers

1 lemon, halved

1 cup fresh flat-leaf parsley leaves

¼ cup fresh marjoram leaves

One of our primary missions in this book is to inspire you to devote more real estate on the grill to vegetables. It's easy and delicious to default to meat and fish when you fire up the grill; but to see truly transformative results, start playing around with vegetables. Time over fire can work magic on plant foods, taking their textures from woody to creamy, their colors from pale to deep, their flavors from bitter or dull to sweet and caramelized. Over the highest heat, edges darken and become crisp right before your eyes, and over low heat, deep, earthy natural flavor slowly reveals itself.

Though Ox probably sounds like a meaty name, we named our restaurant after this hardworking animal primarily because it evokes an image of pulling a plow, tilling the soil to help replenish the land's ability to grow vegetables, fruit, and grains. While we have pledged our undying love for meat, cooking would be kind of monotonous without the magic of the earth's produce coming into and out of season all the time. We think of vegetables, fruit, and grains as the great connectors, not only because people of all diets can enjoy eating them but because they keep us all in more intimate touch with the land and the seasons and the places we live.

CHAPTER 5 **GRILLED VEGETABLES**

Although not much needs to be done to make a properly grilled vegetable delicious, we wanted to take you well beyond a simple squeeze of lemon or coating of olive oil and salt. The recipes that follow will not only inspire creative contrasts in flavors and textures but will also provide a basic education in farm-to-fire technique so that, by flipping through these pages, you can always go to the market, pick up what looks good, and figure out how to maximize its potential. Just as we do at Ox, we encourage you to play around with how you serve vegetables at home—shifting them from side dishes to starters and even to mains. The seasons can guide and influence you, too. Just when you feel like you've tried everything a season offers, a new season will roll in, inspiring you all over again.

GRILLED MAITAKE MUSHROOMS
with smoked sea salt and green onions

For someone who may not eat meat, or just anyone who loves mushrooms, this is an excellent back-pocket grill recipe. The technique is pretty much foolproof, and you can use it on other mushrooms, such as oysters. The maitakes themselves are like a sponge for grill flavor, becoming tender but not overly soft after grilling, and all the wonderful little crags, crevices, and ridges in their tops capturing juices and seasonings. A touch of smoked sea salt amps it up even further.

For the same reason onions pair well with steak—their freshness and spiciness cutting through the intensity of the meat—green onions and grilled mushrooms balance each other deliciously.

Prepare a grill to high heat and be sure to carefully oil the grate.

Trying to keep the mushrooms intact and in large pieces, drizzle with ¼ cup of the oil and season with the kosher salt and pepper. Transfer the mushrooms to the hottest area of the grill, stem side up. Cook until well charred, 3 to 4 minutes; flip and grill on the other side (the stem side). (You do not need to cook the stem fully in this step.)

Transfer the mushrooms, and any small pieces that might have fallen off, into a metal pan, such as a small cast-iron skillet or cazuela that can handle high heat. Place the pan directly onto the coals or atop the hottest area of the grill. Add the water, cover the pan loosely with foil or a lid, and let steam until the stems are tender, about 3 minutes. Remove the lid and cook until the liquid in the pan is mostly reduced, about 2 minutes more. Remove the pan from the heat.

To serve, transfer the mushrooms to plates and drizzle with the juices from the pan. Immediately garnish with the smoked sea salt, green onions, and the remaining 2 tablespoons of the oil.

**SERVES 4 AS A SIDE DISH
OR 2 AS A MAIN DISH**

1 pound maitake mushrooms

6 tablespoons extra-virgin olive oil

1 teaspoon kosher salt

½ teaspoon freshly ground black pepper

½ cup water

1 teaspoon smoked sea salt, homemade (page 242) or store-bought

6 green onions, thinly sliced

GRILLED SPICY GREEN BEANS
with cashews and basil

Because of their slim size, green beans might not be an obvious choice for the grill. But prepared this way—by using a grill basket or crisscrossing grates to prevent them from slipping through—they avoid that blandness and sogginess that boiled or steamed green beans can sometimes have, and take on an edgier flavor from the fire. The vinaigrette adds so much juiciness that it's ideal if the beans are still a little crunchy.

Refreshingly acidic, with a touch of spiciness and a lemony, grassy kick from cilantro, the flavorings of this dish remind us of ceviche. But there is a wonderful umami flavor from fish sauce, a Southeast Asian condiment made from salted, fermented anchovies. It elevates the depth and savoriness in an inexplicable way—and an addictive one.

Serve this dish as a side to all kinds of meat or seafood. Or just spoon the beans over steamed rice with extra chopped cashews for a summery one-bowl meal.

SERVES 4 AS A SIDE DISH

Spicy Citrus Vinaigrette

½ cup extra-virgin olive oil

1 tablespoon sriracha sauce

2 tablespoons fish sauce

2 tablespoons sherry vinegar

2 tablespoons fresh lime juice

¼ cup tangerine juice (or substitute orange juice)

1 teaspoon finely grated tangerine zest (or substitute orange zest)

1 teaspoon kosher salt

⅛ teaspoon freshly ground black pepper

Green Beans

1 pound fresh green beans (preferably haricots verts), trimmed

3 tablespoons extra-virgin olive oil

Kosher salt and freshly ground black pepper

1 pint cherry or grape tomatoes, halved

¾ red onion, thinly sliced

1 to 2 serrano or jalapeño peppers, thinly sliced

½ cup thinly sliced fresh basil leaves, preferably Thai or opal

⅓ cup roasted cashews, coarsely chopped

To make the vinaigrette, combine the oil, sriracha, fish sauce, vinegar, lime juice, tangerine juice and zest, salt, and pepper in a bowl; whisk well to combine.

Prepare a grill to medium-high heat. Place the green beans in a large serving bowl with the oil; season with salt and pepper and toss to combine. Transfer to a grill basket, or, if you don't have one, place a sturdy metal cooling rack upside down on the grill so that the grates run in the opposite direction as those on the grill, forming a crosshatch pattern that should make the green beans harder to slip through. Let the beans cook until lightly charred, about 4 minutes, then either toss the grill basket or gently turn over the beans on the cooling rack to char the other sides. Continue cooking until firm-tender, 6 to 7 minutes (or 10 minutes for a larger-size green bean).

Return the beans to the serving bowl. Add the tomatoes, red onion, and peppers. Add the vinaigrette and toss to coat. Taste and adjust the seasoning, if necessary.

Divide among plates, if desired. Garnish with the basil and cashews.

GRILLED BABY BOK CHOY
with ecuadorian peanut sauce and hard-boiled egg

In Ecuador and other parts of South America, peanuts are used more often in savory preparations than sweet ones, and here they're a delicious complement to earthy hard-boiled eggs and the acidity of fresh lime juice. We paired a peanut butter–based sauce with bok choy, which is naturally light and juicy in contrast. You can serve this dish with anything from the Maple-Brined Pork Chops (page 95) to grilled halibut (page 133) or shrimp, or a more strongly flavored fish like grilled mackerel or sardines.

Prepare a grill to medium-high heat.

To make the peanut sauce, combine the oil, onion, and jalapeño in a small pot over medium heat. Cook, stirring constantly, for about 1 minute. Add the cumin and annatto seed and continue stirring. Stir in the milk and peanut butter until completely incorporated. Add the water and bring to a simmer. Remove from the heat, add the lime juice and salt, and keep warm but not hot.

Drizzle the bok choy on both sides with the oil and season with salt and pepper. Be sure to carefully oil the grate, then place the bok choy, cut side down, on the grill and cook until grill marks form, 4 to 5 minutes. Flip and grill on the other side for 4 more minutes.

To serve, transfer the bok choy to a serving dish. Drizzle with the peanut sauce, then garnish with the egg and cilantro.

How to Hard-Boil an Egg

To hard-boil an egg, put a cold egg in a pot and cover with about 2 inches of cold water. Bring to a boil, then turn off the heat and let sit for 10 minutes. Strain and rinse the egg until cool. When peeled and sliced, it should be fully cooked to firm but with a small area of deeper orange-colored yolk at the center.

SERVES 4 AS A SIDE DISH

Ecuadorian Peanut Sauce

2 tablespoons extra-virgin olive oil

½ small yellow onion, finely chopped

¼ cup minced jalapeño, seeded (unless you like it extra-spicy)

½ teaspoon ground cumin

1 teaspoon ground annatto seed (also known as achiote powder)

¾ cup whole milk

½ cup salted chunky or smooth peanut butter

½ cup water

1 tablespoon fresh lime juice

2 teaspoons kosher salt

Bok Choy

1½ pounds baby bok choy, halved lengthwise

½ cup extra-virgin olive oil

Kosher salt and freshly ground black pepper

2 hard-boiled eggs, peeled and chopped (see Note)

½ cup fresh cilantro leaves

GRILLED ZUCCHINI AND EGGPLANT
with castelvetrano olive–almond salsa

When grilling zucchini or eggplant, people will often stop at salt, pepper, and olive oil for seasoning. But since both zucchini and eggplant are watery, light-flavored vegetables, we think they can use some extra love. By adding the brininess from green olives, the saltiness and crunchiness of Marcona almonds, and the natural spiciness of radish, you can really elevate these pedestrian garden vegetables. You might not think of salsa as contributing a lot of texture to a dish, but between the meatiness of the green olives and the oily goodness of the Marconas, this one does. Choosing smaller zucchini helps them cook quickly without becoming soggy, giving the whole dish a more crunchy texture.

SERVES 4 AS A SIDE DISH

Castelvetrano Olive–Almond Salsa

⅓ cup extra-virgin olive oil

½ cup coarsely chopped pitted Castelvetrano olives or any mild green olives

½ cup coarsely chopped Marcona almonds or toasted slivered almonds

2 tablespoons fresh lemon juice

1 teaspoon finely grated orange zest

1 teaspoon chopped fresh oregano

1 teaspoon crushed chipotle chile flakes or chipotle powder

¼ teaspoon kosher salt, plus more to taste

Grilled Zucchini and Eggplant

2 small green and 2 small yellow zucchini, halved lengthwise

4 small Japanese or Italian eggplants, halved lengthwise

¼ cup extra-virgin olive oil

Kosher salt and freshly ground black pepper

4 small radishes, thinly sliced

Prepare a grill to medium-high heat.

To make the salsa, in a small bowl, combine the oil, olives, almonds, lemon juice, orange zest, oregano, chipotle pepper, and salt; mix well. Taste and adjust the seasoning, if necessary. Let sit at room temperature for up to 1 hour. (The salsa can be made up to 1 day ahead, but leave out the chopped almonds until just before serving to retain their crunch.)

Lay out the zucchini and eggplant on a flat dish or baking sheet. Drizzle with the oil and sprinkle with salt and pepper. Be sure to carefully oil the grate, then grill, cut side down, until grill marks appear, about 2 minutes. Flip and repeat on the second side, then remove the zucchini from the grill and transfer to a serving dish. If needed, turn the eggplant back over to the first side and cook for 2 minutes more, or until tender. Transfer to the serving dish with the zucchini. Drizzle with the salsa and garnish with the sliced radishes.

BLISTERED SNAP PEAS

with "everything" bagel seasoning, chive mascarpone, and smoked salmon roe

Thanks to modern-day grill baskets, cooking peas on a grill doesn't seem like something only a crazy person would do. We toss blistered snap peas with half butter and half sesame oil, which doesn't impart an over-the-top Asian flavor like many dishes with sesame oil do. It's just enough to bring out the nuttiness in the everything-bagel seasoning, which is there for extra flavor, pop, and texture. Double the recipe for the seasoning if you want to have extra during the week for other sides like green beans, roasted potatoes, brussels sprouts, or slices of ripe tomato and avocado.

The peas and seasoning mixture are good on their own, but the creaminess of the mascarpone and saltiness of the smoked salmon roe make this dish sensational. Making mascarpone at home is easy and cost efficient: all you need is cream, lemon, and salt. And if you don't have a smoker or don't want to make the effort to smoke the salmon roe, just marinate the roe as instructed.

Prepare a grill to high heat.

In a serving bowl, toss the snap peas with 2 tablespoons of the oil; transfer to a grill basket. Put the butter and remaining 2 tablespoons oil in the empty bowl and set it nearby.

Place the grill pan directly onto the coals, if using, or over the hottest part of the grill; cook until the outsides of the snap peas start to blister, 45 to 60 seconds. Remove from the heat, then toss or stir the snap peas to flip them and continue cooking for 45 seconds more. Return the snap peas to the bowl with the sesame oil mixture. Lightly season with salt, then stir to coat. Sprinkle with the everything-bagel seasoning; stir again to coat. Taste and adjust the seasonings as needed.

Garnish with a generous dollop of mascarpone, a spoonful of smoked salmon roe, and the chives; serve immediately.

SERVES 4 TO 6 AS A STARTER OR SIDE DISH

1 pound snap peas, stems removed, fibrous strings peeled away

¼ cup toasted sesame oil

2 tablespoons unsalted butter, softened to room temperature

Flaked sea salt

¾ cup "Everything" Bagel Seasoning (recipe follows)

⅓ cup mascarpone cheese, homemade (page 250) or store-bought

3 tablespoons Smoked Salmon Roe (recipe follows)

¼ cup thinly sliced chives

MAKES 1 CUP

2 tablespoons poppy seeds

2 teaspoons nigella seeds

1 teaspoon caraway seeds

¼ cup toasted sesame seeds
(see Note, page 246)

¼ cup roasted sunflower seeds

2 teaspoons dried onion flakes

2 teaspoons dried garlic flakes

1 tablespoon flaked sea salt

"EVERYTHING" BAGEL SEASONING

Toast the poppy, nigella, and caraway seeds, one type at a time, as they each cook at different rates. Place each batch in a small pan warmed over medium heat. Cook, tossing or stirring the seeds constantly until they begin to pop or bounce around the pan from the heat, about 1 minute for each. Remove each batch from the pan quickly to avoid burning, and add to a bowl. Once the seeds have cooled to room temperature, stir in the sesame seeds, sunflower seeds, dried onion, garlic flakes, and salt. If not using immediately, store in a very dry, airtight container up to 2 weeks.

MAKES ¼ CUP

1 (2-ounce) jar cured salmon roe

1 tablespoon mirin (Japanese sweet rice wine)

1 teaspoon soy sauce (gluten-free if desired)

SMOKED SALMON ROE

Put the salmon roe in a small stainless steel pan and sprinkle with the mirin and soy sauce. Transfer to a cold smoker (see sidebar on page 16) and smoke for 15 minutes. Mix gently with a rubber spatula and smoke for 5 minutes more, or until the desired smokiness is achieved. Store in the refrigerator for up to 1 week.

COAL-ROASTED SPAGHETTI SQUASH

with toasted garlic, lemon, and aged goat cheese

So maybe you can't grill pasta, but the flavors and textures in this dish are pretty close to a fire-cooked spaghetti *all'aglio e olio*. When pulled with a fork, spaghetti squash really does look like pasta, so we ran with the theme. The skins, which char beautifully over the fire, make the perfect serving "bowls," and the not-shy accoutrements make an otherwise bland squash a standout.

Much like pasta, this squash is a great dish for a party because it's simple and affordable enough to scale up. You can also get a lot done in advance, like cutting, seeding, and roasting the squash, and making the garlic-lemon oil. Once you get the grill going, it's just a matter of reheating the squash, then letting that cheese cascade down over the top—the best part.

Preheat the oven to 375°F and set a rack in the center of the oven.

Halve the squash lengthwise and scoop out the seeds. Drizzle the interior of the squash with some olive oil and season with salt and pepper. Transfer the halves, cut side down, to a baking sheet, then rub olive oil on the skins. Roast until the flesh is just tender, 30 to 40 minutes.

Remove the squash from the oven and let rest until cool enough to handle. Cut each piece in half again to create wedges. Starting at the top layer, scrape each squash portion with the tines of a fork to loosen up the strands, letting the skins serve as a "bowl." Season again with a drizzle of olive oil and a pinch each of salt and pepper. Keep warm until ready to grill.

Prepare a grill to medium-high heat. If using coals, once the fire has died down and the coals are glowing red, spread them out to create a level surface.

Place a metal cooling rack directly onto the coals, if using, and transfer the squash quarters to the cooling rack, cut side up. If using a gas grill, place the squash over the hottest area and cover the grill. Cook until the squash is heated all the way through, about 15 minutes. (The tough outer skins will get charred but should remain intact.)

Remove from the grill, and place each portion on a plate or in a bowl. Drizzle with the garlic-lemon oil, making sure to divide the garlic slices evenly. Using a fine grater, grate the goat cheese over the top of each squash quarter, distributing it evenly and abundantly. Garnish with chopped parsley.

SERVES 4 AS A SIDE DISH

1 large spaghetti squash (about the length of a football)

5 tablespoons extra-virgin olive oil

Kosher salt and freshly ground black pepper

1 cup Toasted Garlic–Lemon Oil (page 244)

3 to 4 ounces aged, firm goat cheese (we love Briar Rose Creamery's Chevarino Romano, a pecorino-style goat cheese)

2 tablespoons chopped fresh flat-leaf parsley leaves

GRILLED ASPARAGUS
with herbed dungeness crab and crispy capers

Because of their mutual delicateness, spring vegetables tend to go really well with shellfish, without overpowering the seafood's subtle sweetness. Really, any crabmeat would do here, or you could substitute little bay shrimp.

What do provide a concentrated pocket of flavor are the crispy capers, which we dry, then fry, to rid them of their spongy quality and turn them into a crunchy garnish. If you do the frying up to several hours in advance, they'll be ready and waiting when the asparagus is fresh off the grill.

Served alongside any protein or mushroom from the grill, this dish brings a surf-and-turf quality to any meal.

SERVES 4 AS A SIDE DISH OR STARTER

Crispy Capers
¼ cup neutral-flavored vegetable oil

2 tablespoons nonpareil capers

Grilled Asparagus
1¼ pounds skinny asparagus, woody stems snapped off

2 tablespoons extra-virgin olive oil

Kosher salt and freshly ground black pepper

Herbed Crab
¼ cup water

½ cup unsalted butter, cut into 8 pieces

1½ tablespoons fresh lemon juice, plus ½ teaspoon finely grated lemon zest

½ teaspoon ají amarillo powder (or substitute 2 pinches cayenne pepper)

4 ounces Dungeness crabmeat (or substitute blue crabmeat), picked clean of any shells

3 tablespoons thinly sliced chives

1 tablespoon chopped fresh dill

Kosher salt (optional)

To Serve
16 fresh tarragon leaves

To make the crispy capers, heat the vegetable oil in a small pot over medium heat until a deep-fry thermometer registers 350°F. Meanwhile, place the capers on a paper towel to remove excess moisture. Gently drop the capers into the oil and fry until they have opened slightly and dried out, about 2 minutes. Remove from the oil with a slotted spoon and let cool on a paper towel.

Prepare a grill to medium-high heat.

Place the asparagus on a flat surface and drizzle with the olive oil. Season lightly with salt and pepper, and toss to coat evenly. Grill, turning frequently, until just cooked through, 2 to 3 minutes. Transfer to a serving dish and keep warm.

To make the crab, warm a skillet over medium heat on the stove. Add the water and bring to a boil. Reduce the heat to low, then add the butter, piece by piece, swirling the pan to emulsify. Once all the butter has been added and the sauce is thickened, add the lemon juice and zest, the ají amarillo powder, then the crab, swirling the pan constantly. Let cook over low heat until the crab is just heated through, about 1 minute; remove immediately. Stir in the chives and dill. Taste and add salt, if necessary.

To serve, spoon the herbed crab over the warm asparagus. Garnish with the crispy capers and tarragon.

GRILLED PADRÓN PEPPERS
with corn, tomatoes, fried egg, and manchego

Padróns are a Spanish Basque pepper that are similar to a Japanese shishito pepper, and they have a mysterious element: one in every ten or so tends to be spicy, while the others are fairly mild and sweet. Padróns are best served simply, blistered and seasoned with good olive oil and sea salt. Unlike other peppers, they are so thin-skinned and delicate that they never have to be peeled or seeded.

The elements of this dish can be broken down to suit your mood. You can grill the peppers quickly and shave Manchego on top, or just eat the padróns with a fried egg or on their own for a snack. We turned them into a more composed dish that would make a great breakfast, lunch, or dinner side dish, and it takes advantage of two of the best types of summer produce: tomatoes and corn.

If you don't feel like heating the grill, sear the peppers in a hot pan, tossing occasionally, with very little olive oil.

Prepare a grill to medium-high heat.

Place the padróns in a large bowl and drizzle with 2 tablespoons of the oil. Season with salt and toss to coat evenly. Transfer to a grill basket, or, if you don't have one, place a sturdy metal cooling rack upside down on the grill so that the grates run in the opposite direction as those on the grill, forming a crosshatch pattern that should make the peppers harder to slip through.

Grill until the peppers begin to blister, about 2 minutes; shake the grill basket or turn the peppers over and cook for 2 minutes more. Remove from the heat but tent loosely with foil to keep warm.

In a large skillet, melt the butter over medium heat. Add the corn and cook, stirring, about 2 minutes. Add the halved cherry tomatoes and cook until just warmed through, about 1 minute more; season the mixture with salt and pepper. Keep warm while you fry the eggs.

Warm a large nonstick skillet over medium heat. Add the remaining ¼ cup oil, then crack the eggs into the skillet. Raise the heat to medium-high and cook the eggs sunny side up. Baste the egg whites occasionally with the hot oil to help cook them without overcooking the yolks. As soon as the whites have turned from clear to opaque, remove the eggs quickly from the pan. Season the eggs with salt and black pepper.

To serve, divide the corn and tomato mixture among four dishes, then place the eggs on top. Distribute the padrón peppers among the dishes. Garnish with Manchego.

SERVES 4 AS A SIDE DISH, STARTER, OR SMALL MAIN DISH

40 to 50 padrón peppers

6 tablespoons extra-virgin olive oil

Kosher salt

½ cup unsalted butter

Kernels from 2 ears fresh corn

1 pint cherry tomatoes, halved

Freshly ground black pepper

4 eggs

3 ounces Manchego cheese (or your favorite hard cheese, such as Parmigiano-Reggiano), finely grated

GRILLED SWEET ONION
with buttered beets, blue cheese, and walnuts

This dish was inspired by our first trip to Europe together. We rented a cottage on a Provençal vineyard with a little kitchen and set out to the farmers' market, where we picked up all kinds of great produce and cheese. Back at our place, we lit a fire of grapevine clippings in the fireplace and roasted the onion in the hot ashes.

As sharp as an onion can be when it's raw, exposing it to the high level of heat on a grill gives you surprisingly quick caramelization, juiciness, and sweetness, transforming this pungent vegetable almost into a fruit. Still, the onion keeps its savory component in this dish, paired alongside earthy red beets and a strong-flavored cheese. We love that this recipe delivers big, bold flavors without too much richness or heaviness. It is our favorite accompaniment to a rib-eye steak.

Preheat the oven to 350°F.

Spread the walnuts out on a small baking sheet or ovenproof dish and roast until lightly browned and fragrant, 8 to 10 minutes. Remove from the oven and lower the oven temperature to 200°F. Once the walnuts have cooled to room temperature, coarsely crumble or chop them up; set aside.

Prepare a grill to medium heat.

Quarter the onions lengthwise, keeping the root attached so the onion layers don't separate. Drizzle each quarter with a little oil and season with salt and pepper. Transfer, cut side down, to the grill. Cook until dark grill marks form on one side, 3 to 4 minutes, then turn to another cut side and cook for 3 to 4 minutes more. Flip once more so that the onion is curved side down, and cook for 3 to 4 minutes more. If the onion feels tender, remove from the grill. If the inner onion layers still seem raw, transfer to a less hot portion of the grill and continue to cook until just cooked through.

Transfer the onions to four large plates or one large serving platter, separating the onion petals if desired. Crumble the blue cheese on top and keep warm in the oven.

Put the beets in a small skillet or saucepan over medium heat and add the water; season with salt and pepper. As soon as the water begins to simmer, turn the heat to low and add the butter, a couple pieces at a time. Swirl the pan until the butter melts and forms a thick, emulsified sauce. Remove from the heat, adjust the seasoning, if necessary, then spoon the buttered beets over the onions and blue cheese. Drizzle with the saba, then garnish with the walnuts and chives.

SERVES 4 AS A SIDE DISH

10 walnut halves

2 whole sweet onions (such as Walla Walla, Vidalia, or Maui), peeled

2 tablespoons extra-virgin olive oil

Kosher salt and freshly ground black pepper

3 ounces Fourme d'Ambert blue cheese (or any high-quality blue cheese)

2 cups diced roasted beets (page 249) (¼-inch cubes)

¼ cup water

½ cup unsalted butter, cut into ½-inch cubes

3 tablespoons saba (reduced grape must) or store-bought balsamic vinegar glaze

¼ cup thinly sliced chives

GRILLED BUTTERNUT SQUASH
with za'atar and charred green onion yogurt

While you can use pretty much any winter squash for this recipe (other than spaghetti squash), we like that butternut have long necks (as opposed to just skinny, hollow rings) that can potentially be grilled like steaks or fillets. Butternut has a very intense richness that works well on the grill and goes well with strong flavors. To prevent its sweetness from taking over, we pair it with a savory yogurt and some bright spices.

Za'atar is a spice blend used in parts of the Middle East. Everyone's grandma has a different recipe for it, and there can be anywhere from a few spices and herbs to a dozen or so. Usually the spice mix incorporates the toasty nuttiness of sesame seeds as well as the bright flavor of sumac, a berry that when powdered and dried gives a great tanginess. Make your own za'atar (page 246) or buy it premixed at the market.

Preheat the oven to 350°F. Line a baking sheet with parchment paper.

Using a vegetable peeler, peel the butternut squash and slice the neck and bulb parts either crosswise into ¾-inch rounds or lengthwise (like in the photo); scrape out the seeds with a spoon. Transfer to the prepared baking sheet and brush with 4 tablespoons of the oil; season with salt and pepper. Roast until barely softened, 20 to 24 minutes. Remove and let cool to room temperature.

Prepare a grill to medium-high heat. Coat the green onions with the remaining 1 tablespoon oil and sprinkle with salt and pepper. Grill until lightly charred on one side, 2 to 3 minutes. Flip and grill on the other side. Let cool to room temperature.

Finely chop the charred green onions and transfer to a bowl. Add the yogurt, dill, chives, 1 tablespoon salt, and 1 teaspoon pepper; mix well and adjust the seasoning as needed. Refrigerate until ready to use.

Be sure to carefully oil the grate, and place the butternut squash on the grill and cook, turning once, until heated through, 3 to 5 minutes per side. Remove from the grill.

To serve, spread half of the charred green onion yogurt into the middle of a serving platter or four individual plates. Sprinkle each of the grilled squash slices with a heaping teaspoon of za'atar and place them over the yogurt, overlapping slightly if desired. Serve the remaining yogurt sauce in a small bowl on the side.

SERVES 4 AS A SIDE DISH OR 2 AS A MAIN DISH

1 large butternut squash (2½ to 3 pounds)

5 tablespoons extra-virgin olive oil

Kosher salt and freshly ground black pepper

8 green onions, trimmed

2 cups Greek yogurt

2 tablespoons chopped fresh dill, plus coarsely chopped dill for garnishing

2 tablespoons thinly sliced chives

¼ cup za'atar, homemade (page 246) or store-bought

GRILLED PORTOBELLO MUSHROOMS AND HEIRLOOM TOMATO

with faux béarnaise

Béarnaise is essentially a hollandaise sauce with herbs. You see it served with steak in French bistros, and it's delicious with leaner, more mild-flavored cuts of steak because it amps up the richness. Since the traditional recipe requires an arm-numbing amount of whisking, we created this shortcut version with a mayonnaise base.

Think of this recipe as the vegetarian steak dish. Just as steak is so good with tomatoes because they help cut the richness, the same is true in this case of grilled portobellos. The trick to grilling tomatoes without making a mess is to choose a firm fruit and be sure the grill heat is ultrahigh and the grate is oiled and seasoned. Don't fuss around with it much—leave the tomato slices until the point when they naturally release from the grill. You'll know they're close to that stage when you start to see bubbles escaping from the edges, kind of like when pancakes are ready to be flipped on the griddle.

SERVES 4 AS A STARTER OR SMALL MAIN DISH

Faux Béarnaise

1 tablespoon minced shallot

1½ teaspoons tarragon vinegar or champagne vinegar

½ teaspoon coarsely ground black peppercorns

½ cup mayonnaise, homemade (page 243) or good-quality store-bought

2 teaspoons thinly sliced fresh tarragon leaves, or more to taste

Water

Kosher salt

Grilled Portobellos and Tomato

1 large heirloom tomato

¼ cup extra-virgin olive oil

Kosher salt

4 large portobello mushrooms, stemmed, gills removed if desired

1 heaping tablespoon thinly sliced green onion

Prepare a grill to medium-high heat.

To make the béarnaise sauce, in a medium bowl, combine the shallot, vinegar, and peppercorns; let sit for 5 minutes, then whisk in the mayonnaise and tarragon. Whisk in water 1 tablespoon at a time, as needed, until the sauce reaches the desired hollandaiselike consistency. Season with salt to taste.

Slice the tomato crosswise into four thick slices, each about ¾ inch thick. Brush each slice with about 1 teaspoon oil and season generously with salt.

Brush both sides of the portobellos with the remaining oil and season with salt. Be sure to carefully oil the grate, then place the mushrooms stem side down on the grill and cook until they begin to soften and become crisp at the edges, about 3 minutes. Flip the mushrooms, moving them to a slightly less hot part of the grill. Re-oil the grill grates, then place the tomatoes on the hottest part of the grill and cook, turning once, for about 3 minutes total.

Using a metal spatula, place a grilled tomato slice on top of each mushroom cap and top each with a generous dollop of the béarnaise. Cover the grill or top the mushrooms with a large bowl to warm through. Cook for 3 minutes more, then carefully transfer to a platter or plates. Garnish with the green onion and serve.

GRILLED NEW POTATO AND ONION SKEWERS
with bacon-sherry cream

Bacon-sherry cream is one of Greg's favorite sauces to make, and everything we've ever served it with has been so damned delicious—summer corn, brussels sprouts, roasted scallops, lentils. It's incredible on new potatoes, which take on crispy skins when grilled.

Though the sauce is cream-based and rich, it's balanced with black pepper, acid from the sherry vinegar, and juicy sweetness from the grilled onion. You can make the sauce and thread the skewers in advance, then throw the skewers on the grill after your guests settle in.

To make the bacon-sherry cream, put the bacon, butter, and garlic in a nonreactive saucepan over medium heat. Cook, stirring occasionally, until the garlic is lightly browned, 5 to 6 minutes. Add the peppercorns and thyme and cook, stirring constantly, until the thyme stops sputtering. Add the vinegar, scraping up any browned bits from the pan with a wooden spoon. Simmer until the liquid is reduced by half. Add the cream and salt and bring to a boil, then quickly reduce to a simmer to avoid boiling over. Simmer for 20 minutes, then strain through a fine-mesh strainer. Keep warm, reheating to hot just before serving.

Prepare a grill to medium-high heat.

Put the potatoes in a pot and cover with water. Add a heaping tablespoon of salt to the water and bring to a simmer; simmer until completely tender when pierced with a knife, 14 to 20 minutes. Drain and transfer to a baking sheet. Let cool to room temperature.

Place the cooled potatoes in a bowl. (If any are larger than the diameter of a quarter, cut in half.) Cut the onion into 1-inch square chunks and add them to the bowl with the potatoes. Drizzle with the oil, salt, and pepper, and toss gently to coat. Using flat metal skewers, begin to skewer alternating pieces of potato, onion, and bacon, pressing them tightly together.

Once all the vegetables and bacon are skewered, be sure to oil the grate and place the skewers on the grill. Cook until the onions and bacon slices have some char to them and the potatoes are heated through, rotating often, 10 to 12 minutes.

Remove the skewers from the heat and serve with the bacon-sherry cream in a bowl on the side or drizzled over the top of the skewers.

SERVES 4 TO 6 AS A SIDE DISH

Bacon-Sherry Cream

½ cup chopped bacon (from about 2 thick-cut slices), homemade (page 246) or store-bought

¼ cup unsalted butter

3 large cloves garlic, lightly crushed

2 tablespoons black peppercorns, crushed

½ bunch thyme (about 15 sprigs)

½ cup sherry vinegar

4 cups heavy cream

2 teaspoons kosher salt

Grilled Potatoes and Bacon

1½ pounds extra-small new potatoes (preferably no bigger than a ping-pong ball)

Kosher salt

1 small yellow onion

¼ cup extra-virgin olive oil

Freshly ground black pepper

6 to 7 slices thick-cut bacon cut into 1-inch lengths, homemade (page 246) or store-bought

GRILLED BROCCOLINI
with taleggio cream and hazelnuts

Broccolini works surprisingly well on the grill (unlike regular broccoli, which tends to dry out and can take forever to tenderize). You don't have to peel the stems, and the florets have a moisture and looseness to them that helps them crisp up nicely without disintegrating.

Though you can eat this dish in any season, it is ideal for fall or winter grilling. It's lighter than a potato gratin—and does not necessarily require using the oven—but has a similar alpine flavor and feel due to the taleggio, a strongly flavored cheese with some solid funkiness that just so happens to melt really well. If you want to give this dish more of a gratinlike finish, plate the grilled broccolini in gratin dishes and broil until the sauce is bubbly and lightly browned, about 2 minutes.

Prepare a grill to medium-high heat.

Meanwhile, to blanch the broccolini, bring a large pot of salted water to a boil and set a large bowl of ice water next to the stove. Divide the broccolini into three bunches and place one bunch into the boiling water. Cook until bright green and slightly tender, about 1 minute; transfer to the ice water. Repeat with the remaining broccolini bunches. Drain and transfer to a towel to dry.

Pour the heavy cream into a small, heavy saucepan and bring to a simmer over medium heat. Reduce the heat to low. Add the taleggio pieces and whisk slowly into the hot cream until melted. Add the nutmeg, then season with salt and white pepper to taste. Remove from the heat and keep warm.

Coat the blanched broccolini with the oil and season with salt. Transfer to the grill, using a grill basket if desired, and cook until the florets begin to char lightly, 2 minutes. Flip and cook on the other side for 1 minute.

To serve, place the broccolini on one large or four small plates. Spoon the taleggio cream over the broccolini, dividing it evenly. Garnish with the chopped hazelnuts.

SERVES 4 AS A SIDE DISH

1 pound broccolini, trimmed

Kosher salt

1½ cups heavy cream

6 ounces taleggio cheese, rinds trimmed away, cheese cut into ½-inch pieces

¼ teaspoon freshly grated nutmeg

Freshly ground white pepper

3 tablespoons extra-virgin olive oil

½ cup toasted hazelnuts, coarsely chopped

PART 3 **FROM THE GARDEN**

In the meat-driven *parrilla* culture of Argentina, the salad can often be somewhat of an afterthought. Frequently served as a side to beef or other proteins from the grill, salads rarely are more complex than one or two types of crisp lettuce and the occasional tomato or onion. Nonetheless, we appreciate seeing them on the table, because there is nothing quite like the relief and delight your mouth gets when switching from hearty grilled meats to crisp, cooling vegetables.

We say "vegetables" because, to us, salads don't necessarily need to be made of greens. In fact, the characteristics of a great salad can vary depending on the time of year, as well as what else you're serving in the meal. The best versions do have a few things in common, however. They offer punch, whether it's delivered through bracingly bitter greens or a generous dose of acidity from citrus or vinegar. Secondly, salads offer the power to relieve the palate and provide contrast to the other items on the table, be they grilled meats or platters of warm vegetables or grains. And finally, the best salads also offer a variety of textures and contrasts within themselves, from juicy to crunchy, sweet to bitter, and beyond.

CHAPTER 6　# SALADS

There is an essential leap between even the most perfect-looking produce and a delicious salad, and that is a sensational dressing. Whether you're going Italian countryside–style with little more than a bottle of really good olive oil and salt, or you've whipped up a more inspired or complex vinaigrette, ultimately a great dressing is one of the main factors that transforms simple ingredients into something more. Many qualities are in play here: creaminess, saltiness, acidity, and sweetness.

As you'll see in the recipes that follow, we love to add a little something special to our salads—a garnish that might be considered luxurious, some cooked elements, or an ingredient that's not what you might typically use in your everyday repertoire. A little flair is worth it in the end. Because, to us, the measure of a great bowl of greens is simply this: how much fun have you added to it?

KALE AND RADICCHIO SALAD

with miso-lemon dressing, feta, and crispy red onion rings

We have no problem admitting that we really dig Caesar salads. To capture the unabashed creaminess and pungent characteristics of a Caesar while taking the flavor to a new or unexpected place, we base the dressing here on miso paste, which has salty, fermented flavors, then mellow it out with a house-made mayonnaise and brighten it up with lemon juice and zest. The dressing recipe makes double what you'll need, and remainders keep for at least 2 weeks in the fridge. It tastes equally amazing on a spinach or romaine salad, or used as a glaze or marinade for chicken or fish before grilling.

As far as salad "greens" go, kale and radicchio are fibrous, chewy, and typically not very juicy on their own. But their intense flavors and textures stand up well to creamy dressings.

If you don't have time to fry the onion rings or just want to keep it simple, thinly sliced red onions are a tasty alternative; just soak them in water for a few minutes before adding to soften their harsh bite.

SERVES 4 TO 6 AS A STARTER OR SIDE DISH

1 large bunch curly kale, stems removed, leaves torn into bite-size pieces (about 8 cups)

2 small heads radicchio, torn into bite-size pieces (about 8 cups)

¾ cup Miso-Lemon Dressing (recipe follows), plus more as needed

4 ounces feta cheese, crumbled (about 1 cup)

2 tablespoons thinly sliced chives

Crispy Red Onion Rings (recipe follows) (or substitute thinly sliced red onion)

Combine the kale and radicchio in a large serving bowl and drizzle with ¾ cup of the dressing; toss with your hands, scrunching up the kale with your fingers and massaging the dressing into it. Taste and add more dressing, if desired, and continue tossing until evenly coated.

Divide among plates or serve family-style. Garnish with the feta, chives, and onion rings.

MISO-LEMON DRESSING

MAKES ABOUT 2 CUPS

5 tablespoons white miso

¼ cup fresh lemon juice

Zest of ½ lemon, finely grated

½ small garlic clove, finely grated or minced

2 cups mayonnaise, homemade (page 243) or store-bought

¾ teaspoon freshly ground black pepper

In a large bowl, whisk together the miso, lemon juice, lemon zest, and garlic until well combined. Whisk in the mayonnaise and pepper until the mixture is smooth. Cover and keep chilled until ready to use, up to 2 weeks.

CONTINUED

MAKES ENOUGH TO GARNISH
6 SALADS (ABOUT 2 CUPS)

2 to 3 cups neutral-flavored vegetable oil, for shallow frying

1 cup well-shaken buttermilk

1 small red onion, sliced into ⅛-inch-thick rings

1 cup rice flour

Kosher salt and freshly ground black pepper

CRISPY RED ONION RINGS

Pour the oil into a pot (it should measure 1½ to 2 inches up the sides of the pot); heat over medium heat until the temperature registers 375°F on a deep-fry thermometer.

Preheat the oven to 200°F. Line a plate with paper towels.

Pour the buttermilk into a bowl and add the onions; separate the rings with your fingers, swirling them until well-coated.

Pour the flour into another bowl. Transfer the onion rings to the flour in small batches, tossing to coat evenly. Transfer the rings, tapping off any excess flour, to a baking sheet or large platter.

Carefully add six to eight onion rings at a time into the oil and cook until lightly browned on one side, 30 to 60 seconds. Turn quickly and gently using tongs, chopsticks, or a slotted metal spoon; cook for 30 to 60 seconds more. Place on the prepared plate to drain any excess oil and season immediately with salt and pepper. Fry the remaining onion rings. Keep warm in the oven until ready to use.

SIMPLE GREEN SALAD

Reminiscent of the straightforward, unfussy green salads that we were so grateful to have been served alongside large platters of meat in Argentina and Uruguay, this version is perfect for those times when you just need something light, fresh, and easy to serve with a meal—especially a rich one. In the summer, you can add additional fresh vegetables such as tomato or cucumber, or embellish the greens with fresh herbs such as chervil, cilantro, basil, or chives.

In a large bowl, combine the lettuces and onion and drizzle with the oil and vinegar. Season with the salt and a couple pinches of pepper and toss gently to combine and distribute seasoning. Taste and adjust the seasoning, if necessary.

Cut the avocado into ¾-inch pieces. Serve the salad in a large serving bowl or divide among four individual bowls or plates. Garnish with the avocado and serve immediately.

SERVES 4 AS A SIDE DISH

8 cups loosely packed baby lettuce leaves, such as Little Gem, red or green leaf, or baby romaine (8 ounces total)

¼ onion, halved through the stem and thinly sliced against the grain

¼ cup extra-virgin olive oil

1 tablespoon plus 1 teaspoon red wine vinegar

½ teaspoon kosher salt, plus more as needed

Freshly ground black pepper

1 avocado, halved, pitted, and peeled

LITTLE GEM LETTUCES
with mozzarella milanesa and fried anchovy vinaigrette

SERVES 4 AS A STARTER, SIDE DISH, OR SMALL MAIN DISH

Fried Anchovy Vinaigrette

¾ cup extra-virgin olive oil

1½ tablespoons chopped garlic

¼ teaspoon red pepper flakes

1 tablespoon chopped oil-packed anchovies (2 or 3 fillets)

1 tablespoon sherry vinegar

1 tablespoon fresh lemon juice

Kosher salt and freshly ground black pepper

Mozzarella Milanesa

2 (4-ounce) balls fresh mozzarella, drained and halved

1 egg

¼ cup milk

5 tablespoons all-purpose flour

½ teaspoon kosher salt

¼ teaspoon freshly ground black pepper

¾ cup dried bread crumbs

¾ cup finely grated Parmigiano-Reggiano

About 4 cups neutral-flavored vegetable oil, for deep-frying

Salad and Garnishes

4 quarts loosely packed Little Gem lettuce leaves

⅓ cup chopped Marcona almonds

2 tablespoons coarsely chopped pickled red peppers

Kosher salt and freshly ground black pepper

1 medium-large avocado, peeled and cut into ¾-inch chunks

2 tablespoons thinly sliced chives

In Latin America just as in Italy, Milanesa-style is a preparation you often find with meats—pounded thin, lightly breaded, then pan-fried. We love that tradition, but since we're so smitten with grilling our meats, we wanted to adapt the Milanesa technique to other ingredients, and a ball of fresh mozzarella seemed the perfect fit.

The salad it sits on is a flattering accompaniment for grilled seafood, lamb, poultry, and steak. It covers the salad must-haves: crunch (almonds), creaminess (avocados), and sweet-spiciness (pickled peppers).

To make the vinaigrette, in a medium nonreactive pot over medium-low heat, add ¼ cup of the olive oil, the garlic, and the red pepper flakes; cook until the garlic is lightly browned, 3 to 4 minutes. Add the anchovies and stir until mostly dissolved, 45 to 60 seconds. Add the vinegar and lemon juice and bring to a simmer. Season generously with salt and pepper and remove from the heat. Whisk in the remaining ½ cup olive oil. Taste and adjust the seasoning, if necessary. Let cool to room temperature before using. (At this point, the vinaigrette can be refrigerated for up to 10 days; bring back to room temperature before using.)

To make the mozzarella Milanesa, dry the mozzarella on a paper towel for about 5 minutes. In a small bowl, whisk the egg and milk. Add the flour, salt, and pepper, and whisk just until smooth. In a separate bowl, combine the bread crumbs and the Parmigiano-Reggiano.

Working with one piece at a time, completely coat the mozzarella in the egg mixture. Transfer to the bowl of bread crumbs, rolling to coat all sides (press gently if needed to help the bread crumb mixture adhere). Chill for at least 20 minutes or up to 12 hours before frying.

In a heavy large pot, heat the vegetable oil over medium heat until it registers 375°F on a deep-fry thermometer.

Shortly before the oil comes up to temperature, make the salad. In a large bowl, combine the lettuce, almonds, and pickled peppers; drizzle with ⅔ cup of the vinaigrette, toss well, and season to taste, adding more dressing, if needed. Distribute the salad among four plates. Sprinkle a bit of salt and pepper on the avocado chunks and divide them among the salads.

Set a paper towel–lined plate next to the stove. Carefully transfer the mozzarella balls into the heated oil; fry until the bread crumbs are golden brown, 1½ to 2 minutes. Gently turn and cook on the second side for 1 minute more; transfer to the paper towel–lined plate. Season with salt. Place a freshly fried mozzarella half-ball on top of each salad and garnish with chives. Serve immediately.

BELGIAN ENDIVE SALAD

with pecans, fresh cherries, dijon vinaigrette, and stilton blue

Say what you will about endive, to us, it's just the right degree of bitter and a juicy, easy-to-work-with salad green. It does benefit from either something creamy or smoky to contrast its bitterness, which is why it's one of our favorite things to serve or eat with a steak, and also why we add the blue cheese. Between the fresh fruit and the crunch, plus the rich crumbled blue cheese, this salad has the same elements as a cheese plate but in reverse proportions.

Endive is available almost year-round, but if it's not cherry season quite yet, you can swap in thin slices of apple or pear.

SERVES 4 AS A STARTER OR SIDE DISH

1 cup raw pecan halves

4 small heads Belgian endive

Dijon Vinaigrette (recipe follows)

Kosher salt and freshly ground black pepper

1¼ cups pitted fresh sweet cherries, sliced

4 ounces Stilton blue cheese, crumbled (about 1 cup)

2 tablespoons thinly sliced chives

¼ cup Bing Cherry Puree (recipe follows)

Preheat the oven to 350°F.

Place the pecans on a rimmed baking sheet and roast until toasty and sweet, 6 to 9 minutes. Remove from the oven and let cool completely.

Separate the leaves of the endive by slicing off ¼ inch from the stem end and letting the leaves fall away, then separating with fingers. Transfer to a large bowl and drizzle with ½ cup of the vinaigrette; season with salt and pepper and toss to coat. Add more dressing, if desired.

Divide the endive among four plates or serve on one large platter, leaning and stacking the leaves atop each other. Carefully garnish each stack with the pecans, cherries, and Stilton. Sprinkle with chives. Drizzle the cherry puree around or atop the salad.

DIJON VINAIGRETTE

MAKES ¾ CUP

2 tablespoons Dijon mustard

1 tablespoon apple cider vinegar

1 tablespoon champagne vinegar

½ teaspoon sugar

½ teaspoon kosher salt

¼ teaspoon freshly ground black pepper

½ cup extra-virgin olive oil

In a bowl, combine the mustard, vinegars, sugar, salt, and pepper. Slowly add the oil, whisking constantly. Taste and adjust the seasoning, if necessary. The dressing can be stored in the refrigerator for up to 3 weeks.

MAKES 1¼ CUPS

1 cup pitted fresh Bing cherries, halved

1 cup sugar

½ teaspoon kosher salt

Freshly ground black pepper

BING CHERRY PUREE

In a small nonreactive saucepan, combine the cherries, sugar, salt, and pepper and bring to a boil over medium-high heat. Reduce to a high simmer and cook until cherries are cooked through, about 10 minutes. Transfer to a blender and blend until completely smooth. Serve chilled or at room temperature. The puree can be stored in the refrigerator for up to 2 weeks.

CUCUMBER AND STRAWBERRIES
with calabrian chile and cured black olive relish, pine nuts, and chèvre

Unlike many salads that hinge largely on the season and what's fresh and available, this is a dish you can extend through the year with a few small tweaks. The dressing—which isn't so much a classic vinaigrette as a rustic chopped chile condiment—packs a ton of flavor, but the dish is still cool and refreshing enough to give relief from richness in other parts of the meal. In the spring, we make it with chilled snap peas instead of cucumbers, and through the winter, it works perfectly with jicama batons and sprigs of watercress. Take out the chèvre if you want to make the dish vegan.

Calabrian chiles are hot peppers from the south of Italy known for their unique fruity and briny flavors and the incredible heat they pack for their size. While you may see them in dried, flake form, for this recipe you want to use the jarred chiles packed in oil, which you can find in Italian or specialty markets.

Preheat the oven to 325°F.

To make the relish, mix together the olives, chiles, vinegar, oil, and salt, whisking until the salt is dissolved. Set aside.

On a flat dish or pan, spread out the pine nuts and roast until they are several shades darker but not yet browned, 5 to 7 minutes. Remove and transfer to another dish; let cool completely.

Peel the cucumbers and slice into 2½-inch logs. Quarter the logs, then remove the seeds. Halve each spear lengthwise. Divide the cucumber spears among six plates or serve on one platter, stacking them slightly. Scatter the sliced strawberries over the top, then drizzle with the relish, evenly distributing the olives and chiles. Garnish with the chèvre, pine nuts, and mint. Sprinkle lightly with sea salt.

SERVES 6 AS A STARTER OR SIDE DISH

Calabrian Chile and Cured Black Olive Relish

½ cup pitted, chopped cured black olives

¼ cup seeded, chopped Calabrian chiles in oil

¼ cup champagne vinegar

¾ cup extra-virgin olive oil

¼ teaspoon kosher salt

Cucumber and Strawberries

¼ cup pine nuts

2 salad or English cucumbers

1 pint fresh strawberries, hulled and sliced crosswise into rounds

4 ounces chèvre cheese, crumbled (½ cup)

12 mint leaves, very thinly sliced

Flaked sea salt

HEIRLOOM TOMATOES
with shaved sweet onion, capers, bottarga, and cress

We could be very happy eating a tomato any time of day or night—breakfast, dessert, whenever—but especially when a steak is on the table. Few things work as well as ripe summer tomatoes to cut through the intense flavors of grilled beef.

Tomatoes also have a kinship with salt and salty ingredients, which is why we pair them in this dish with bottarga—a salt-cured fish roe enjoyed all around the Mediterranean. Also, because we can't put anchovies in everything (even though Gabi would like to), we use bottarga, which is very similar in flavor and brings the same briny and bold qualities to a dish. If you have trouble sourcing bottarga in time (you can buy it online or in specialty markets), feel free to substitute anchovies. Finally, a touch of sweet onion—which is amazing with grilled meat as well—pops up every few bites to add pungency.

Sprinkle the tomato slices with a modest amount of sea salt and a generous amount of pepper. Arrange them on a large serving platter so they slightly overlap. Scatter the onion slices over the tomato, then scatter the celery slices, watercress leaves, and capers on top. In a small bowl, mix the lemon zest into the oil. Evenly drizzle the oil over the whole salad. Thinly shave or finely grate the bottarga, tasting it to gauge its level of saltiness; distribute the bottarga atop the salad to taste. Grind some more pepper over the salad, and, only if needed, sprinkle a little bit more sea salt over the whole dish.

SERVES 4 AS A STARTER OR SIDE DISH

3 to 4 heirloom tomatoes, cored and sliced ½ inch thick

Flaked sea salt and freshly ground black pepper

1 small sweet onion (such as Walla Walla, Vidalia, or Maui), thinly sliced on a mandoline or with a sharp knife

2 large ribs celery, thinly sliced on a bias

Leaves from 1 small bunch watercress

1½ tablespoons capers, rinsed and drained

1 teaspoon finely grated Meyer lemon zest (or substitute regular lemon zest)

¼ cup extra-virgin olive oil

1 ounce bottarga or minced oil-packed anchovies

GRILLED RADICCHIO AND CORN
with mt tam triple cream and roasted tomato vinaigrette

Since we are lovers of a good bitter leaf, we always find a way to serve radicchio throughout the seasons, be it baked with cream in a wintry gratin or in this summery preparation with tomatoes and corn. Together with a bloomy-rind cheese, the summer vegetables add sweetness, and just the prettiest colors.

Certain fibrous, robust leafy vegetables gain a juiciness and lusciousness on the grill. Radicchio is a prime example, and a smoky char from the fire works beautifully with the leaves' bitter flavors. You can grill up to 1 day ahead, then serve the radicchio at room temperature or rewarmed in the oven or a pan just before serving.

Preheat the oven to 400°F.

To make the vinaigrette, spread the tomatoes in a single layer on a baking sheet and drizzle with 2 tablespoons of the oil; sprinkle with 1 teaspoon of the salt and roast until lightly dehydrated, 12 to 15 minutes. Remove from the oven.

Meanwhile, in a medium bowl, combine the vinegar, the remaining 10 tablespoons oil, the remaining 1 teaspoon salt, and the pepper; add the roasted tomatoes and toss gently to combine. Let sit 10 minutes, then taste and adjust the seasoning, if necessary.

Prepare a grill to medium-high.

Place the radicchio quarters and corn cobs on a baking sheet and drizzle with oil, tossing to coat all sides; season with salt and pepper. Transfer the corn to the grill and cook, turning occasionally, until the kernels are tender and lightly browned, with just a touch of darker char, 10 to 12 minutes. Remove and let cool slightly. Slice the kernels off, keeping the strips intact, and set aside.

Place the radicchio on the grill with one of the cut sides down. Cook until the leaves start to wilt and lightly char, 3 to 4 minutes. Turn each piece onto its other flat side and repeat. Remove and let cool slightly. Slice away the stems so the leaves no longer hold together.

On a large serving platter or individual plates, arrange the radicchio and arugula leaves, then top with the corn kernels. Spoon the vinaigrette over the top, making sure to evenly distribute the tomatoes. Garnish with the cheese wedges and the slices of shallot.

SERVES 6 TO 8 AS A STARTER OR SIDE DISH

Roasted Tomato Vinaigrette

1 pint cherry or grape tomatoes

¾ cup extra-virgin olive oil

2 teaspoons kosher salt, or more to taste

½ cup balsamic vinegar

½ teaspoon freshly ground black pepper, or more to taste

Radicchio and Corn Salad

2 heads radicchio, quartered lengthwise through the stems

4 ears corn, husks and silk removed

½ cup extra-virgin olive oil

Kosher salt and freshly ground black pepper

4 cups arugula, loosely packed

8 ounces bloomy-rind triple-cream cheese (such as Mt Tam, Brillat-Savarin, or Délice de Bourgogne), sliced into thin wedges

1 medium-large shallot, thinly sliced

You've now heard us sing the praises of vegetable dishes throughout this book, from our love of crisp, cool, and textural salads to our lust for smoky, caramelized grilled vegetables. For those times when the grill is full or you simply want to feature some nongrilled items for contrast, this section offers ideas for every appetite, season, and scenario. Some may inspire you to bypass meat or fish altogether and make a meal around one or more of these vegetable offerings. To us, a baking dish filled with bubbling, creamy vegetables and golden-brown bread crumbs can be just as satisfying as a Sunday night steak.

CHAPTER 7   # WARM VEGETABLE DISHES

At long last, eating vegetables is no longer considered a chore in this country, and few things are more motivational in the kitchen than dreaming up ways to cook with them. The spectrum of colors, textures, and tastes is vast and exciting, as are the many cuisines from which you can draw inspiration. Just walking through the farmers' market fuels anticipation—talking to growers, smelling, lifting, and prodding the produce, taking in all the mesmerizing scents and colors.

Part of our strategy behind devising the recipes in this section is the simple practice of matching up foods we love to techniques that suit them, and vice versa. Among some you'll discover: baking tomatoes in a salt crust as a way to intensify flavor and juiciness, cooking mushrooms in rendered foie gras fat, and more. On their own or as part of a grill-focused feast, these recipes offer flavors as unique as the vegetables themselves.

SALT-CRUSTED HEIRLOOM TOMATOES
with basil, oregano, and grilled bread

It's amazing how drastically a little bit of salt can awaken the flavors hidden in tomatoes. Encapsulating them in a salt crust does not, as you might think, intensify the saltiness, but rather it concentrates the flavors of the fruit while lightly seasoning its outer layers. Since egg white is used to suspend the salt into a crust, once you carefully chisel away that outer layer, each bite inside bursts with sweetness.

This makes a lovely family-style starter or side dish, one that we enjoy eating with our Baked Ricotta (page 43). If you have any leftovers, chop them up into a hot bowl of pasta the next day.

Preheat the oven to 400°F.

Using a paring knife, core the tomatoes, then score the bottom of each tomato with a 1-inch-long "X." Place the tomatoes, core side down, into a baking dish just small enough to crowd the tomatoes but tall enough to cover their sides completely. Tuck the basil leaves and half of the oregano leaves in between the tomatoes as well as on top. Drizzle with the oil.

In a large bowl, whisk the egg whites until frothy, then add the remaining half of the oregano. Stir in the salt and peppercorns to form a paste. Tightly and firmly pack the salt paste around the tops of the tomatoes to form the shape of a dome.

Transfer the dish to a baking sheet and bake for 25 minutes. Remove from the oven and let rest for 5 to 10 minutes. Use a knife to cut around the edge of the salt crust and gently remove it, ideally in one piece. If it breaks up, carefully lift away the pieces, including the smaller ones that may oversalt the tomatoes.

Break the tomatoes up a bit with a spoon and serve with the grilled bread.

SERVES 4 AS A STARTER OR SIDE DISH

6 heirloom tomatoes

12 basil leaves

Leaves from 3 sprigs oregano

¼ cup extra-virgin olive oil

4 egg whites

3 cups kosher salt

1 teaspoon cracked black peppercorns

Grilled Bread (page 250), for serving

ROASTED CAULIFLOWER

with spicy golden raisin vinaigrette, mint, and sesame

A perennial favorite at the restaurant, this caramelized cauliflower is also likely to be a favorite at home. The spiciness and saltiness of the vinaigrette, pops of sweetness from the raisins, and bracing freshness of the mint help cut through any fatty grilled meats and contrast with the smoky flavors of the grill. We find its sweet-sour style reminiscent of a Chinese sauce or Sicilian-style *agrodolce*.

For a little added grandeur in presentation, you can roast the cauliflower head whole in a 400°F oven until tender, about an hour. But cutting the cauliflower into smaller pieces as directed allows a quicker cook time. While the cauliflower bakes, you can prepare your garnishes.

Preheat the oven to 450°F.

To make the vinaigrette, combine the oil, garlic, and red pepper in a saucepan over medium heat. Cook, stirring often, until the garlic is golden brown and smells toasty, 3 to 4 minutes. Add the vinegar, soy sauce, raisins, and salt. Remove from the heat and adjust the seasoning, if necessary. Keep warm.

Add the cauliflower and oil to a large bowl, season with salt and pepper, and toss well; transfer to a baking sheet. Roast until golden brown and just tender, 15 to 20 minutes.

Wipe out the large bowl and add some of the vinaigrette. Add the cauliflower and toss to coat; taste and adjust the seasoning, if necessary.

Divide the cauliflower among four plates or serve on one large serving dish, making sure to distribute the raisins and remaining vinaigrette evenly. Garnish with the mint, chives, and sesame seeds.

SERVES 4 AS A SIDE DISH

Spicy Golden Raisin Vinaigrette

¼ cup extra-virgin olive oil

2 tablespoons finely chopped garlic

1 teaspoon red pepper flakes

½ cup unseasoned rice vinegar

¼ cup soy sauce (gluten-free, if desired)

¾ cup golden raisins

1½ teaspoons kosher salt

Roasted Cauliflower and Garnishes

1 head cauliflower (about 1½ pounds), broken into florets the size of ping-pong balls

¼ cup extra-virgin olive oil

Kosher salt and freshly ground black pepper

¼ cup coarsely chopped mint

1 tablespoon thinly sliced chives

1 tablespoon toasted sesame seeds (see Note, page 246)

SAUTÉED MUSHROOMS

with foie gras, sweet onion, and wilted spinach

Buttery sautéed mushrooms are very common on steak house menus. Our reinterpretation involves using the rendered fat from foie gras to sear and flavor the fungi. In particular, shiitake mushrooms really carry the taste of the foie gras and have a similar, complementary texture.

In some parts of Spain, it's common to see sautéed spinach, foie gras, or mushrooms served simply with a fried egg on top. Try that here—since this sauté is a combination of all three ingredients—or serve this dish as a luscious accompaniment to steak, pork, chicken, or fish.

Quarter the shiitake mushrooms, unless they're small, in which case you should leave them whole or cut them in half (they should be bite-sized); transfer to a small bowl. Separate the oyster mushrooms from each other by removing as little of the stem as you need for them to fall away from each other; add to a separate bowl. Quarter or halve the button mushrooms into bite-sized pieces; add to a separate bowl.

In a large skillet over medium heat, warm 2 tablespoons of the oil and add ½ teaspoon of the garlic; cook, stirring occasionally, until the garlic starts to brown lightly, about 1 minute. Immediately add the shiitakes and 2 tablespoons water, stirring the pan to deglaze. Add ½ teaspoon salt and a pinch of pepper and cook until the mushrooms are softened and the water has evaporated, about 3 minutes. Transfer to a bowl and set aside.

Wipe out the sauté pan and place it back over medium heat. Repeat the cooking process with the oyster mushrooms, using the same amounts of oil, garlic, water, salt, and pepper. Remove the oyster mushrooms from the pan and set them aside with the shiitakes.

Wipe out the sauté pan one more time and place it back over medium heat. This time, warm the remaining 3 tablespoons oil with the remaining 1 teaspoon garlic. Cook until the garlic is lightly browned, about 1 minute, then stir in the button mushrooms. Add the wine, stirring to deglaze the pan. Season with ½ teaspoon salt and a pinch of pepper. Cook until the wine evaporates and the mushrooms are tender, 3 to 4 minutes, then remove the button mushrooms from the heat; set them aside with the other mushrooms.

Wash out the skillet, then warm the pan over high heat. Season the foie gras slices with salt and pepper and quickly place them into the searing-hot pan. Cook, without disturbing, until the foie begins to render and brown on one side, about 45 seconds. Remove the pan from the heat and shake once to help dislodge the foie; transfer the foie to a plate, leaving behind the rendered fat. Store the plate in a warm, but not hot, place.

SERVES 4 TO 6 AS A SIDE DISH

8 ounces shiitake mushrooms, stemmed

8 ounces oyster mushrooms

8 ounces button mushrooms

6 tablespoons extra-virgin olive oil

2 teaspoons finely chopped garlic

¼ cup water

1½ teaspoons kosher salt, plus more to taste

Freshly ground black pepper

½ cup white wine

4 ounces foie gras, cut into ½-inch slices

½ sweet onion, halved through the stem and thinly sliced into slivers

4 cups firmly packed spinach leaves

¼ cup thinly sliced chives

Add the sweet onion slices to the hot pan with the rendered fat and return the pan to medium-high heat. Cook, stirring the onions occasionally, until browned on one side, about 1 minute, then add all of the mushrooms back to the pan; stir. Let cook without stirring for 2 minutes to help the mushrooms sear and warm through, then toss once and cook 2 minutes more without stirring. Add the spinach to the pan, half at a time, gently tossing or stirring to wilt. Taste and adjust the seasoning, if necessary. Remove from the heat.

Divide the mushrooms and spinach among individual plates or serve on one large serving dish. Cut each slice of foie gras into three pieces and distribute evenly over the mushrooms (the foie will warm through from the heat of the mushrooms). Garnish with the chives.

MAPLE-GLAZED HEIRLOOM CARROTS
with chèvre and truffle-salted pistachios

Glazing root vegetables in a mixture of butter and sugar is a classic French technique, and it works very well with carrots. Greg's Vermont roots and consequent love of maple syrup led us to try this dish with a maple twist. The warmth and candylike flavor is comforting, but the addition of chèvre (fresh goat cheese), tarragon, and pistachios adds a tanginess, texture, and sophistication to this dish.

You can offer this preparation through the seasons because carrots are always available. In the spring or whenever possible, we try to use baby heirloom varietals. But you can use larger carrots cut into oblique pieces as well.

Place a large pot or pan wide enough to contain the carrots in one to two layers over medium heat and add the butter, maple syrup, and water; cook until the butter is melted and the mixture starts to boil. Add the carrots, kosher salt, and white pepper and stir with a spoon or heat-resistant rubber spatula; cover and lower the heat to bring the mixture to a simmer. Steam the carrots until firm-tender, 5 to 7 minutes. Uncover the pan and raise the heat to bring the mixture to a boil; cook, stirring frequently, until the liquid is reduced to a thick glaze for the carrots. Taste and adjust the seasoning, if necessary.

Divide the carrots among four plates or place on one large platter. Garnish with the chèvre, pistachios, tarragon, and sea salt to taste.

Tip: If using full-sized carrots instead of baby carrots, cut 1 pound into even 1-inch pieces on the diagonal by using the roll-cut method: Beginning at the small end of each carrot, place your knife about ½ inch from the end and cut through the carrot at a 45-degree angle. Roll it a quarter turn towards you so that the cut angle is now facing you, then place your knife about ½ inch up the carrot and cut again at a 45-degree angle. Continue the roll-cut through the entire carrot and repeat with the remaining carrots.

SERVES 4 AS A SIDE DISH

½ cup unsalted butter

½ cup maple syrup, preferably grade B

¼ cup water

1 pound baby heirloom carrots (or substitute large carrots, see Tip), peeled

2 teaspoons kosher salt

¼ teaspoon freshly ground white pepper

3 ounces chèvre, crumbled

⅓ cup Truffle-Salted Pistachios (page 248)

20 tarragon leaves

Flaked sea salt

HORSERADISH AÏOLI

1 cup mayonnaise, homemade (page 243) or store-bought

⅓ cup firmly packed, finely grated fresh horseradish, or more to taste

2 tablespoon extra-virgin olive oil

1 tablespoon unseasoned rice vinegar

⅛ teaspoon finely grated or minced garlic

Kosher salt and freshly ground black pepper

In a medium bowl, whisk together the mayonnaise, horseradish, oil, vinegar, and garlic; season with salt and pepper and whisk again to combine. Taste and adjust the seasoning, if necessary, adding more freshly grated horseradish, if you prefer it spicier. Refrigerate for up to 3 days.

FRIED POTATOES
with horseradish aïoli and dill

It would just be wrong to serve steak at a restaurant without a potato and some horseradish to go with it. Of all the delicious potato preparations out there, we wanted something that was crispy on the outside and creamy and pillowy on the inside, reminiscent of a steak fry.

Roasting the potatoes before frying them achieves this crispy-soft harmony beautifully. You can do the roasting a day in advance and make the aïoli 2 or 3 days in advance. Come serving time, the potatoes take just 4 to 5 minutes to fry.

Preheat the oven to 400°F.

Cut the potatoes into 1¼-inch cubes and transfer to a large baking sheet. Toss with the oil, salt, and pepper, then spread the potatoes out as much as possible (divide between two baking sheets, if needed, to avoid stacking the potatoes). Bake for about 20 minutes, then gently stir to promote even cooking. Continue to bake until the potatoes are just cooked through, 10 to 20 minutes longer, then remove. The potatoes can be baked 1 day ahead of time and refrigerated until ready to fry.

Lower or preheat the oven to 225°F. Line a baking sheet with paper towels and set next to the stove. In a large pot, heat the vegetable oil over medium heat until it reaches 375°F on a deep-fry thermometer.

Using a spider or wide wire skimmer, carefully lower about one-third to one-half of the potatoes into the oil; cook until golden brown and crispy, 4 to 5 minutes. Remove and transfer to the paper towel–lined baking sheet. Once some of the oil has been absorbed, remove the paper towels and transfer the baking sheet to the oven to keep the potatoes warm. Repeat with the remaining potatoes.

Once all of the potatoes are fried, place them in a large bowl and season with salt and pepper to taste. Place in a serving dish or divide among four plates, then spoon the horseradish aïoli over the top. Garnish with dill.

SERVES 4 AS A SIDE DISH

1¾ pounds russet potatoes, peeled

¼ cup extra-virgin olive oil

1 tablespoon kosher salt, plus more to taste

1 teaspoon freshly ground black pepper, plus more to taste

8 cups neutral-flavored vegetable oil, for deep-frying

1 cup Horseradish Aïoli (recipe opposite)

3 tablespoons coarsely chopped fresh dill, for garnishing

STEWED HEIRLOOM HOMINY

with fava beans, pork belly, and fried duck egg

This dish was inspired by a traditional northern Argentinian stew called *mote con habas* (hominy with favas) that typically contains different kinds of stewed pork and/or beef. You can make it anytime, even when favas aren't in season, by omitting the beans altogether. Though it's typically a one-pot dish, we break up the components in ours so we can cater to guests with different diets. The stew can be vegan or vegetarian if you prefer something lighter.

If you decide to go the meaty route, pork belly braised with maple syrup and beer takes the heartiness up a level, turning it into a great breakfast or light meal on its own.

To blanch and peel the fava beans, bring a small pot of water to a boil, and season generously with salt (the water should taste like seawater). Set a large bowl of ice water next to the stove. Add the fava beans to the boiling water and cook for about 1 minute. Transfer to the ice bath, let chill for 3 minutes, then drain. Peel the fava beans of their outer skins and place in a clean bowl.

Slice the braised pork belly into 1-inch-wide strips, then into ½-inch-thick slices. Warm a large pot over medium-high heat and add the pork belly slices to lay flat (work in batches, if necessary, and drain any excess fat between batches). Cook without disturbing until the fat begins to render and one side begins to brown, 2 to 3 minutes; flip and brown the other side. Add the pork braising liquid, deglazing the pot. Let cook until the liquid is reduced to a couple of tablespoons, then add the fava beans and hominy; bring to a simmer. Keep warm.

Warm a large nonstick frying pan over medium heat. Add the oil, then crack 4 duck eggs into the pan. Raise the heat to medium-high and cook the eggs sunny-side-up until the edges are crispy, about 2 minutes. Baste the egg whites occasionally with the hot oil to cook them through without overcooking the yolks. Season the eggs with salt and pepper and remove from the pan. Repeat with the remaining 4 duck eggs.

Divide the hominy among 8 warm serving bowls, then place 1 duck egg on top of each. Garnish with the green onions, jalapeños, and cilantro.

CONTINUED

SERVES 8 AS A SIDE DISH OR A SMALL MAIN DISH

Kosher salt

2 cups shelled fava beans (about 2 pounds in the pod)

1 pound Beer-Braised Pork Belly (page 247), chilled, plus 1 cup of its braising liquid

6 cups Stewed Hominy (recipe follows)

¼ cup extra-virgin olive oil

8 duck eggs (or substitute chicken eggs)

Freshly ground black pepper

4 green onions, thinly sliced, for garnish

2 jalapeños, thinly sliced, for garnish

1 cup tightly packed cilantro leaves, for garnish

MAKES 6 CUPS

MAKES 6 CUPS

1½ cups dried heirloom hominy, soaked in cold water for 12 hours

Kosher salt

5 medium ripe tomatoes

3 tablespoons extra-virgin olive oil

2 teaspoons finely chopped garlic (from about 3 cloves)

1½ cups diced yellow onion (½-inch pieces)

¾ cup diced celery (½-inch pieces)

¾ cup peeled and diced carrot (½-inch pieces)

1 tablespoon ground annatto seed (also known as achiote powder)

2 jalapeño peppers, seeded and diced into ¼-inch pieces (¼ cup total)

STEWED HOMINY

Drain the hominy and transfer to a large pot. Fill the pot with water so that it's covering the hominy by 3 inches, then lightly salt the water. Bring to a simmer over high heat, then reduce the heat to low and simmer for about 3 hours, checking the pot regularly and continuing to top off with water as needed, so that the hominy is submerged at all times. When the hominy is soft and most of the kernels (90 percent) have burst, it is ready.

Meanwhile, add the tomatoes to a high-powered blender and puree until smooth, at least 1 minute; strain through a fine-mesh strainer to remove the seeds.

Combine the oil and garlic in a large pot over medium-high heat. Cook, stirring, until the garlic is lightly browned, 1 to 2 minutes, then add the onion, celery, and carrot. Cook until the onion begins to soften, about 5 minutes. Add the annatto seed and stir for 1 minute more to toast it lightly. Add the tomato puree and bring to a simmer; season with salt and add the jalapeños. Remove the tomato mixture from the heat and set aside until the hominy is completely cooked.

Remove enough water from the hominy so that the kernels are just poking up out of the water. Add the tomato mixture and stir well. Taste and adjust the seasoning, if necessary. The stew can be made up to 4 days in advance and stored in the refrigerator.

SAVORY APPLE AND ROASTED ONION CRUMBLE
with walnut-thyme streusel

We have always liked the idea of transforming what would normally be considered a dessert into a savory dish, and vice versa. Apples really are more acidic than sweet, and it's only when you add sugar to them that they become a dessert. Here they are treated more like vegetables, topped with a savory crumb made with fresh thyme and toasty walnuts. For a touch of sweetness, we caramelize the onions in the apple filling.

A dish that skews fall and winter, this can be spooned alongside fattier items such as foie gras, pork chops, ribs, or steak. It is also excellent beside a large roast, and merits a spot on the holiday table.

SERVES 4 TO 6 AS A SIDE DISH

Walnut-Thyme Streusel

1 cup rolled oats

½ cup unsalted butter, at room temperature

½ cup chopped, roasted walnuts

3 tablespoons all-purpose flour

1 tablespoon sugar

2 teaspoons chopped fresh thyme leaves

1 teaspoon kosher salt

½ teaspoon coarsely ground black pepper

Apple Filling

1 pound small cipollini onions, peeled

2 tablespoons extra-virgin olive oil

Kosher salt and freshly ground black pepper

3 cups peeled, sliced apples (about 1 pound), preferably Honeycrisp, Granny Smith, or Fuji

4 tablespoons unsalted butter

8 sage leaves

½ cup marsala wine

1 tablespoon plus 1 teaspoon all-purpose flour

To make the streusel, in a stand mixer fitted with the paddle attachment, combine the oats, butter, walnuts, flour, sugar, thyme, salt, and pepper; mix until just combined (do not overmix). Chill for at least 30 minutes.

Preheat the oven to 400°F. Line a baking sheet with parchment paper.

To make the apple filling, in a large bowl, combine the cipollinis and oil, and season with salt and pepper; toss, then transfer to the prepared baking sheet. Roast until lightly caramelized and tender, about 25 minutes. Remove and let cool; transfer to a large bowl and add the apple slices. Reduce the oven temperature to 375°F.

In a small skillet or saucepan over medium heat, melt the butter. Continue cooking until the butter turns deep brown and smells sweet and nutty, 4 to 5 minutes. Remove from the heat and add the sage (the leaves will snap and crackle). Pour in the marsala and season with salt and pepper. Immediately pour the sage butter over the apples and onions; sprinkle with the flour and season with salt and pepper, then toss gently to combine. Pour the mixture into a 10-inch or 12-inch baking or gratin dish, spreading and pressing into an even, flat layer. Crumble the streusel over the top in small pieces (no larger than a small marble).

Bake until the streusel topping is toasted and the filling is bubbling, 35 to 45 minutes. Serve hot or warm.

GRATIN OF WHITE BEANS
with grilled escarole, sunchokes, and bagna cauda cream

We love this dish so much that we have a hard time taking it off the menu at Ox. Luckily, each season offers a new set of ingredients to change it up. In the summer, we swap the white beans for fresh pocha or Tarbais beans from a nearby farm, and add roasted zucchini and fresh cherry tomatoes. In the fall and winter, we add a grilled bitter vegetable such as escarole or radicchio, and roasted broccoli or sunchokes. The sunchokes infuse the cream with a delicate artichoke flavor.

The sauce was inspired by our love of classic Italian bagna cauda and the way its strong flavors work so wonderfully with vegetables. The garlic and anchovy flavors are very sharp in a traditional bagna cauda, but the addition of cream mellows and rounds out the intensity. The sauce is a bit lighter than it lets on: in place of flour, it has richness and creaminess from pureed white beans. Skip the bread crumbs if you want to make this dish entirely gluten-free.

SERVES 4 AS A SIDE DISH

Bagna Cauda Cream

2 tablespoons unsalted butter

2 tablespoons finely chopped garlic

1 teaspoon red pepper flakes

8 to 10 oil-packed anchovies (1½ ounces)

½ cup white wine

1 cup cooked, drained Seasoned White Beans (recipe follows) (or substitute canned white beans such as cannellini)

3 cups heavy cream

Kosher salt and freshly ground black pepper

Gratin

2 cups scrubbed and cubed sunchokes (about ¾-inch pieces)

¼ cup extra-virgin olive oil

Kosher salt and freshly ground black pepper

1 small head escarole, halved lengthwise

2½ cups cooked, drained Seasoned White Beans (recipe follows) (or substitute canned white beans such as cannellini)

⅓ cup Toasted Garlic Bread Crumbs (page 250)

1½ ounces Parmigiano-Reggiano cheese, finely grated (⅓ cup firmly packed)

1 tablespoon chopped fresh flat-leaf parsley leaves

To make the bagna cauda cream, melt the butter in a medium saucepan over medium heat. Add the garlic and red pepper and cook, stirring, until the garlic is lightly browned, about 2 minutes. Add the anchovies, breaking them up with a wooden spoon to help them dissolve, and continue to stir. Add the wine and let cook until reduced by about one-quarter, 2 to 3 minutes. Add the beans and bring the mixture to a boil. Add the cream and bring back to a boil. Immediately decrease the heat to a simmer and cook for 10 minutes. Taste and adjust the seasoning, keeping in mind that the anchovies will add considerable salt to the sauce once it's pureed. Remove from the heat and transfer to a blender; blend until smooth, then strain through a fine-mesh strainer. Keep warm until ready to serve, or store in the refrigerator for up to 5 days.

Preheat the oven to 375°F.

To make the gratin, on a baking sheet, spread out the sunchokes and drizzle with 2 tablespoons of the oil; season with salt and pepper and toss to combine. Roast until softened and cooked through, about 20 minutes. This can be done up to 1 day ahead.

Prepare a grill to high heat.

Drizzle each escarole half with 1 tablespoon oil and season lightly with salt and pepper, then place cut side down on the grill. Cook until the leaves start to char slightly, 2 to 3 minutes. Flip and repeat on the other side. If the inner leaves are densely packed and did not get cooked, separate the leaves from each other and place the undercooked leaves directly on the grill; remove when lightly charred. Let the leaves cool slightly, then cut into bite-size (2- to 3-inch) pieces and discard the stem. The escarole can be prepared up to 1 day ahead.

Preheat the broiler.

In a large pot over medium heat, combine the sunchokes, grilled escarole, beans, and bagna cauda cream. Bring to a simmer and cook, stirring constantly, until heated through; transfer to a large baking or gratin dish. In a small bowl, stir together the bread crumbs and Parmigiano-Reggiano; sprinkle over the gratin to cover. Broil until the cheese and bread crumbs are lightly browned, 3 to 5 minutes. Garnish with parsley.

Tip If you don't feel like firing up the grill, you can roast the leaves of escarole in the oven. Drizzle with extra-virgin olive oil and sprinkle with kosher salt and freshly ground black pepper. Roast at 425°F until browned around the edges, 12 to 15 minutes.

SEASONED WHITE BEANS

MAKES ABOUT 3½ CUPS

1½ cups dried white beans, such as cannellini

2 tablespoons extra-virgin olive oil

1 teaspoon finely chopped garlic

½ teaspoon red pepper flakes

1 teaspoon kosher salt, plus more to taste

Soak the white beans in cold water for 8 to 12 hours; drain. (You can skip this step if needed, but it will shorten the cooking time considerably.)

In a large pot over medium heat, combine the oil, garlic, and red pepper. Cook, stirring with a wooden spoon, until the garlic is lightly browned, 1 to 2 minutes, then immediately add the white beans. Add the salt and enough water to cover, and bring to a simmer. Lower the heat to maintain a low simmer and skim away any froth that forms. Cook until the beans are tender, adding water as needed so that the beans are always completely submerged. The total cook time will vary greatly depending on the freshness of the dried beans and whether they were soaked or not, so check the beans every 30 minutes. Once the beans are tender, remove from the heat, taste, and adjust the seasoning, if necessary. Store refrigerated for up to 4 days.

PART 4 **SWEETS AND DRINKS**

Just like hearty, juicy meats and bright, vibrant vegetables, desserts are essential to any proper grilled feast. After you've enjoyed all the smoky, savory notes, it's fun and satisfying to end on something at least relatively sweet. Though the two of us debate chocolate versus fruit desserts and which are better, we agree on the necessity of at least a little something to wrap up a good meal.

By making your own desserts at home, you can approach them with the same eye to balance and flavor as you do your savory courses. To us, having contrasts of sweet and salty as well as a mix of textures and temperatures are as important in the last course as they are in the first. Desserts made from scratch also give us the freedom to tweak recipes and cater to all types of eaters—including gluten-free and dairy-free (and both chocolate lovers and fruit lovers alike).

CHAPTER 8 # DESSERTS

Our obsession with seasonality carries over into desserts, whether there is a glut of some wonderful berry or stone fruit in summer or it's the height of orchard season, say. But dessert can also be a time to take advantage of the convenience staples in your pantry and fridge. Recipes like our Hazelnut Brown Butter Torte (page 210) and Parmesan Pound Cake (page 218) do just that. We've even found use in our recipes for a few savory-turned-sweet ingredients, like fresh summer corn and herbs.

It's interesting that a part of the meal that can bring such childlike pleasure to everyone can sometimes be complicated to prepare. Of course, desserts can be complex, and if you have a love of showing off with them, you will find your share of dazzling displays in this chapter. But we urge you to keep things as simple as you like, remembering the wow factor that a stand-alone scoop of homemade fruit sorbet or a few bites of one perfect cookie can deliver. Feel free to break down these recipes into individual elements as you desire.

Speaking of keeping things simple, do your best to make these recipes ahead of time, as much for your own sanity as for your own enjoyment when it's time to sit down and dig into dessert.

WARM HAZELNUT BROWN BUTTER TORTE
with "honeycomb" candy and honey-chamomile ice cream

Almost like a nutty blondie, this torte is a gluten-free dessert that never leaves anyone wanting. You can smell the brown butter and vanilla with each chewy bite. We add loads of hazelnuts (and the "honeycomb" candy) for contrast and crunch and top it with ice cream for creaminess.

This is a dish where the whole is so much greater than the sum of its parts, and while most of our dessert recipes can be broken down and appreciated as their individual components, we urge you to go the distance and serve everything together here, down to the ice cream and the drizzle of olive oil. The combination of chewy textures and sweet and savory flavors has made this dessert a house favorite that will always be on the menu at Ox.

Preheat the oven to 350°F.

In a food processor, combine the hazelnuts and confectioners' sugar; process until finely ground. Transfer to a large bowl; add the almond flour and salt. Stir to combine and set aside.

In a small saucepan over medium heat, warm the butter with the vanilla bean pod and seeds; cook, swirling the pan, until the butter has melted. Reduce the heat to low and continue to cook, being careful to avoid splatters as the moisture evaporates. Cook the butter until the milk solids have turned toasty and golden brown, the butter is foamy, and the aroma is nutty, about 10 minutes. Let cool for about 10 minutes. Remove the vanilla bean pod and discard.

Brush the bottom of a 10-inch round springform pan (or a 10-inch square cake pan) with 1 tablespoon of the vanilla brown butter.

In a large bowl or the bowl of a stand mixer fitted with the whisk attachment, whisk the egg whites for about 30 seconds (or until frothy). With the motor running, slowly add the granulated sugar. Whisk at medium speed until stiff peaks form. Gently fold the whipped egg whites into the dry ingredients with a rubber spatula. Mix in the remaining vanilla brown butter until fully incorporated.

Pour the torte batter into the prepared pan.

Bake until a toothpick inserted in the center of the cake comes out clean, 45 to 60 minutes. Let cool on a wire rack for 30 minutes, then release from the pan (alternatively, slice the cake straight from the pan).

Serve the cake slightly warm with a scoop of the honey-chamomile ice cream, and crumble the honeycomb candy on top. Garnish with a drizzle of oil and some seasonal berries, if available.

CONTINUED

SERVES 8 OR 9

Hazelnut Brown Butter Torte

1¼ cups toasted hazelnuts

1⅓ cups confectioners' sugar

⅓ cup almond flour

1 teaspoon kosher salt

1 cup plus 1 tablespoon unsalted butter

½ vanilla bean, seeds scraped

5 egg whites

3 tablespoons granulated sugar

To Serve

Honey-Chamomile Ice Cream (recipe follows)

"Honeycomb" Candy (recipe follows)

Extra-virgin olive oil

Seasonal berries, for garnish (optional)

HONEY-CHAMOMILE ICE CREAM

MAKES JUST OVER 1 QUART

1½ cups heavy cream

1 cup milk

¼ cup honey

⅓ cup dried chamomile flowers

6 egg yolks

3 tablespoons sugar

¼ teaspoon kosher salt

In a medium, heavy pot, combine the cream, milk, and honey; bring to a simmer over medium heat, then remove from the heat. Add the chamomile flowers and let steep for 10 minutes; strain.

In a medium bowl, whisk together the egg yolks, sugar, and salt. Slowly pour the cream mixture into the yolk mixture, whisking constantly. Transfer the mixture back to the pot and cook over low heat, stirring constantly with a heat-resistant rubber spatula. As soon as the custard thickens (and before the egg scrambles), strain through a fine-mesh strainer. Chill to cool completely before transferring to an ice cream maker; spin and freeze according to the manufacturer's directions. Store for up to 1 month in a covered freezer-safe container.

"HONEYCOMB" CANDY

SERVES 8 TO 10

Neutral-flavored vegetable oil, for greasing the pan

1½ cups sugar

¼ cup honey

¼ cup water

1 tablespoon baking soda

Rub or spray a baking sheet or silicone baking mat with vegetable oil.

In a large, heavy nonreactive pot, heat the sugar, honey, and water over medium-high until the mixture registers 300°F on a candy thermometer. Immediately remove from the heat and whisk in the baking soda. Quickly pour the mixture onto the prepared baking sheet, but do not smash it down or you will lose the air pockets that make this candy so light and crispy. Let cool to room temperature for about 15 minutes, then break off shards of the candy, crumbling some and leaving others in larger pieces.

GRILLED BANANA
with malted chocolate semifreddo and sunchoke chips

The semifreddo is a chocolate mousse recipe that we stuck in the freezer one day—we went crazy for the chewy texture it developed. A bonus of this recipe is that it won't melt at room temperature like ice cream will. You can refrigerate the dessert instead of freezing it if you're not in the mood for a frozen confection. Serving it with fried sunchoke chips adds a crunch reminiscent of crispy shards of salted caramel.

To make the semifreddo, in a large bowl using a whisk or in the bowl of a stand mixer fitted with the whisk attachment, begin whisking the cream and one-third of the malted milk powder until incorporated. Add half of the remaining powder to the cream mixture, and whisk again until incorporated. Finally, whisk in the remaining powder. Continue to whip the cream until stiff peaks form. Refrigerate until ready to use.

Fill a medium pot with 1 inch of water and bring to a simmer. Place a heatproof bowl on top (the water should not touch the bottom of the bowl). Add the chocolates and let melt, stirring frequently.

In a mixing bowl using a whisk or in the bowl of a stand mixer fitted with the whisk attachment, beat the egg whites until frothy. Add the cream of tartar and salt; slowly begin adding the sugar 1 tablespoon at a time, whisking constantly. Continue to beat until stiff peaks form. Whisk in the melted chocolate. This will deflate the egg and make it look like cake batter. Refrigerate until chilled, about 1 hour.

Add the whipped cream to the chilled chocolate mixture in three additions. For the first third, use a whisk and mix aggressively. For the second third, whisk less aggressively. For the final third, use a spatula and gently fold the whipped cream in until fully incorporated. Transfer the mixture to an appropriately sized storage container and freeze for at least 6 hours. (Alternatively, refrigerate for at least 6 hours to serve the mixture as a chocolate mousse instead.)

Prepare a grill to high heat.

Just before you are ready to serve, peel the bananas and slice in half crosswise, then lengthwise; rub gently with the oil. Be sure to carefully oil the grate, then transfer the bananas to the grill and cook just long enough for one side to pick up grill marks and become lightly caramelized, about 3 minutes. Gently flip the bananas and grill for 2 minutes more. With a metal spatula, carefully remove and place two (or more) pieces of banana in each bowl (banana split–style) and add a scoop or two of the semifreddo. Garnish with the sunchoke chips.

SERVES 4 TO 6

1 cup heavy cream

½ cup malted milk powder (3 ounces)

8 ounces milk chocolate, chopped into small pieces

2 ounces dark chocolate, chopped into small pieces

¼ cup egg whites

¼ teaspoon cream of tartar

½ teaspoon kosher salt

¼ cup sugar

4 firm bananas (without brown spots)

3 tablespoons extra-virgin olive oil

2 to 3 cups Sunchoke Chips (page 250)

VANILLA BEAN TRES LECHES CAKE
with marionberry ice cream

Tres leches cake is a traditional Latin American dessert served in many parts of the continent. Essentially a cream-soaked cake, it's unparalleled in richness and puddinglike texture. You can definitely serve it alone, but it also goes really well with seasonal fruit like strawberries, tart lemon curd, citrus sorbet, or coffee ice cream.

In the summertime, we love to serve this cake with fresh berries and marionberry ice cream. Marionberries are a breed of blackberries that were originally developed in Oregon and come into season in July in the Pacific Northwest. They are a deep purple-black color, glossy, plump, and wonderfully juicy and tart. They also have a more concentrated, robust, caramelized-sugar sweetness than other blackberries. If you can't find them, you can substitute ripe blackberries.

SERVES 12

Vanilla Bean Tres Leches Cake

1 cup all-purpose flour

1½ teaspoons baking powder

½ teaspoon kosher salt

5 eggs, separated

1 cup granulated sugar

⅓ cup whole milk

1 teaspoon vanilla extract

Soaking Liquid

1 (14-ounce) can sweetened condensed milk

1 (12-ounce) can evaporated milk

1 cup heavy cream

2 tablespoons dark rum

1 vanilla bean, seeds scraped

Kosher salt

Sweetened Whipped Cream

2 cups heavy cream

¼ cup confectioners' sugar

To Serve

Alfajor Cookies with Dulce de Leche (page 217) (optional)

Marionberry Ice Cream with additional Marionberry Puree (recipe follows)

Preheat the oven to 350°F. Butter a 9 by 13-inch cake pan.

To make the cake, in a large bowl, whisk together the flour, baking powder, and salt; set aside.

In the bowl of a stand mixer fitted with the paddle attachment (or using a handheld electric mixer), beat the egg yolks on high speed with ¾ cup of the granulated sugar until thickened and pale in color, 5 to 8 minutes. Add the milk and vanilla and mix until combined. Using a spatula, fold in the dry ingredients until just incorporated (do not overmix).

In a clean bowl of a stand mixer fitted with the whisk attachment, beat the egg whites on high speed until frothy. With the motor running, slowly add the remaining ¼ cup granulated sugar. Continue beating on high until stiff peaks form, about 2 minutes. Fold the egg white mixture into the cake batter with the spatula until just combined (do not overmix). Pour the batter into the prepared pan.

Bake for 12 minutes. Rotate the pan 180 degrees and continue baking until a toothpick inserted into the center of the cake comes out clean, 12 to 15 minutes more. The cake will be golden brown and the edges will start to pull away from the sides. Remove from the oven and let cool slightly on a wire rack.

To make the soaking liquid, in a large bowl, whisk together the condensed milk, evaporated milk, cream, rum, vanilla bean pod and seeds, and a pinch of salt; remove the vanilla bean pod.

With the cake still in the pan, prick the cake all over with a fork (about 2 dozen times), then drizzle half of the soaking liquid over the cake.

CONTINUED

Refrigerate for 30 minutes, then drizzle the rest of the soaking liquid over the cake and refrigerate until absorbed, about 2 hours.

To make the whipped cream, in a large bowl or the bowl of a stand mixer, whisk the cream and confectioners' sugar until soft peaks form.

To serve, garnish the tres leches cake with the whipped cream, and the cookies with dulce de leche, if desired. Serve with the marionberry ice cream and a drizzle of marionberry puree.

MARIONBERRY ICE CREAM

MAKES 1½ QUARTS ICE CREAM, PLUS ½ CUP PUREE

Vanilla Ice Cream Base

1½ cups heavy cream

1½ cups whole milk

½ vanilla bean, seeds scraped

6 egg yolks

¾ cup sugar

¼ teaspoon kosher salt

Marionberry Puree

1 pound marionberries

1 cup sugar

2 tablespoons fresh lemon juice

Kosher salt

To make the ice cream, combine the cream, milk, and vanilla bean pod and seeds in a heavy nonreactive pot and bring to a simmer over medium heat. Remove from the heat and let steep for 10 minutes.

Whisk together the egg yolks, sugar, and salt in a bowl. Slowly whisk the cream mixture into the yolk mixture until combined. Transfer the mixture back to the pot and cook over low heat, mixing constantly with a heat-resistant rubber spatula, until the mixture thickens (and before the egg scrambles), 8 to 10 minutes. Strain through a fine-mesh strainer and transfer to the refrigerator or an ice bath to cool completely.

To make the marionberry puree, heat the berries, sugar, lemon juice, and a pinch of salt in a medium stainless steel pot over medium-high heat until the sugar dissolves and the mixture becomes juicy and begins to boil. Reduce heat to simmer for 10 minutes more. Remove from the heat and strain through a fine-mesh strainer, firmly pressing the mixture through with the back of a small ladle. Stir the puree, then chill.

Combine 1 cup of the chilled marionberry puree with the chilled ice cream base and mix well. Taste and add more puree or lemon juice, if needed. If not, save the extra puree (ideally ½ cup) to garnish the plate or drizzle over the marionberry ice cream. Transfer to an ice cream maker; spin and freeze according to the manufacturer's directions. Store for up to 1 month in a covered freezer-safe container.

ALFAJOR COOKIES
with dulce de leche

While alfajores may appear plain or simple on their own, the combination of these crumbly, buttery, cornstarch-based cookies and the rich, caramelized dulce de leche they sandwich is to die for. Originally from Spain, alfajores are found all over Latin America, where there are entire cafés dedicated just to them. Enjoy them filled, or savor the cookies on their own with coffee at the end of a meal. You could also substitute the dulce de leche filling with fruit preserves or peanut butter.

Preheat the oven to 350°F. Line a large baking sheet with parchment paper or a silicone baking mat.

In a medium bowl, sift the flour, cornstarch, baking powder, and salt.

In a large bowl or the bowl of a stand mixer fitted with the paddle attachment, cream the butter, granulated sugar, and vanilla seeds until light and fluffy, about 5 minutes. Add the egg yolks one at a time and mix until incorporated. Add the brandy and mix well. Add the dry ingredients in three batches, mixing each time until just incorporated and the dough just comes together (do not overmix). Wrap the dough in plastic wrap and refrigerate for 10 to 20 minutes.

Using a rolling pin, roll out the dough between two pieces of parchment paper to a thickness of ¼ inch. Cut out cookies to 1½-inch squares or your preferred size and shape, and transfer to the prepared baking sheet, leaving at least ½ inch of space between each cookie. Refrigerate the dough as needed to keep it cool while working with it. Do not reroll scraps of dough more than once. Chill for 10 minutes.

Bake on the middle rack of the oven for 7 minutes, then rotate 180 degrees and bake until the cookies are barely starting to brown at the bottom (tops should still be pale), 6 to 8 minutes more (or longer if the cookies are cut larger). Set on a wire rack to cool completely.

If making sandwich cookies, carefully place a heaping teaspoon of dulce de leche (or more as desired) on the flat bottom side of half of the cookies; sandwich with the other half of the cookies. Dust the cookies with confectioners' sugar before serving. Serve soon after adding the dulce de leche to prevent the cookies from softening.

MAKES ABOUT 28 1½-INCH-SQUARE COOKIE SANDWICHES OR 56 REGULAR COOKIES

1¼ cups all-purpose flour

1 cup cornstarch

1 teaspoon baking powder

½ teaspoon kosher salt

½ cup unsalted butter, at room temperature

¾ cup granulated sugar

½ vanilla bean, seeds only

2 egg yolks

1 tablespoon brandy

¾ cup Dulce de Leche (page 251)

Confectioners' sugar, for dusting

WARM PARMESAN POUND CAKE
with whipped mascarpone, raspberries, and basil sugar

This cake is our version of a Salvadorian cake called a *quesadilla*—which is not to be mistaken for the Mexican tortilla-based dish, although it does get its name because it contains cheese. It's a decidedly less sweet, more dense and buttery cake (similar to a pound cake) that is classically served as a snack in the afternoon with coffee. While the cheese used in the traditional recipe is comparable to a fresh farmers' cheese, we substitute a generous amount of Parmigiano-Reggiano, which adds umami and an interesting crystalline texture. Mascarpone whipped with sour cream brings a little tanginess and lift. Saba, which you can find online and at some gourmet markets and which is used as a garnish here, is basically a reduction of grape juice that hasn't yet been fermented into wine, so that adds a great acidic kick and marries well with the fruit. If you can't find it, substitute a good-quality, aged balsamic vinegar or a balsamic glaze.

SERVES 12 TO 15

Whipped Mascarpone

2¼ cups mascarpone, homemade (page 250) or store-bought

¾ cup sour cream

3 tablespoons confectioners' sugar

Parmesan Pound Cake

2 cups all-purpose flour

2 teaspoons baking powder

½ teaspoon finely ground sea salt

5 ounces Parmigiano-Reggiano cheese, finely grated (1¼ cups firmly packed)

1 cup unsalted butter, softened to room temperature

2 cups granulated sugar

6 eggs, lightly beaten

1 cup mascarpone

1 cup sour cream

To Garnish

3 pints fresh raspberries

Basil Sugar (recipe follows)

¼ cup saba (reduced grape must) (or substitute a thick, aged balsamic vinegar)

To make the whipped mascarpone, whisk together the mascarpone, sour cream, and confectioners' sugar until well combined. Cover and keep chilled until ready to serve.

Preheat the oven to 350°F. Butter and lightly flour a 9 by 12-inch cake pan, tapping out any excess flour.

To make the cake, sift the flour, baking powder, and salt into a large bowl. Whisk in the grated cheese.

In the bowl of a stand mixer fitted with the paddle attachment, cream the butter and granulated sugar over high speed for about 5 minutes, stopping to scrape down the sides of the bowl with a rubber spatula as needed. Reduce the speed to medium and slowly drizzle in the beaten eggs; mix thoroughly. Add the mascarpone and mix again until smooth. Reduce the speed to low and alternate adding one-third of the flour mixture and one-third of the sour cream until both are nearly incorporated. Stop the machine and finish mixing the ingredients using a spatula to avoid overmixing. Transfer the batter to the prepared cake pan and spread evenly into the pan.

Bake in the middle rack of the oven until a toothpick inserted into the center of the cake comes out clean, 45 to 55 minutes. Transfer to a wire rack to cool. Serve warm, topped with whipped mascarpone and fresh berries. Sprinkle some of the basil sugar over everything, then drizzle the berries and the plate with the saba.

½ cup sugar

¼ cup firmly packed fresh basil leaves

BASIL SUGAR

In a coffee grinder, spice grinder, or micro food processor, combine half of the sugar and half of the basil; pulse until the basil leaves have been chopped up finely and the sugar has taken on the color and scent of the basil. Repeat with the remaining sugar and basil. Store in an airtight container for up to 3 days.

CHOCOLATE OLIVE OIL CAKE
with molasses cream and fudge sauce

This chocolate cake is our go-to birthday cake recipe every year. Along with the molasses cream and fudge sauce, the frosting or accompaniments change based on the honoree's preference. One favorite is mint ice cream, but this cake also pairs extremely well with lightly sweetened mascarpone whipped with a little dark rum (the resulting flavor is reminiscent of tiramisù). The molasses cream adds a savory note to this dessert, and the fudge sauce—somewhat like a glaze—is a nice alternative to an intensely sweet, buttery frosting.

In place of a neutral-flavored vegetable oil, we use olive oil in this cake to impart a mild fruitiness and a good degree of moisture.

Preheat the oven to 350°F. Butter or oil and flour a 9 by 13-inch cake pan, tapping out any excess flour.

In a large bowl, whisk together the flour, granulated sugar, brown sugar, cocoa, baking soda, baking powder, and salt. In a separate bowl, whisk together the eggs, sour cream, coffee, oil, and vanilla. Add the wet ingredients to the dry and whisk just to incorporate (some small remaining lumps are okay). Transfer the batter to the prepared cake pan.

Bake for 10 minutes, then rotate the pan 180 degrees and bake for another 10 minutes, or until a toothpick inserted into the center of the cake comes out clean. Remove from the oven and cool in the pan on a wire rack.

To serve, cut the cake (while still in the pan) into 3-inch squares or disks using a square cookie cutter or ring mold. Place a couple of spoonfuls of the molasses cream onto each serving dish. Place a portion of cake into the center of the cream, then drizzle the cake with the fudge sauce and sprinkles. Serve with peppermint ice cream, if desired.

CONTINUED

SERVES 12

1¾ cups all-purpose flour

1 cup granulated sugar

1 cup firmly packed light or dark brown sugar

1 cup unsweetened cocoa powder

2 teaspoons baking soda

1 teaspoon baking powder

1½ teaspoons kosher salt

2 eggs

1 cup sour cream

1 cup hot brewed coffee

½ cup extra-virgin olive oil

1 teaspoon vanilla extract

Molasses Cream (recipe follows), for serving

Lissa's Fudge Sauce (recipe follows), for serving

Chocolate croquant sprinkles, for serving (optional)

Peppermint ice cream, for serving (optional)

MOLASSES CREAM

MAKES JUST OVER 2 CUPS

2 cups heavy cream

¼ cup blackstrap molasses

3 tablespoons sugar

Kosher salt

In a small saucepan over low heat, combine the cream, molasses, sugar, and a pinch of salt; bring to a boil, keeping the heat low and stirring often. Immediately remove from heat and pass through a fine-mesh strainer. Let cool completely, then briefly whisk before serving. This sauce can be refrigerated for up to 5 days.

LISSA'S FUDGE SAUCE

MAKES JUST UNDER 2 CUPS

4 ounces bittersweet chocolate

¼ cup light corn syrup or cane syrup

7 tablespoons water

¼ cup sugar (2½ ounces)

⅓ cup unsweetened cocoa powder (2½ ounces)

½ teaspoon kosher salt

Fill a medium pot with 1 to 2 inches of water and bring to a simmer. Place a heatproof bowl on top of the pot (water should not touch the bottom of the bowl). Add the chocolate and let melt, stirring frequently.

In a small saucepan, combine the corn syrup and water; bring to a boil over medium-high heat, then turn off the heat.

In a large bowl, whisk together the sugar, cocoa powder, and salt in a large bowl. Slowly whisk in the corn syrup mixture, then whisk the cocoa–corn syrup mixture into the melted chocolate. Strain through a fine-mesh strainer and let cool completely before using. This sauce can be stored in the refrigerator indefinitely.

PINEAPPLE-CUCUMBER SORBET

A generous scoop of this sorbet is a light, refreshing way to end a big meal any time of year. Even as bright and bracing as the cucumber and fruit flavors are, the texture remains surprisingly creamy. In part, that's due to the addition of glucose syrup (available online), which helps prevent an icy mouthfeel. But if you don't have any on hand, substitute either Lyle's Golden Syrup or light corn syrup.

In a high-powered blender, combine the pineapple, cucumber, glucose syrup, and salt; process until smooth. Add the sugar and blend on medium-high until fully dissolved, about 3 minutes. Taste and add more sugar if needed for sweetness, keeping in mind that the sweetness mellows once the sorbet is frozen. If more sugar is added, blend all ingredients together again. Strain through a fine-mesh strainer, pushing through with the back of a small ladle.

Refrigerate the mixture until fully chilled, then transfer to an ice cream maker. Spin and freeze according to the manufacturer's directions. Store for up to 1 month in a covered freezer-safe container.

MAKES ABOUT 2 QUARTS

2 pounds peeled pineapple, cut into cubes

1 pound peeled cucumber, sliced

¾ cup glucose syrup (or substitute Lyle's Golden Syrup or corn syrup, preferably organic)

½ teaspoon kosher salt

1 cup granulated sugar, plus more if needed

GRILLED PEACHES
with maple-sweet corn panna cotta

The rustic presentation of this dessert brings up a bit of a chicken-and-egg scenario: since you can serve yourself as much as you want of either the juicy, fire-kissed peaches or the luscious, light panna cotta, *you* can choose which one is the star of this dessert plate. While either can certainly hold its own as dessert, why not have a bit of both?

Anytime you are going to serve a grilled food at dessert, remember to keep your grill fire going after dinner, or to get the grilling done during dinner prep. In that case, enjoy your grilled dessert at room temperature later.

To make the panna cotta, in a nonreactive pot, whisk together the cream, milk, mascarpone, corn, maple syrup, vanilla bean pod and seeds, and salt. Bring to a boil over medium heat, then let steep for 10 minutes. Discard the vanilla pod and transfer the mixture to a blender; puree until smooth, then strain through a fine-mesh strainer into a bowl.

Put the gelatin in a small bowl and add enough cold water to cover it completely; let sit until "bloomed," about 3 minutes. Remove the softened gelatin from the water, gently squeeze out any excess water, then whisk the gelatin into the hot cream mixture, making sure it melts and incorporates completely. Transfer to a storage container and cover with plastic wrap, pressing it against the surface of the mixture to prevent a skin from forming. Chill for at least 8 hours before serving.

When ready to serve, whisk the panna cotta briefly to loosen it up into a puddinglike consistency, then transfer to a large serving bowl or individual bowls.

Prepare a grill to medium-high heat and be sure to carefully oil the grate. Rub the peach halves with oil and transfer, cut side down, to the hot grill. Let cook, undisturbed, until grill marks form, 2 to 3 minutes. Flip and cook for 2 minutes more, then remove from the grill and place on a serving plate, cut side up. Drizzle the peach halves with the syrup and sprinkle with sea salt. Serve family-style, alongside the panna cotta, so your diners can help themselves.

SERVES 4 TO 6

Maple-Sweet Corn Panna Cotta

1 cup heavy cream

½ cup whole milk

½ cup mascarpone, homemade (page 250) or store-bought

1 cup corn kernels (from about 1 large cob), plus scrapings from the cob

½ cup plus 1 teaspoon maple syrup, preferably Grade B

½ vanilla bean, seeds scraped

½ teaspoon kosher salt

3 sheets gelatin

Grilled Peaches

3 large firm-ripe peaches, halved and pitted

2 tablespoons extra-virgin olive oil

2 tablespoons maple syrup, preferably Grade B

Flaked sea salt

STRAWBERRY-CHERRY SORBET
with chocolate "magic shell" and crushed pistachios

Since icy sorbets can often be overlooked as the diet-friendly cousins of more exciting sweets like ice cream, we wanted to make one that could give more decadent desserts a run for their money. In late spring or early summer, when strawberries are at their prime here in Oregon and cherries are starting to hit the market, we let the flavors of the fruits shine and simply do what we can to help them along. Cooking the cherries before we blend them into the sorbet does just this, adding intensity and dimension.

Since strawberries and cherries go undeniably well with chocolate, we top this sorbet with a hard chocolate shell—like the ones at the ice cream shops of our childhood. It's a bit nostalgic and lends more texture than a typical fudge sauce.

**MAKES JUST OVER
1½ QUARTS, SERVES 4 TO 6**

Strawberry-Cherry Sorbet

1 quart pitted and halved sweet cherries (from about
1½ pounds cherries)

1½ cups sugar, plus more as needed

1 pound ripe strawberries, hulled

1 teaspoon kosher salt

To Garnish

½ cup roasted pistachios, chopped

Bittersweet Chocolate "Magic Shell" (recipe follows)

Flaked sea salt

In a nonreactive stainless steel pot, bring the cherries and sugar to a simmer over medium-high heat. Simmer until the cherries are just cooked through, 10 to 12 minutes. Remove from the heat, transfer to a blender, and puree until completely smooth. If your blender does not produce a perfectly smooth puree, strain the mixture through a fine-mesh strainer, using the back of a ladle to help push it through. Add the fresh strawberries to the blender and puree until smooth (do not bother to strain). Add to the cooked cherries.

Taste and adjust the sugar content, if necessary. If the sorbet base needs more, place some of the mixture back into the blender with another ¼ cup sugar and blend until the sugar dissolves. Mix it all together and taste. Repeat the process, if necessary.

Chill the mixture completely, then transfer to an ice cream maker. Spin and freeze according to the manufacturer's directions.

To serve, sprinkle some pistachios into small serving bowls. Place a scoop or two of the sorbet in each bowl, then drizzle with warm chocolate sauce. Sprinkle the remaining pistachios and a few grains of sea salt over the chocolate. Let the shell harden for about 1 minute.

BITTERSWEET CHOCOLATE "MAGIC SHELL"

MAKES ABOUT 1 CUP

8 ounces bittersweet chocolate

2 tablespoons plus ½ teaspoon virgin coconut oil

Kosher salt

Fill a medium pot with 1 to 2 inches of water and bring to a simmer. Place a heatproof bowl on top of the pot (water should not touch the bottom of the bowl). Add the chocolate and let melt, stirring frequently. Stir in the coconut oil and a pinch of salt. Keep warm until ready to use, or refrigerate for up to 3 weeks. Reheat gently in a double boiler.

We tend to drink how we eat: we like our cocktails balanced and usually bold. If and when they are part of our meal, the two of us gravitate towards classic cocktails or riffs on the classics—as these tend to avoid being overly sweet or fruity and typically go well with food.

CHAPTER 9 **COCKTAILS**

But there is a place for almost every kind of cocktail in a meal. Many of the versions we chose for this book are the result of collaboration from various bartenders and managers who have worked with us at Ox or its adjoining cocktail bar, the Whey Bar. Behind both bars, we carry a mix of locally produced and international distillates—from Argentina, Brazil, France, Italy, and more. A few of the drinks that follow can be made simply using these ready-made ingredients, while others incorporate from-scratch syrups, seasonal juices, or other contributions from your kitchen. These elements, which can be made in advance, are not only fun to concoct but are also great to have in your cupboard or refrigerator so that, whenever company calls, you are only a few steps away from stellar homemade drinks. If you go so far as to pre-mix a batch of cocktails that are ready to be shaken and poured when guests arrive, you're that much more ahead of the game.

Just as there are no strict rules for which dishes we serve as starters, mains, or sides in this book, there are no real requirements for when or in which order to serve or consume these drinks. But there are a few that we do think work well for getting the appetite going at the beginning of a meal or party, and others that are darker, richer, and make a nice note to end on. As long as you're enjoying what you're drinking and having a good time, that's all that really matters.

DIRTY GRANDMA AGNES
unfiltered vodka, grandma agnes's pickles, vermouth

Our riff on a dirty martini and one of the most popular drinks on our menu, this sipper uses the brine of our favorite homemade pickles to tame down the vodka instead of jarred olive juice. The pickles were Greg's grandma's recipe, which he grew up with and loved as a child, and the addition of garlic and crushed red pepper gives the brine a light spiciness. We put a pickle spear in it for a bit of crunch and a fun presentation.

Here's to you, Grandma Agnes.

In a mixing glass, combine the vodka, brine, and vermouth; fill the glass three-quarters of the way with ice and stir the mixture for 30 to 45 seconds. Strain into a champagne coupe or martini glass. Garnish with the pickle spear.

MAKES 1

1½ ounces unfiltered vodka, such as Belvedere brand

¾ ounce brine, plus 1 pickle spear from Grandma Agnes's Spicy Dill Pickles (page 248), for garnishing

½ ounce dry vermouth, such as Dolin brand

Ice

CALIMOCHO
mulled wine, fernet branca, cola

MAKES 1

Ice

3 ounces Mulled Red Wine (recipe follows)

About 4 ounces Coca-Cola, preferably Mexican, for topping

¾ to 1 ounce Fernet Branca (optional)

Lime slice, for garnishing

Calimocho is a cheap and cheerful drink seen around Argentina and elsewhere in South America and Spain, and it typically consists of red wine mixed with Coca-Cola. It's commonly served over ice there, but first we warm and flavor the wine using mulling spices. Later, we top it with a Fernet Branca float. It's our spiced-up twist on the classic—and a really fun drink to serve at a party.

Pour the mulled wine into an ice-filled pint glass; top with Coke. Add the Fernet Branca, if using, to the top of the cocktail (this is called a "float" in the bar world). Garnish the glass with the lime slice.

MAKES ABOUT 3¾ CUPS (ENOUGH FOR 10 COCKTAILS)

1 (750ml) bottle inexpensive Cabernet Sauvignon or Malbec

½ cup honey

15 black peppercorns

6 whole cloves

3 sticks cinnamon

1 bay leaf

Zest of 1 orange

¼ cup brandy

MULLED RED WINE

In a small pot, combine the wine, honey, peppercorns, cloves, cinnamon sticks, bay leaf, and orange zest. Bring to a boil, then immediately reduce the heat to low; let simmer for 10 minutes. Remove from the heat, add the brandy, and let rest for 30 minutes for the flavors to marry. Strain, then refrigerate until ready to use.

THINGS DONE CHANGED

pisco, smoked lemon, jalapeño oil, egg white

Egg whites give a smoothness and richness to a cocktail's texture, and we like that about this drink because it means the texture can stand up to the smokiness and pepperiness of its flavors. First, you do a dry shake without ice, which helps break apart the membrane and albumen of the egg white and gives it a silky texture. You then do a second shake with ice to chill the drink and create an airy foam on top.

That foam is classic in a pisco sour, and this is our spicier, more complex version. The smoked lemon syrup really makes it, but if you don't have the means to make smoked lemon rinds, skip the smoking step and make a lemon simple syrup (not smoked), then swap ½ ounce of the pisco for ½ ounce mezcal (such as Del Maguey Vida brand) for smokiness.

MAKES 1

1½ ounces pisco

¾ ounce Smoked Lemon Syrup (recipe follows)

1 ounce fresh lemon juice

½ ounce egg white (about ½ of an egg's worth)

¼ ounce Jalapeño Oil (recipe follows)

Kosher salt

Angostura bitters, for garnishing

In a cocktail shaker (with no ice), combine the pisco, lemon syrup, lemon juice, egg white, jalapeño oil, and a pinch of salt. Make sure the shaker is closed tightly (eggs tend to leak out and create a mess), and shake until the egg white is frothy, 30 to 45 seconds. Open the shaker and fill it with ice; shake for 10 to 15 seconds. Double strain the mixture through a Hawthorne strainer and a fine-mesh strainer into a champagne coupe or martini glass. Garnish with an Angostura swirl: Using a dropper, gently drop 3 to 4 drops of Angostura bitters onto the top of the cocktail. Using a toothpick, zig-zag through the drops, then do one final pull through the line of drops to create a flower design (optional).

MAKES 3 CUPS (ENOUGH FOR 32 COCKTAILS)

1 lemon, zest peeled into 7 to 10 strips

6 ounces vodka (100 proof)

18 ounces (2¼ cups) simple syrup (1:1 sugar to water)

SMOKED LEMON SYRUP

Prepare a smoker with mesquite wood for cold smoking (see sidebar on page 16), or skip the smoking-related steps if making nonsmoked lemon syrup. Spread the lemon zests on a wire rack and transfer to the prepared smoker. Smoke for 1 hour, making sure the zests do not get dry or crispy. Transfer the zests to the vodka and let sit for 2 days; strain out the zests. The syrup will keep indefinitely when stored in the fridge.

JALAPEÑO OIL

2 jalapeños, coarsely chopped

1 cup neutral-flavored
vegetable oil

In a medium nonreactive pot, cook the jalapeños in the oil over medium-low heat until they start to discolor, 10 to 15 minutes (do not cover the pot, as this could cause the oil to boil over). Cool, then strain through a fine-mesh strainer, pressing on the jalapeños with the back of a ladle to extract all the juice. Store in a sterilized sealed container in the refrigerator for up to 2 weeks.

LA YAPA

rye, fernet branca, velvet falernum, house grenadine

All over Argentina—and coincidentally in Portland, too—people love Fernet Branca, a type of Italian amaro, or bitter herbal liqueur. In Argentina they drink it simply and at a variety of times and occasions, often either straight or mixed with cola.

This cocktail blends Fernet well, without leaving behind any overpowering medicinal quality. The name comes from an old Andean term from which the Creole *lagniappe* is derived: it refers to a little something extra that a shop owner gives to a customer to complete a purchase, or something one gives as a bonus—similar to getting a thirteenth treat after buying a dozen, or one for the road.

You can serve this cocktail at the beginning or end of a meal (or enjoy it all afternoon long).

MAKES 1

1 ounce rye, such as Old Overholt brand

1 ounce fresh lemon juice

1½ ounces La Yapa Mix (recipe follows)

2 dashes Angostura bitters

Ice

In a cocktail shaker, combine the rye, lemon juice, La Yapa Mix, and bitters; fill the shaker with ice and shake for 10 to 15 seconds. Double strain through a Hawthorne strainer and a fine-mesh strainer into an ice-filled rocks glass or old-fashioned glass.

LA YAPA MIX

MAKES 16 OUNCES (ENOUGH FOR 12 COCKTAILS)

4 ounces grenadine, homemade (recipe follows) or store-bought

4 ounces Fernet Branca

4 ounces John D. Taylor's Velvet Falernum

In a mixing glass, combine the grenadine, Fernet, and Falernum; stir well to mix. Store in a sealed container in the refrigerator. Will keep indefinitely.

HOUSE GRENADINE

MAKES ABOUT 4 CUPS

2 cups pomegranate juice

2 cups sugar

2 ounces pomegranate molasses

1 teaspoon orange blossom water (optional, but strongly suggested)

In a small nonreactive pot, combine the pomegranate juice and sugar and heat over medium heat (do not boil) until the sugar dissolves, 4 to 5 minutes; remove from the heat. Stir in the pomegranate molasses and orange blossom water. Let cool completely. Store in a sterilized sealed container for up to 1 month in the refrigerator.

THE WHEY OF THE GUN

aged rum, bourbon, whey, lime, demerara

MAKES 1

1¼ ounces dark Jamaican rum, such as Appleton brand

¼ ounce bourbon, such as Evan Williams brand

1 ounce whey (see Homemade Ricotta, page 251)

¾ ounce fresh lime juice

½ ounce Demerara Syrup (recipe follows)

Ice

Lime slice, for garnishing

We make our own ricotta at Ox and end up with a lot of leftover whey—the milky liquid left behind once the cheese curds form. We started to use it in cocktails, realizing it adds a viscosity and texture without overwhelming the drink with a heavily creamed flavor. Now we have a whole series of cocktails that include whey (as well as an adjoining lounge called the Whey Bar), and with that, a slew of horribly punny cocktail names.

This one is a rum-based cocktail, and the natural acidity and saltiness of the whey plays well with rum's dark, syrupy sweetness.

In a cocktail shaker, combine the rum, bourbon, whey, lime juice, and demerara syrup; fill the shaker with ice and shake for 10 to 15 seconds. Double strain through a Hawthorne strainer and a fine-mesh strainer into an ice-filled rocks glass. Garnish with a lime slice.

MAKES ABOUT 1 CUP

½ cup demerara sugar

½ cup water

DEMERARA SYRUP

In a small saucepan, combine the demerara sugar and water and cook over medium-high heat, stirring constantly, until the sugar dissolves, 3 to 4 minutes. Let cool to room temperature before using. Store in the refrigerator for up to 1 month.

OX BLOOD
bourbon, beet syrup, tarragon

MAKES 1

1½ ounces bourbon, such as Buffalo Trace brand

1 ounce Beet Syrup (recipe follows)

¾ ounce fresh lemon juice

Kosher salt

Ice

1 sprig fresh tarragon

The first thing people notice about this drink is its incredible color, so deep and unique it immediately makes you want to drink one. The source is fresh red beet juice, which has sweetness and earthiness that plays brilliantly with bourbon. To round out the juiciness, fresh tarragon adds a light bitterness and licorice flavor.

In a cocktail shaker, combine the bourbon, beet syrup, lemon juice, and a pinch of salt; fill with ice, seal, and shake for 10 to 15 seconds. Double strain through a Hawthorne strainer and a fine-mesh strainer into an ice-filled rocks glass. Garnish with the tarragon sprig.

MAKES ABOUT 10 OUNCES (ENOUGH FOR ABOUT 10 COCKTAILS)

1 cup red beet juice (from about 2 medium beets)

⅓ cup cane sugar

BEET SYRUP

In a small nonreactive pot over medium heat, cook the beet juice and cane sugar, stirring constantly, until the sugar dissolves, 4 to 5 minutes. Let cool completely. Store in a sterilized sealed container in the refrigerator for up to 1 week (though the syrup is best when used right away).

BASIC RECIPES

In both our restaurant and home kitchens, we try to make as much from scratch as possible. Not only does this allow us to know exactly what goes into each dish, it also gives us control over the seasoning, balance, and appearance of these ingredients, and allows us to improvise as needed.

EMPANADA PASTRY

This pastry is intended for fried empanadas and will not work when baked. The recipe is actually an old Ecuadorian version, and due to the absence of vegetable shortening or lard, it's surprisingly nongreasy (yes, even when deep-fried). Once it's been rolled into disks, you can store it in the freezer and fill the thawed disks with almost any leftover meat or vegetable and cheese filling.

MAKES 1¾ POUNDS (ENOUGH FOR 9 TO 11 SIX-INCH-LONG EMPANADAS)

3 cups all-purpose flour

1½ teaspoons kosher salt

1 teaspoon baking powder

½ cup chilled unsalted butter, cut into 8 pieces

¾ cup chilled soda water

In the bowl of a food processor, combine the flour, salt, and baking powder and pulse briefly to mix. Add the butter piece by piece, pulsing after each addition. With the motor running, slowly add the soda water. Turn off the food processor as soon as the pastry begins to clump together.

Turn out the pastry onto a flat surface and knead gently just to form a ball. Shape the dough into a disk and wrap tightly in plastic wrap. Let rest at room temperature for about 1 hour. If making in advance, store in the refrigerator for up to 24 hours. Return to room temperature (still wrapped in plastic) before rolling it out.

SMOKED SEA SALT

We finish many of our meats and some vegetables off the grill with this lightly smoked salt, which enhances and carries on the flavors of the fire. This recipe makes a big batch, but it keeps for 1 month.

MAKES 1 CUP

1 cup flaked sea salt

Prepare a smoker with mesquite chips and bring it up to a full rolling smoke. Spread out the sea salt in a shallow metal pan and transfer to the smoker. Turn off or snuff out the heat source and let smolder for 20 to 25 minutes (stopping the heat here will help prevent the smoke from taking on a bitter, acrid taste). Stir the salt to redistribute the smoky crystals, then add new chips as needed to return the smoker to full rolling smoke; turn off or snuff out the heat source again. Let smoke until the salt takes on a light brown hue, at least one or two more 20- to 25-minute cycles. Store in a jar or airtight container for up to 1 month.

HOMEMADE KETCHUP

Making your own ketchup is easier than it sounds, plus you get to control the spices and ingredients. You start with a can of tomato paste, simmer it with seasonings, cool, and store.

MAKES ABOUT 3 CUPS

1 (12-ounce) can tomato paste

½ cup Lyle's Golden Syrup (or substitute light corn syrup)

1 cup distilled white vinegar

½ cup firmly packed dark brown sugar

1 teaspoon garlic powder

1 teaspoon onion powder

1 tablespoon kosher salt

½ teaspoon freshly ground black pepper

1 teaspoon Hungarian sweet paprika

1 cup water

In a medium nonreactive pot, combine the tomato paste, Golden Syrup, vinegar, brown sugar, garlic and onion powders, salt, pepper, paprika, and water; whisk until smooth. Bring to a simmer over medium heat, then reduce the heat to low and simmer for 15 minutes. Taste and adjust the seasoning, if necessary; let cool completely. Refrigerate for up to 1 month.

HOMEMADE MAYONNAISE

The most important part of making fresh mayonnaise is the emulsification step. To help ensure a thick, creamy result and prevent the mayo from breaking, start drizzling the oil in slowly and in very small increments.

MAKES JUST UNDER 2½ CUPS

2 egg yolks

1 teaspoon kosher salt

¼ teaspoon freshly ground white pepper

1 tablespoon unseasoned rice vinegar

1 tablespoon Dijon mustard

¼ cup water

2 cups neutral-flavored vegetable oil

In a bowl or in a food processor or blender, combine the egg yolks, salt, pepper, vinegar, mustard, and water; whisk by hand or process until blended. (If using a blender, blend on medium speed.) While still whisking or with the motor running, drizzle in the oil in very small increments until the mixture is emulsified. Refrigerate for up to 1 week.

CHIMI MAYO

As a condiment, this mix of chimichurri and mayo is the best of both worlds in one bite—the mayonnaise delivers creaminess and richness, but it's cut by the acidity and zing from lemon juice, fresh

herbs, and raw onion. Red pepper flakes and raw garlic add a subtle spicy kick.

MAKES 1 CUP

½ cup mayonnaise, homemade (left) or store-bought

¼ cup extra-virgin olive oil

3 tablespoons chopped fresh flat-leaf parsley leaves

2 tablespoons minced onion

1 tablespoon fresh lemon juice

1½ teaspoons chopped fresh oregano leaves

1 teaspoon kosher salt

¼ teaspoon finely grated or minced garlic

¼ teaspoon red pepper flakes

In a small bowl or medium jar, mix all the ingredients well until combined. Store for up to 3 days.

MINT AÏOLI

Traditional Provençal aïoli is simply flavored with garlic and olive oil. The addition of fresh mint, a little Dijon, and some rice vinegar gives this one lightness and zip. It's delicious dolloped on a seafood stew, but it's also good on potatoes or with roasted or grilled fish or lamb.

MAKES ABOUT 1 CUP

¼ cup fresh mint leaves

¼ cup fresh flat-leaf parsley leaves

1 small clove garlic

1 tablespoon unseasoned rice vinegar

1 tablespoon Dijon mustard

1 egg yolk

Kosher salt and freshly ground black pepper

½ cup extra-virgin olive oil

In a blender, combine the mint, parsley, garlic, vinegar, mustard, egg yolk, and a pinch each of salt and pepper. Blend at medium speed to chop up the herbs, then stop to scrape down the sides of the blender with a rubber spatula. Blend at medium speed again, slowly trickling in the oil, until emulsified. Use immediately or refrigerate for up to 5 days.

CITRUS-SOY VINAIGRETTE

The addition of salty, umami-rich soy sauce and sweet orange juice makes an otherwise common citrus vinaigrette wonderfully more complex. This dressing is great drizzled over sliced avocado, cucumber, tomato, or melon.

MAKES ¾ CUP

¼ cup fresh orange juice plus 1 teaspoon finely grated orange zest

2 tablespoons fresh lemon juice plus ½ teaspoon finely grated lemon zest

1 tablespoon soy sauce (gluten-free if desired)

¼ cup extra-virgin olive oil

½ teaspoon kosher salt

¼ teaspoon freshly ground black pepper

In a medium bowl, whisk together the orange juice and zest, the lemon juice and zest, the soy sauce, oil, salt, and pepper until the salt is dissolved. When ready to use, re-whisk to evenly disperse the ingredients. Refrigerate for up to 1 week.

ORANGE-CHILE OIL

This chile oil can be used on almost anything, but it's particularly good drizzled on any sashimi-grade fish with a dash of soy sauce or a pinch of sea salt, or used as a base for a vinaigrette.

MAKES ABOUT 2 CUPS

⅓ cup dried hot chiles, such as Thai, pequín, or arbol, stemmed

2 to 2⅓ cups neutral-flavored vegetable oil

1 tablespoon kosher salt

¼ cup Hungarian sweet paprika

Finely grated zest of 3 oranges

In a dry skillet, toast the whole chiles until slightly darkened but not blackened, about 3 minutes. Transfer to a food processor, then pulse to chop.

In a small, heavy nonreactive pot over medium-low heat, combine 2 cups of the oil, the salt, and the chopped chiles. Once the oil starts to shimmer

and the chiles start moving around, remove from the heat and add the paprika and the orange zest. If the oil is too hot and the paprika starts to sizzle and burn, be ready to cool it off quickly by adding the remaining ⅓ cup of vegetable oil.

Let the mixture cool to room temperature, then strain through a fine-mesh strainer lined with a few layers of cheesecloth. This oil will keep indefinitely when stored in the refrigerator.

TOASTED GARLIC-LEMON OIL

Toasting the garlic until lightly browned sweetens it and adds a nutty quality to the oil. Halve the recipe for smaller uses, or use any leftovers as a tangy pasta sauce or over grilled, roasted, or steamed seafood or vegetables.

MAKES ABOUT 1¼ CUPS

1 cup extra-virgin olive oil

¼ cup thinly sliced garlic

6 tablespoons fresh lemon juice

1 teaspoon kosher salt

¼ teaspoon freshly ground black pepper

Combine the oil and garlic in a small nonreactive pot over medium heat; cook, stirring, until the garlic turns light brown and toasty, 4 to 6 minutes. Remove it from the heat and immediately add the lemon juice; season with salt and pepper. Serve warm. Store in the refrigerator for up to 1 week.

SOY DASHI

Dashi is a savory Japanese broth typically made from dried kelp or fish. It is commonly used as the base for miso soup, but you can use it in other soups and sauces, or as a broth for poaching chicken, fish, or mushrooms.

MAKES ABOUT 3 CUPS

1 sheet kombu seaweed (measuring about 4 inches square), wiped clean with a damp cloth

4½ cups cold water

1 cup dried bonito flakes

6 tablespoons soy sauce (gluten-free if desired),
or to taste

In a small pot, submerge the kombu in the water
and refrigerate overnight.

The next day, bring the pot to a gentle simmer
over medium heat. Reduce the heat to low (if the
water boils, the stock will not be totally clear)
and just barely simmer for 5 minutes. Stir in the
bonito flakes. Turn off the heat and let stand for
2 minutes to allow the bonito flakes to settle.
Skim off any foam.

Line a strainer with cheesecloth and set it over
a large bowl; carefully ladle the dashi through
to strain. Discard the kombu and bonito flakes.
Add the soy sauce to taste.

BROWN VEAL STOCK

Roasting the bones and vegetables before simmering
gives the stock its dark color and full flavor.

MAKES ABOUT 4 CUPS

3 pounds veal bones

1 large yellow onion, cut into chunks

1 large carrot, peeled and cut into chunks

2 large celery ribs, cut into chunks

8 cups water, plus more as needed

2 tablespoons tomato paste

4 cloves garlic, unpeeled

1 tablespoon black peppercorns

2 sprigs thyme

2 bay leaves

Preheat the oven to 450°F.

Spread out the veal bones in a large roasting pan
and roast until they reach a deep golden brown,
about 1 hour. Add the onion, carrot, and celery
and roast for 30 minutes more. Remove the pan
from the oven, add 4 cups of the water to the
pan, and let sit for 5 to 10 minutes. (This will help
remove all the good roasty bits from the bottom
of the pan.)

In a large pot, combine the tomato paste, garlic,
peppercorns, thyme, bay leaves, the remaining
4 cups water, and the contents of the roasting
pan. Add more water, if needed, to just cover the
bones, and bring the mixture to a boil. Reduce to
a very low simmer. Simmer for at least 6 hours,
but preferably up to 10 hours.

Strain the stock through a fine-mesh strainer; let
cool to room temperature, then refrigerate until
ready to use. Before using, remove and discard the
fat cap. Refrigerate for up to 5 days or store in
the freezer for up to 3 months.

HERBED SALMUERA (BASTING LIQUID)

Salmuera is a well-seasoned brine that's often used
in South America to baste fire-cooked meats as they
cook. It moistens, seasons, and evenly distributes
color on large cuts of meat and other items that take
some time on the grill, such as large steaks or whole
tenderloins, sweetbreads, or pork and veal chops.
Customize the herbs and seasonings to your liking,
or substitute beer or wine for some of the water.

MAKES ABOUT 4 CUPS

4 cups water

8 cloves garlic, smashed

¼ cup kosher salt

2 teaspoons freshly ground black pepper

2 tablespoons chopped fresh rosemary leaves, plus
6 sprigs rosemary, at least 6 inches long

2 tablespoons fresh thyme leaves, plus 6 sprigs thyme,
at least 6 inches long

2 tablespoons fresh oregano leaves, plus 6 sprigs oregano,
at least 6 inches long

In a small pot, bring the water to a boil. Remove
the pot from the heat and add the garlic, salt,
and pepper; let sit for at least 10 minutes, stirring
from time to time to help the salt dissolve. Add
the chopped rosemary leaves, thyme leaves, and
oregano leaves. Tie the sprigs of rosemary, thyme,
and oregano together with twine so that the
herbs can serve as a "brush" for basting. Store the
salmuera for up to 2 days, but fashion the fresh
herb brush right before basting.

MAPLE BRINE

Brining meats—especially lean ones—before grilling or roasting them helps them retain their moisture and adds seasoning before cooking. The length of brining time depends on the size of the cut you use.

MAKES 6 CUPS

¼ cup kosher salt

¼ cup maple syrup, preferably Grade B

2 tablespoons sugar

2 tablespoons dried thyme

1 teaspoon black peppercorns

2 bay leaves

1 head garlic, sliced in half crosswise

6 cups water

In a medium pot, combine the salt, maple syrup, sugar, thyme, peppercorns, bay leaves, garlic, and water; bring to a boil. Remove from the heat and let steep for 30 minutes; strain. Let cool completely before using. Refrigerate for up to 2 weeks.

DRY CURE

Like any dry cure, this one is partly for seasoning meat (such as bacon) and partly for preserving it or lightly drying it out. We urge you to follow the proportions exactly—which means weighing the ingredients, especially the pink salt—as pink salt can be toxic if used in the wrong quantities.

MAKES ABOUT 2 CUPS

½ pound kosher salt (1½ cups)

4 ounces sugar (½ cup)

1 ounce pink salt (sodium nitrite–based preservative)

2 teaspoons dried thyme leaves

2 teaspoons freshly ground black pepper

In a medium bowl, combine the kosher salt, sugar, pink salt, thyme, and black pepper; stir to combine. Store at room temperature in an airtight container for up to 3 months.

ZA'ATAR

Homemade za'atar is great with roasted meats or vegetables, sprinkled on avocado, or mixed with extra-virgin olive oil as a dip for bread or pita.

MAKES ¾ CUP

¼ cup sumac

¼ cup toasted sesame seeds (see Note)

1 tablespoon dried thyme

2 teaspoons dried marjoram

1 teaspoon kosher salt

Combine the sumac, sesame seeds, thyme, marjoram, and salt in a spice grinder or mini food processor and pulse on and off for about 30 seconds to combine (the texture will be coarse). Store in an airtight container for up to 2 weeks.

Note You can often find toasted sesame seeds in the Asian foods aisle of the supermarket. If you can't find the toasted ones, toast raw sesame seeds by warming them up in a small pan over medium heat, then tossing or stirring until they turn a light brown color, 2 to 3 minutes. Remove them from the pan quickly so they don't burn.

HOMEMADE BACON

Bacon by definition is always cured and sometimes smoked, but to us it's worth the extra flavor to smoke it. Since you'll be taking the time to smoke it, we suggest making the full quantity of this and storing it for later use, either in the fridge or freezer.

MAKES JUST OVER 4 POUNDS

5 pounds pork belly, skin removed

2 ounces Dry Cure (opposite)

Put the pork belly in a stainless steel or glass pan large enough to fit the pork in one single layer, and coat all sides of the pork with the prepared dry cure. Cover the pan with plastic wrap and refrigerate for 6 days to cure. Three days into the curing process, flip the belly over to ensure even seasoning.

On day 6, rinse the cure off the belly, then pat it dry with paper towels. Place on a wire rack set in a rimmed baking sheet (this will help promote even airflow) and refrigerate for 24 hours, uncovered, to form a pellicle (dry outer layer).

Prepare a smoker with mesquite chips and preheat to 160°F. When the wood chips are smoldering, put the pork belly, fat side up, in the smoker. Immediately close the door or lid and unplug the smoker (if electric). Smoke for four 30-minute cycles. After the first 30 minutes, remove the condensation from the top of the belly by tilting the rack it is on so as to avoid touching the meat. Pour off the condensation, then return the rack to the smoker and repeat the process three more times. Add more mesquite chips as needed to keep the smoker full of smoke. (Reminder: Be sure to remove and replace chips before they have blackened completely to avoid acrid flavors in the meat.)

Just before the final round of smoking is complete, preheat the oven to 325°F.

Transfer the belly (it will be smoky but not completely cooked) to a wire rack set on a baking sheet. Roast in the oven until the belly is cooked through and a meat thermometer inserted into the deepest part registers 150°F, 25 to 45 minutes. Remove and let cool to room temperature.

Wrap the bacon well and refrigerate until ready to use. The bacon can be stored in the refrigerator for up to 1 week, or in the freezer for 3 months.

BEER-BRAISED PORK BELLY

Bacon (usually cured and/or smoked pork belly) has been so universally loved for ages, it's fun to finally see uncured raw pork belly in so many butcher shops and markets. This braised preparation turns out pork that is tender and moist rather than crispy or smoky.

The recipe makes more braised belly than you will need for the hominy stew (page 200), but you will want to snack on it from the moment it comes out of the oven. Leftovers can be used in stews or baked beans. And of course you can also slice and broil or sauté the pieces and serve plain, with breakfast, or as part of the best sandwich ever.

MAKES ABOUT 2 POUNDS

3 pounds fresh pork belly, skin removed

1 tablespoon kosher salt, plus more to taste

1 tablespoon smoked sweet Spanish paprika (also called pimentón dulce)

½ cup maple syrup, preferably Grade B

6 cloves garlic, peeled

1 (12-ounce) can beer such as lager or pilsner (nothing too bitter)

Water

Preheat the oven to 325°F and set a rack in the center of the oven.

Place the pork belly in a pan that leaves just an inch or two of space around the sides (choose a pan that also can be placed on the stovetop burners). Season the belly on all sides with a generous amount of salt and paprika. Drizzle the belly with the maple syrup, scatter the garlic cloves around the pan, then pour enough beer all over the belly so that it reaches about halfway up the thickest sides. Add enough water to the pan so that the liquid reaches about three-quarters of the way up the sides of the belly.

Place the pan on the stove over low heat. Bring the liquid to a simmer, gently jiggling the pan around from time to time so that the belly doesn't stick to the pan. (If you do this over high heat, the syrup may cause the belly to scorch, so be sure the heat is very low.) As soon as the liquid is simmering, turn off the heat and cover the pan with a lid or aluminum foil; transfer to the oven.

Bake for about 2 hours, then check for tenderness: Uncover the belly and use a sharp knife to pierce the thickest part. If the knife releases very easily, the belly is done. If not, cover again and return it to the oven for an additional 30 to 90 minutes, depending on its thickness (check every 30 minutes).

Once the belly is tender, remove from the oven and, using a metal spatula or two, gently transfer the belly to a wire rack set on a baking sheet. Reserve the braising liquid. Raise the temperature of the oven to 425°F and place the baking sheet with the belly in the middle of the oven. Cook until browned across the top, 10 to 15 minutes. Remove and let cool to room temperature, then chill until cold in the refrigerator (this will make it easier to slice more uniformly). Wrap tightly in plastic to store (up to 1 week refrigerated).

Meanwhile, taste the braising liquid and adjust the seasoning, if necessary (if it's too salty, add a bit more water). Strain the braising liquid through a fine-mesh strainer and let cool until ready to use. Skim away any fat that settles on the top before using the liquid. Refrigerate for up to 1 week, or freeze for up to 1 month.

POACHED OCTOPUS

When it comes to octopus, we prefer the size of the ones from Spain, and we like that its population is currently stable and sustainable. To us, frozen octopus yields the best results—the process of freezing and thawing helps tenderize it. Here we poach it in saltwater until it's completely tender and not chewy. You can prepare this octopus up to 4 days in advance of serving.

MAKES 3 TO 5 POUNDS

3 to 5 pounds frozen cleaned Spanish octopus, thawed in cold water

Kosher salt

In a large nonreactive pot, cover the octopus with warm water; bring to a boil. Season lightly with salt, then reduce to a simmer, weighing down the octopus to completely submerge it. Simmer until tender, 1½ to 2 hours. Start testing for doneness after 45 minutes and every 20 minutes after: poke the octopus with a skewer or toothpick until the skewer comes out with no resistance (but before the octopus begins to disintegrate or lose its

skin). Remove from the heat and let cool in the cooking liquid.

Transfer to the refrigerator (still in the cooking liquid) until ready to use, up to 4 days. To store the octopus longer than 4 days, remove from the poaching liquid and freeze in an airtight plastic bag.

TRUFFLE-SALTED PISTACHIOS

These nuts make an incredible snack with cocktails as well as a great garnish or cheeseboard accompaniment. Double the recipe to have extras on hand.

MAKES 1 CUP

1 cup raw shelled pistachios

1 tablespoon extra-virgin olive oil

2 teaspoons good-quality truffle salt

Preheat the oven to 325°F.

Spread the pistachios in a single layer in a baking dish and bake until roasted, up to 10 minutes; check the nuts after 6 minutes and continue to check every minute until they are fragrant and just toasty. Remove from the oven and immediately transfer them into a bowl. Add the oil and truffle salt and toss well to combine, then immediately place the nuts onto a flat surface to cool. Store refrigerated for up to 1 month.

GRANDMA AGNES'S SPICY DILL PICKLES

This is a pretty standard process for pickling, but the recipe is special. It comes from Greg's late Grandma Agnes, who made pickles throughout his childhood. Back in the day, they used to keep the pickles crunchy by adding alum (a pickling preservative) before canning them, but we prefer to keep ours in the refrigerator instead, to ensure a good, crisp texture.

In addition to the classic dill pickle spicing, the brine has garlic and red pepper flakes for a bit of heat. If you can get ahold of some fresh cherry peppers, throw those in as well. Grandma Agnes would be proud.

MAKES 3 QUARTS

8 cups water

4 cups distilled white vinegar

1 cup kosher salt

3 pounds pickling cucumbers

4 cloves garlic

2 ribs celery, cut into 4-inch pieces

2 teaspoons red pepper flakes

1 bunch fresh dill

In a large nonreactive pot, combine the water, vinegar, and salt and bring to a boil. Turn down the heat and simmer for 5 minutes.

Meanwhile, put the cucumbers, garlic, celery, red pepper, and dill in a storage container with an airtight lid. Once the brine has simmered for 5 minutes, pour it over the cucumber mixture to cover. Weigh down the cucumbers in the container with a dish so that they are completely submerged in the brine. Refrigerate the pickles for at least 2 weeks before eating. Will keep indefinitely in the refrigerator.

PICKLED RED ONION

Quickly cooking the onion rings in a salty-sweet vinegar mixture gives them a vibrant pink color and sweet-sour taste.

MAKES 1½ CUPS

¾ cup champagne vinegar

¼ cup sherry vinegar

⅓ cup water

1 tablespoon sugar

1 tablespoon kosher salt

½ teaspoon red pepper flakes

1 small red onion, sliced into ⅛-inch rounds

In a large nonreactive pot, combine the vinegars, water, sugar, salt, and red pepper; bring to a simmer. Put the onions in a heatproof storage container. Pour the hot liquid over the onion. Wrap the container tightly in plastic wrap or cover with a heatproof lid to let the onions steam. Refrigerate for at least 12 hours before serving. Keep covered and store in the refrigerator for up to 2 weeks.

ROASTED BEETS

Roasting beets, as opposed to boiling them, helps concentrate their flavor. Here we roast them covered so that they essentially steam in their skins. You may want to wear gloves when you handle red beets so that they don't temporarily stain your hands.

MAKES 2 WHOLE BEETS, OR ABOUT 2 CUPS DICED BEETS

2 medium beets

1 teaspoon extra-virgin olive oil

Kosher salt and freshly ground black pepper

Preheat the oven to 350°F.

Scrub the beets and place them in a snug-fitting baking dish. Drizzle with the oil and season generously with salt and pepper. Cover with foil, wrapping it tightly around the dish so that no steam escapes. Cook for about 45 minutes, then check to see if the beets are cooked through by piercing through one of them, foil and all, with a skewer or a long toothpick; the skewer should release easily from the beet. Remove from the oven and uncover, allowing them to cool.

Once they are cool enough to handle, peel the beets by slicing off the root end, then peeling the skin away with a paper towel or dishcloth in your hands (the added friction helps you grab the skin of the beets). Use immediately, or refrigerate peeled beets for up to 5 days.

SUNCHOKE CHIPS

Sunchokes—which come from the root of a plant related to a sunflower and have a mildly sweet, artichoke-like flavor—make a great snack in chip form. The fried chips can be used as a garnish for anything savory, like salads or soups, as well as on sweet, creamy desserts.

MAKES 4 CUPS

3 cups neutral-flavored vegetable oil, for deep-frying

5 small to medium sunchokes, scrubbed clean (2 to 3 ounces)

Kosher salt

In a small pot, heat the oil until it registers 300°F on a deep-fry thermometer. Line a small baking sheet with paper towels.

Meanwhile, very thinly slice the sunchokes (preferably on a mandoline) to a thickness no greater than $1/16$ inch. Discard the thicker pieces from either end of the sunchoke. Using a slotted spoon or spider skimmer, carefully lower the sunchoke slices into the oil and stir gently to separate and prevent sticking. Let cook until lightly golden brown, about 1 minute. Remove immediately using the slotted spoon or spider skimmer and spread out onto the paper towel–lined pan; sprinkle with salt. The chips will keep in an airtight container for up to 1 day.

GRILLED BREAD

If you don't feel like lighting the grill just for this, broil sliced bread until it's crunchy and light golden brown. Check the slices after 2 minutes in the oven to be sure they don't burn or become too hard.

SERVES 4

4 (¾-inch-thick) slices levain-style bread (about 7 inches long) or any other artisan-style sourdough loaf

3 tablespoons extra-virgin olive oil

1 large clove garlic

Prepare a grill to medium heat.

Drizzle or brush both sides of the bread with the oil and transfer to the grill. Cook 2 to 3 minutes or until the bread is lightly browned but the only actual char is the grill marks. Turn the bread over and repeat on the second side, 1 to 2 minutes more.

Remove from the grill. Rub both sides of the bread with the garlic and serve warm.

TOASTED GARLIC BREAD CRUMBS

A fun way to add flavor to plain homemade or store-bought bread crumbs, this recipe keeps for up to a week. Sauté a batch—or a few—in advance, and you can sprinkle them on everything from salads to gratins to pastas.

MAKES ½ CUP

½ cup plain, coarse dried bread crumbs

½ teaspoon finely grated or minced garlic

⅛ teaspoon kosher salt

2 teaspoons extra-virgin olive oil

Preheat a heavy pan over medium heat. Add the bread crumbs, then sprinkle in the garlic and salt and drizzle the oil on top. Reduce the heat to low and cook, gently stirring the bread crumbs with a heat-resistant rubber spatula, making sure to scrape down the sides often. Continue cooking until the bread crumbs have turned a golden-brown color and the garlic smells toasty, 7 to 8 minutes. Remove from the heat and immediately transfer to a large dish or cake pan to prevent burning; let cool completely. Store in an airtight container in the refrigerator for up to 1 week.

HOMEMADE MASCARPONE

Mascarpone, technically a cream-based cheese from Italy, is easy and inexpensive to make at home—don't ever spend five dollars on a small container at the store. It works well with both sweet and savory preparations, lending a rich creaminess and natural sweetness.

MAKES 3¾ CUPS

6 cups heavy cream (not ultrapasteurized)

6 tablespoons fresh lemon juice

1½ teaspoons kosher salt

In a small, heavy nonreactive pot, bring the heavy cream up to a simmer over medium-low heat. Once the cream comes to a full simmer, stir well with a heat-resistant rubber spatula, then add the lemon juice. Continue stirring for 5 minutes and maintain a simmer. You will most likely need to keep altering the heat level so that the cream doesn't boil over.

Remove from the heat and stir in the salt. Let cool to room temperature in the pot for at least 45 minutes.

Place a large coffee filter in a small colander and slowly pour the mascarpone cream into it, being careful not to let it go over the sides. Place the strainer over a bowl and wrap tightly with plastic wrap. Refrigerate for at least 12 hours and up to 24 hours.

The next day, scrape the thickened mascarpone into a clean, dry storage container. Press a layer of plastic wrap over the top of the mascarpone, then cover with an airtight lid. Refrigerate for up to 5 days.

HOMEMADE RICOTTA

Making ricotta yourself leaves you with a bonus ingredient, whey, which you can use to marinate meats or give body and flavor to cocktails.

MAKES 2 CUPS

4 cups whole milk

1¼ cups heavy cream (not ultrapasteurized)

2 tablespoons distilled white vinegar

2 teaspoons kosher salt

In a medium, heavy nonreactive pot, heat the milk and cream over medium heat, stirring occasionally. As soon as the mixture comes to a boil, remove from the heat and stir in the vinegar and salt; the mixture should separate into curds and whey immediately. Let sit for 20 minutes.

Line a strainer with a few layers of cheesecloth and set it over a bowl, then pour in the cheese. Let sit over the bowl for at least 1 hour and up to 3 hours, until the liquid has drained. Refrigerate the cheese until ready to use, for up to 1 week. Save the whey in a covered container in the refrigerator for other uses, or discard it.

DULCE DE LECHE

This caramelized milk confection is used in sweets all over Latin America. At times during our travels there, family dinners would end in kids and adults alike lapping it up straight out of the jar. It's also delicious swirled into coffee, as a topping for ice cream, or as a frosting for cake. Traditionally, it's made from milk and sugar cooked over very low heat until reduced to a thick caramelized jam. This recipe is somewhat of an easier, cheater's version, but it does demand attention: you must be sure to keep the can of condensed milk completely submerged with water. If the water evaporates, the can has the potential of dangerously exploding. Using a heavy lid on the pot helps to prevent this.

MAKES 1¾ CUPS

1 (14-ounce) can sweetened condensed milk

½ teaspoon kosher salt

Place the unopened can of milk in a medium pot and add water to cover by at least 3 inches. Cover with a lid. Bring to a boil, then reduce the heat to low to maintain a low simmer; cook for 4 hours, adding more water as needed to keep the can covered by at least 2 inches of water at all times. Remove the can carefully with tongs and let the can cool to room temperature. Transfer its contents to a bowl and whisk in the salt. Use immediately or refrigerate for up to 1 month.

ACKNOWLEDGMENTS

We would like to thank our Ox Restaurant staff, both past and present.

To our back-of-the-house team—the cooks, chefs, prep, and dishwashers who have put blood, sweat, and tears into making our food taste great every day: we cannot thank you enough for your commitment and hard work. You are all the reason people want to eat at Ox, and you continue to impress us every day. Without you, there is no Ox.

If it were not for our insanely talented and hardworking kitchen management team, we would never have been able to take on this project. Thanks to our sous chefs, "Sweet Baby" Kyle Burgess, Jeffrey Newman, and Travis Lowry, our guests hardly noticed when we were out of the kitchen and buried deep in recipe notes while making this book. That is the biggest compliment two chefs could hope for and a testament to your high standards.

To Cory Rom, our CDC, who has become a talented chef in his own right: your help with the production and logistics of executing this book are not lost on us. Cory, you have our loyalty and respect forever. We look forward to celebrating your successes in the future. Thank you!

We would also like to give special thanks to our two prep superwomen who have been with us since before Day One of Ox. Paula Bello and Carolina Barbosa, you are amazing and we are so lucky you are part of our team.

Thank you to our front-of-the-house team for their professionalism, knowledge, enthusiasm, and ability to project our vision to our guests. You are the true face of Ox.

And to all the managers of Ox Restaurant, present and past: Dani Weiner, Blythe Freeman, and Andrew Moore; RJ Hodde, Adam Smith, Marisa Mitchell, Justin Díaz, Patrick "Mecos" Martinez, Andrew Rivera-Myers, Ryan Whyte, Jamal Hassan, and Natalie Obeso. You are the reason Ox thrives today, and we could not have endeavored to take on this project without your hard work and dedication to making Ox a better place for our diners and our staff.

To the people who invested their trust in us, Sara Parker and Scott Thurman, Cindy Emmet, and Marc Visnick, your contributions will never be forgotten. Thank you!

To our partners: Jeff Jones and Donna Wax, Stephen and Tanya Doubleday, and Kurt Huffman. Thank you for believing in us. With your guidance and support, we continue to push ourselves to be better chefs, restaurant managers, and business owners every day.

To the Portland restaurant community: together we continue to grow and impress the world. We couldn't be more proud to be a part of this city. Keep Portland real! To the local farms that supply our produce and meats: thank you for making us look good. To our local winemakers, brewers, and distillers: you make us grateful to live in (and thrilled to drink in) the Pacific Northwest.

We have worked for many chefs in our lives, and without them we would not be the people and chefs we are today. We would like to give a special thank you to Hiro Sone and Lissa Doumani of Terra for hiring us at the same time and inspiring us to this day. You took a chance on both of us and we hope we made you proud!

Words cannot convey our heartfelt gratitude to the friends we made in Argentina and Uruguay. You welcomed us into your homes and lives and were so generous with your time and lessons around the fire. Your hospitality will forever be a part of us. At La Araucana in Capitán Sarmiento: Felipe Menéndez, Angie, and el maestro Rafa. At Sucre Restaurant and all across Buenos Aires: Fernando Trocca. In Buenos Aires: Juliana Lopez May, Cesar Eugenio Sagario, and Armando Cadoppi. At Finca Cosima in Sierras de Garzón and Café Misterio in Montevideo: Juan Pablo Clérici and Silvina Tocchetti. In Montevideo: Santiago Garat. And in José Ignacio: Clo Dimet, Martín Pittaluga, Gustavo Barbero, and Guzmán Artagaveytia. Thank you!

Stacy Adimando, thank you for letting us through your door at *Every Day with Rachael Ray* magazine to pitch you on how awesome Portland is. Who knew that that meeting would be the beginning of this wild ride?! Thank you for your kindness, friendship, and incredible talent. We are so lucky to have such a great writer as our co-author. Cheers to you and to our partnership!

To our photographer, Evan Sung: we don't pretend to understand how you project emotions into your photos the way you do. You gave our book life and vision. We cannot thank you enough for being our photographer and friend. Thank you, Jeanna, for letting us borrow him!

Kira Corbin, we did not think we needed a prop stylist. Then we saw our book photos and realized how wrong we were. Thank you for helping us tell our story! And a special thanks to Dan Kunnecke for lending us your beautifully made ceramicware.

Sincere thanks to our editor, Emily Timberlake, designer Ashley Lima, and the team at Ten Speed Press, for giving us the opportunity to share our passions on these pages.

We really wanted to make sure the recipes in this book could work in home kitchens and backyards. Thank you to all of the people who helped us test our cookbook recipes: Shirley Mattingly and Bruce Ward, RJ Hodde, Dani Weiner, Cory Rom, "Sweet Baby" Kyle Burgess, Travis Lowry, Camilo Schaser-Hughes, Cooper Wathey and Jordana Beh, Michael Davis, Britney Marr, John Figgatt, Winnie Ng, James Mendez, Uriel Miguel, Paula Bello, Alex and Sonya Mielnik, Joe Wilson and Jaimee Bremner, Rachael Steifbold, Kyle "Butch" O'Brian, and Kat Powers. A very special thank-you goes to Erin Keller (and her friends and housemates), who took on a mountain of responsibility when it came to testing our recipes. You went above and beyond, and we cannot express enough gratitude for your squeezing this all into your very busy life. We are so happy to have you in our lives. Thank you, Keller!

One more special thank-you goes to our bar man, Andrew Moore, who not only tested several of these recipes but also singlehandedly spearheaded the entire cocktail section. We would have been lost without your help.

Finally, thank you to the customers of Ox. We could not be in this position without your walking through our doors, waiting for our tables, and paying us with your hard-earned money. All of us here at Ox realize your importance to our successes in the past and in the future. We will continue to strive to give you the best we have every day.

Thank you!

—GREG AND GABI

Shirley Mattingly, you have been the best mother, friend, and editor that a girl could have, and your undying belief in me and my dreams has not only comforted me but has also pushed me to be where I am today. I couldn't be more grateful. Thank you for showing me that the ultimate reward for hard work is happiness.

Thanks to my stepdad, Bruce Ward, for sharing your grill and your love of good food, wine, and travel with us. Many of our Sunday suppers around your grill have inspired the dishes in this book and how we live our lives.

To my father, Jose Ignacio Quiñónez: you shared your passion for a good dining adventure from the moment I was old enough to strap into the passenger seat, and you showed me that no trek was ever too long or far for a good plate of *fritada*, *hornado*, or *asado*. Thank you.

To my grandmother, Rosario Albuja, who worked so hard for most of her life just to put food on the table and then spent the rest of her life making sure our family was always well cared for: thank you for keeping traditions alive with treats from your kitchen, patience, and love. Your memory lives on in the kindness of the sons and daughters you raised.

And to my partner in everything, Greg Denton, thank you for saying yes to this project even though you knew it would be much more difficult than I was willing to admit. Working by your side every day and night makes even the toughest jobs not only manageable but really, really fun. Thank you for keeping a smile on my face and laughter in my heart. I love and cherish you always.

—GABI

By the age of four, I knew I wanted to be a chef, so acknowledging everyone who has influenced me would need to be a book of its own. If I forget to call out someone I have met on this amazing journey, I would like to apologize, but please understand that I have been influenced in one way or another by every person with whom I have worked and spent time. Thank you!

I first would like to thank my wife, partner, co-chef, and best friend, Gabi. Without you, my life would be an O without an X.

I would like to thank my brothers, Travis, Chad, and Channing, for their support—sarcastic at times, but I still feel the love.

Thanks to my mom, who continues to impress me with her courage to change in the pursuit of happiness.

Thanks to Terry, my second dad and my father's husband, whose wisdom, kindness, loyalty, and laugh will always be kept near and dear to my heart.

To my Grandma Agnes, who taught me how to love food made from the heart and to always make sure everyone is taken care of before myself: I love and miss you!

And to my father, Gregory A. Denton, thank you for teaching me how to be a man, a manager, and a person who treats people fairly. Luv ya!

I would also like to thank Bruce Ward and Shirley Mattingly for raising such an amazing woman, my wife, Gabi. You both have helped me open my eyes to a world of food, love, and kindness. I am blessed to be a part of your wonderful lives! Thank you for everything!

Finally, I would like to thank the restaurants and chefs who let me look behind the curtain, let me intrude on their spaces as a stage, let me apprentice with them, and taught me as a student or allowed me to become an employee. The days, weeks, and years have infused in me more than you would ever know.

—GREG

INDEX

Published in the United States by Ten Speed Press, an
imprint of the Crown Publishing Group, a division of
Penguin Random House LLC, New York.
www.crownpublishing.com
www.tenspeed.com

Ten Speed Press and the Ten Speed Press colophon are
registered trademarks of Penguin Random House LLC.

Library of Congress Cataloging-in-Publication Data
Denton, Greg.
  Around the fire : recipes for inspired grilling and seasonal
feasting from Ox Restaurant / Greg Denton and Gabrielle
Quinonez Denton ; with Stacy Adimando ; photography by
Evan Sung. — First edition.
     pages cm
  Includes bibliographical references and index.
 1. Outdoor cooking. 2. Barbecuing. 3. Cooking, Latin
American. 4. Cooking, Argentine. I. Quinonez Denton,
Gabrielle. II. Adimando, Stacy. III. Title.
  TX823.D46 2016
  641.5'78—dc23

                              2015032700

Hardcover ISBN: 978-1-60774-752-9
eBook ISBN: 978-1-60774-753-6

Printed in China

Design by Ashley Lima

10 9 8 7 6 5 4 3 2 1

First Edition